CRYPTOCURRENCY
AND DIGITAL ASSET REGULATION
A PRACTICAL GUIDE FOR COUNSEL

ABA®
AMERICAN BAR ASSOCIATION
Tort Trial and Insurance
Practice Section

Editors: Deborah R. Meshulam and Michael Fluhr

Cover design by Cory Ottenwess/ABA Design

Printed in the United States of America.

26 25 24 23 22 5 4 3 2 1

ISBN: 978-1-63905-030-7
e-ISBN: 978-1-63905-031-4

Discounts are available for books ordered in bulk. Special consideration is given to state bars, CLE programs, and other bar-related organizations. Inquire at Book Publishing, ABA Publishing, American Bar Association, 321 North Clark Street, Chicago, Illinois 60610.

www.ShopABA.org

Contents

About the Contributors xi
Introduction xv

1 Introduction to Blockchain-Based Assets 1

Michael Fluhr and Deborah Meshulam 1

Introduction 1
Traditional Digital Assets 2
Digital Asset Ecosystems 3
The Problem of Trusted Third Parties 4
Enter the Blockchain 5
Case Study: Bitcoin 5
An Interesting Aside on the Unknown Origin of Bitcoin 8
Other Blockchains 9
Common Types of Blockchain Assets 10
Cryptocurrencies 10
Stablecoins 12
Utility Tokens 13
Rights-Based Tokens 14
Non-Fungible Tokens (NFTs) 14
The Blockchain Industry 15
Other Potential Uses for Blockchain 16
Introduction to Blockchain Regulation 16

2 Blockchain-Based Assets as Securities 19

Deborah Meshulam and Michael Fluhr 19

Introduction 19

Introduction to Securities and Their Regulation 20

What Are Securities? 20

Securities Laws Relevant to Blockchain-Based Securities 21

What Blockchain Assets Are Securities 24

Investment Contracts and Howey 24

What Assets Are Not Securities? 27

Application of Howey *to Blockchain-Based Assets* 29

The DAO Report 30

Utility Tokens and SAFTs 31

Early Enforcement Actions 32

Registration Failures 35

SEC Statement on Digital Asset Securities Issuance and Trading 37

April 2019 SEC Framework for "Investment Contract" Analysis of Digital Assets 38

No-Action Letters 44

Certain 2020 Enforcement Litigation 46

Analysis of Particular Blockchain-Based Assets 50

Other Howey *Issues as Applied to Blockchain Assets* 55

A Note on "Notes," Reves and Decentralized Finance 59

Securities Regulation of Other Activities Related to Blockchain-Based Assets 61

Unregistered Broker-Dealers 61

Investment Companies and Investment Advisers 64

Exchanges 65

Special Problems Involving Blockchain-Based Securities 67

3 Commodity Futures Trading Commission Regulation of Blockchain-Based Assets 71

Daniel Nathan, Jonas Robison, and S. Chris Min 71

Introduction 71

CFTC's Jurisdiction over Blockchain-Based Assets 72
Types of Blockchain-Based Digital Assets 72
The Commodity Exchange Act Definition of Commodity 73
The Divide Between CFTC's and SEC's Jurisdiction 77
Position Taken by CFTC to Date 78
Application of Commodity Interest Definitions to Virtual Currencies and Other Digital Assets 79
Independent Exchanges and Self-Regulatory Organization Regulation of Trading in Commodity Interests 82
Overview of Various CFR CFTC Requirements 84
Certain Categories of Market Participants 84
Certain Requirements Applicable to All OTC Swap Market Participants 85
Exchange-Traded Markets 87
Designated Contract Markets and Swap Execution Facilities 88
Derivatives Clearing Organizations 88
Futures Commission Merchants, Introducing Brokers, and Associated Persons 88
Enforcement Efforts and Litigation 89
Enforcement Actions Involving Off-Exchange Trading 90
Actions Involving Fraudulent Conduct 93
Other Significant Actions Brought by the CFTC 98
Offshore Enterprises 98
Trade Practice Cases 99
Anti–Money Laundering Cases 99
Liability of Developers, Miners, and Other Parties Involved in a Distributed Ledger Network 101
Private Rights of Action Under the CEA 102
Representative Cases 102
Conclusion 103
Appendix 104

4 Federal Taxation of Virtual Currencies 107

Sarah-Jane Morin and Alexander Reid 107

IRS Guidance 107

IRS Notice 2014-21: IRS Virtual Currency Guidance 107

2017 IRS Reminder 113

2019 IRS Frequently Asked Questions 113

Hard Forks and Airdrops: Revenue Ruling 2019-24 115

Basis, Holding Period, and Character Considerations of Blockchain-Based Assets 116

Like-Kind Exchanges of Blockchain-Based Assets 118

Donations of Blockchain-Based Assets 119

Tax Implications of Cryptocurrency "Hard Forks" 122

Initial Coin Offerings 125

Reporting Blockchain-Based Asset Transactions 128

Highlights of Additional Federal Guidance Addressing Blockchain-Based Asset Tax Issues 129

2016 Treasury Inspector General for Tax Administration (TIGTA) Guidance 129

2016 Department of Justice Actions 130

LB&I Compliance Campaigns 131

2020 Government Accountability Office (GAO) Report 132

2021 Financial Crimes Enforcement Network Notice 132

5 Digital Assets as Payment and Money Transfer Systems 133

Margo Tank and Andrew W. Grant 133

FinCEN Regulation of Virtual Currency Money Transmission 134

FinCEN's Guidance Addressing Convertible Virtual Currency 136

Persons or Activities That FinCEN Deems to Be Engaged in "Money Transmission Services" 138

Persons or Activities That Do Not Constitute Money Transmission 143

Status of Decentralized Token or Virtual Currency Developers 145

The Status of Initial Coin Offerings 146
Financial Action Task Force Approach to Virtual Currency Money Transmission 147
State Regulation of Virtual Currency Money Transmission 149
General Overview of State Money Transmission Laws 149
New York BitLicense 153
The Uniform Law Commission's Uniform Regulation of Virtual-Currency Businesses Act 155
The Electronic Fund Transfer Act and Digital Assets 157
Conclusion 159

6 Anti–Money Laundering for Digital Assets 161

Alma Angotti and Elizabeth Sisul 161
Bank Secrecy Act/Anti–Money Laundering Act Overview 161
AML Requirements 163
BSA/AML Program 163
Know Your Customer/Customer Due Diligence 165
Recordkeeping and Reporting 166
Transaction Monitoring 170
Digital Assets' Susceptibility to AML Risks 171
Three Stages of Money Laundering 171
Placement 171
Layering 172
Integration 172
Cryptocurrency Characteristics that Facilitate Money Laundering 172
Cryptocurrency Characteristics that Assist with AML Detection and Prevention 179
Participants in the Cryptocurrency Business Ecosystem 179
Cryptocurrency Miners 180
Cryptocurrency Exchanges 180
Bitcoin Teller Machines 180
Cryptocurrency Structuring and Mixers/Tumblers 181

Digital Commodities and Securities 181
Digital Asset Managers 182
Buyers and Sellers of Digital Assets 183
Ransomware Firms 183
Financial Institutions' Adoption of Cryptocurrency 183
Stablecoins 184
Risks for Financial Institutions 185
Money Laundering in Cryptocurrency Transactions 185
Understanding Cryptocurrency Risk 187
Mitigating Cryptocurrency Risk 188
Risk Assessment 189
Know Your Customer 189
Training 190
AML Controls 190
Regulator Engagement 190
Identifying Red Flags in Cryptocurrency Transactions 191
Prohibition/Blocking of Anonymous Trading Tools 192
Conclusion 192

7 Sanctions Compliance for Cryptocurrency Transactions 195

Alma Angotti, Adam Klauder, and Elizabeth Sisul 195
Sanctions—Overview 195
Cryptocurrency's Susceptibility to Sanctions Risks 197
Pseudo-anonymity 198
Cross-Border Transactions 199
Exchanges and a Path to Fiat Currency 200
Immutability 200
Privacy-Focused Cryptocurrencies 201
Ability to Be Mixed or Tumbled to Obscure the Source of Funds 201
Ease of Creating New Cryptocurrencies 202
Online Activity 202
Foreign Nations' Use of Cryptocurrency to Evade US Sanctions 202

Iran 203

Venezuela 204

Russia 205

North Korea 206

Regulatory Regime Guidance 208

Enforcement Actions 209

Cryptocurrency Addresses as Identifiers 210

Strategies for Compliance 211

Risk Assessment 212

Know Your Customer Assessment and Update 212

Transaction Screening and Surveillance 213

Training 213

Conclusion 213

8 Selected Issues in Litigation 215

Michael Fluhr and Deborah Meshulam 215

Introduction 215

Fraud, Conversion, and Misappropriation of Trade Secrets 215

I am Nakamoto: Kleiman v. Wright, *No. 18-cv-80176 (S.D. Fla.)* 215

The Fall of Mt. Gox 217

Blockchain and Trademark 218

Contract Issues: Forked Currencies 221

Anonymity on the Blockchain 223

Valuing Cryptocurrency Loss 226

Location of Blockchain Transactions 228

What Do These Cases Mean? 229

About the Contributors

ABOUT THE EDITORS

Deborah R. Meshulam is a partner at DLA Piper LLP (US) where she is one of the leaders of the firm's Securities Enforcement practice. She has a broad regulatory practice that includes defending clients facing claims of securities law violations and conducting cross-border investigations for multinational corporations. She regularly advises clients on compliance matters and litigation avoidance and counsels them on a wide range of regulatory matters including the application of the federal securities laws to digital assets. She advises exchanges, digital asset issuers, and regulated entities on these issues. Ms. Meshulam has published multiple articles related to the Securities and Exchange Commission's (SEC) regulation of digital assets and is a sought-after speaker on this and related topics. She has been repeatedly recognized by legal industry publications including most recently by Who's Who Legal Investigations 2021 as a global leader in investigations and by the Legal 500 for her work in securities litigation defense. She is a past recipient of the Burton Award for Legal Achievement, run in alliance with the Law Library of Congress. She is also recognized as a Washington, DC, Super Lawyer in Securities Litigation. She formerly served as Assistant Chief Litigation Counsel in the SEC's Division of Enforcement.

Michael Fluhr practices at DLA Piper LLP (US), where he counsels and defends companies in a wide variety of complex, commercial disputes. Mr. Fluhr focuses his practice on the financial sector, including the blockchain and digital asset space, where he advises and defends exchanges, issuers, and related companies. Sought after for his deep understanding of the space and technology, he has been quoted in media and regularly publishes and speaks about issues germane to blockchain and digital assets, including securities analysis, intellectual property rights, and regulation of the non-fungible token (NFT) space.

ABOUT THE AUTHORS

Alma Angotti is a managing director and cohead of the Global Investigations and Compliance practice for Guidehouse. With over twenty-five years of experience in regulation and enforcement, Angotti has held senior enforcement positions at the US Securities and Exchange Commission (SEC), US Department of the Treasury's Financial Crimes Enforcement Network (FinCEN), and the Financial Industry Regulatory Authority (FINRA). In these positions, she was responsible for investigations and enforcement of the Bank Secrecy Act, the federal securities laws, and FINRA rules. At FinCEN and FINRA, she designed and led the anti–money laundering enforcement programs.

Andrew W. Grant advises on the full spectrum of legal and regulatory matters related to the use of electronic signatures and records to enable digital transactions (including smart contracts) in the online and mobile environment in compliance with the federal Electronic Signatures in Global and National Commerce Act (ESIGN Act) and state adoption of the Uniform Electronic Transactions Act (UETA) across multiple sectors. Further, he advises financial institutions, such as banks, nonbank lenders, money transmitters, blockchain and digital currency companies, and other related entities on regulatory compliance matters related to consumer financial services.

Adam Klauder is a senior director in Guidehouse's Global Investigations and Compliance practice in Washington, DC, where his practice is focused on compliance matters involving economic sanctions, export controls, anticorruption, cryptocurrency, and other cross-border regulatory regimes. He publishes and speaks regularly at industry events on sanctions, financial crime compliance, and digital assets.

S. Chris Min is of counsel in the New York City office of Orrick Herrington & Sutcliffe LLP. She is a member of Orrick's structured finance group and has experience in a variety of structured finance transactions. She was also a core member of the Finance, Securitization and Smart Contracts working group of the Mobility Open Blockchain Initiative (MOBI), lending her securitization expertise to MOBI's work of assessing the potential value proposition of blockchain to finance and securitization transactions and standardization for its practical application.

Sarah-Jane Morin is a tax partner based in the San Francisco, California, office of Morgan, Lewis & Bockius LLP. She focuses her practice on representation of public and private companies, private equity funds, venture capital funds, real estate funds, portfolio companies, and alternative investment vehicles in the tax aspects of complex business transactions and fund formations, including domestic and cross-border investment strategies, sponsor investment strategies, limited partner investment strategies, mergers, acquisitions, integrations, buyouts, recapitalizations, debt and equity restructurings, and ongoing operations and tax compliance issues.

Daniel Nathan is senior counsel in the Washington, DC, office of Orrick, Herrington & Sutcliffe LLP, where he is in the White Collar, Investigations, Securities Litigation & Compliance practice group, and cohead of the firm's Blockchain Working Group and Commodity Futures Trading Commission (CFTC) Regulation Working Group. He represents US and international financial institutions and individuals before financial regulators, including the Securities and Exchange Commission (SEC), CFTC, and the Financial Industry Regulatory Authority (FINRA), and provides regulatory and compliance advice. Prior to entering private practice, he was a senior enforcement official with the SEC, CFTC, and FINRA.

Alexander Reid is a partner at Baker & Hostetler LLP (BakerHostetler) where he conducts a broad-based tax practice that includes tax controversy, tax planning, and tax transactional matters. He previously served as legislation counsel to the Joint Committee on Taxation, US Congress, and as a Fellow at the Office of Tax Policy, US Department of the Treasury. Reid represents taxpayers of all types under audit and at Internal Revenue Service (IRS) appeals and counsels taxpayers seeking administrative guidance from the IRS and US Department of the Treasury. He also provides advice to clients under investigation and advice regarding legislative tax matters being considered by Congress. Alex also serves as national team leader of BakerHostetler's Tax Exempt Organizations and Charitable Giving Team. In that role, he works with numerous types of tax-exempt organizations, including colleges and universities, charities, foundations, museums, and other nonprofits and provides advice regarding planning, structuring, governance, investigations, tax compliance, and transactional matters.

Jonas Robison is a senior associate in the New York office of Orrick Herrington & Sutcliffe LLP. He has a broad financial regulatory practice, including regularly advising on derivatives and bank regulatory requirements. He also negotiates a broad range of derivatives products and, in addition, represents underwriters and issuers in commercial mortgage loan and other types of securitizations.

Elizabeth Sisul is an associate director at Guidehouse in Washington, DC, in the Global Investigations and Compliance practice. She has significant experience working on anti–money laundering (AML) and sanctions engagements, including end-to-end assessments of financial institutions' and digital asset companies' AML and sanctions compliance programs, as well as investigations into potential violations or misconduct. She has published multiple thought leadership pieces in the digital assets space and has conducted trainings on AML and sanctions compliance for digital assets companies. She is a member of the Anti–Human Trafficking Intelligence Initiative's Cryptocurrency Consortium.

Margo Tank is the US cochair of DLA Piper LLP's (US) Financial Services Sector and cochair of the Financial Regulatory, Payments and Digital Group. She advises on the full spectrum of legal and regulatory matters related to the use of electronic signatures and records to conduct business digitally in compliance with the federal Electronic Signatures in Global and National Commerce Act (ESIGN Act), the Uniform Electronic Transactions Act (UETA), and various Uniform Commercial Code (U.C.C.) articles enabling digital transactions, including Article 9-105. She also advises businesses on the use of smart contracts and blockchain technologies, the laws enabling money transmission, and laws related to privacy and data security matters. She coauthored nine editions of Thomson Reuters' *The Law of Electronic Signatures and Records*, and three editions of *Standards and Procedures for Electronic Records and Signatures* (SPeRS). Tank is ranked in Chambers FinTech and Legal 500 Fintech and was named to the *National Law Journal*'s list of Legal Technology Trailblazers.

Introduction

Deborah Meshulam and Michael Fluhr

Over a decade ago, an individual going by the name Satoshi Nakamoto released the first known version of Bitcoin software, mined the genesis block, and created the first 50 Bitcoins in existence. As of the time this book is published, almost two million Bitcoins have been mined. People and institutions across the globe buy and sell Bitcoin on various cryptocurrency exchanges. The price of a Bitcoin on various markets rose to over $50,000 in late 2021, giving Bitcoin a global valuation of over $1 trillion. Bitcoin might draw more attention than any other single asset. To date, Satoshi Nakamoto's true identity remains unknown.

Satoshi's vanishing act is not the only strange story in this new blockchain world. In 2010, early adopter Laszlo Hanyecz convinced an individual on a Bitcoin forum to deliver two pizzas to him in exchange for 10,000 Bitcoins, now worth over $250 million.[1] In 2019, cryptocurrency exchange QuadrigaCX allegedly lost over $250 million worth of customer assets when its CEO and founder died (also allegedly) together with the passwords needed to retrieve the assets.

Bitcoin was built and exists on a blockchain, which stores information such as account balances and transfers across a community of decentralized users. Individuals and institutions all over the world trade a menagerie of digital assets built on an endless variety of blockchains (of which Bitcoin is merely one). These assets have a fascinating variety of features. Filecoin allows you to store data with unknown storage providers—securely. With MANA, you can buy plots of virtual real estate in a place called Decentraland and trade the digital plots on

1. Pictures of the $250 million pizzas are allegedly viewable at http://heliacal.net/~solar/bitcoin/pizza?.

exchanges. Elon Musk has claimed that the economy on Mars will run on cryptocurrency.[2]

The proliferation of these new assets and technologies raises a host of legal questions. Are there regulatory restrictions on the creation, sales, and trading of these assets? What safeguards must industry participants employ to prevent and avoid participating in misuse of the assets? How are purchases, trades, and investments in these assets taxed? What will courts think of them? Answering all of these questions requires applying existing law to new technology.

Navigating these legal issues presents a challenge. Blockchain does not implicate one particular area of the law or even a single industry. Blockchain is simply a novel way to store information; the content and use of the stored information impact what laws apply. Blockchain-based securities will implicate securities laws. Blockchain-based commodities derivatives and swaps will implicate commodities laws. Blockchain-based assets used as forms of currency may implicate anti–money laundering regulations and money services and transmitter laws. And the list goes on.

This book is intended to provide an overview of some of the most common legal issues that arise in the world of blockchain-based assets. It is intended to help the practitioner understand their client's issues and to provide a starting point for additional research or referral.

Because the legal areas and issues implicated by blockchain technology span diverse practice areas, the chapters of this book have different authors, each with expertise in the area of law covered by the chapter. As a result, the tone, style, format, and structure of the chapters vary, and there is some overlap in the subject matter, though the editors have tried to minimize this. This book presents only some of the myriad of legal topics applicable to digital assets. Because the law in this area is constantly evolving, by the time you read this book, there may have been additional legal developments in the areas discussed.

Chapter 1 is an introduction to blockchain technology and assets. This chapter's intent is to familiarize the reader with the basic technological underpinnings of blockchain-based assets sufficient to understand the impetus for blockchain technology, the technology itself, and the unique challenges in applying existing laws.

---

2. Anthony Cuthbertson, *Elon Musk Says Mars Economy Will Run on Cryptocurency*, The Independent, December 29, 2020, https://www.independent.co.uk/life-style/gadgets-and-tech/elon-musk-mars-cryptocurrency-marscoin-b1779456.html.

Chapter 2 covers securities laws as applied to blockchain-based assets. As discussed in this chapter, application of securities laws presents vexing and unresolved challenges in the blockchain-based asset space. The chapter first addresses the question of which blockchain assets are securities, which remains the biggest legal issue in the industry. This chapter then addresses other topics such as what other securities industry activities are regulated and the future of blockchain-based securities.

Chapter 3 covers commodities laws. Commodities regulation presents similar issues to securities regulation, such as regulation of sales and trading of certain commodities-related assets. This chapter discusses, among other things, how the US commodities regulators have approached blockchain-based assets much more favorably than the securities regulators have approached them.

Chapter 4 discusses taxation with respect to blockchain-based assets. Blockchain-based assets can serve a variety of functions, such as payment mechanisms or investments. The federal tax code treatment of such assets may be nuanced and case specific.

Chapter 5 addresses blockchain-based digital assets as payment mechanisms. A variety of state and federal banking laws regulate the conduct of financial institutions, including money services business and money transmitters. This chapter explores the situations in which entities in the blockchain-based asset space may be considered financial institutions, subject to this regulation, and introduces the main types of regulation governing their conduct.

Chapter 6 complements Chapter 5 and focuses on regulations specifically intended to combat money laundering and terrorism financing, as applied to blockchain-based assets. This chapter covers a number of regulatory requirements and related compliance programs, including those concerning transaction reporting, suspicious activity monitoring, and customer due diligence.

Chapter 7 concerns the related field of compliance with federal laws restricting business with known bad actors and sanctioned countries. This chapter discusses how certain features of blockchain-based assets both facilitate and complicate compliance with sanctions restrictions.

Finally, Chapter 8 discusses blockchain-based assets in litigation not otherwise covered in prior chapters. Once again, blockchain-based assets have features that add twists on myriad traditional legal principles, and this chapter explores cases in which such issues have arisen.

1 Introduction to Blockchain-Based Assets

Michael Fluhr and Deborah Meshulam

INTRODUCTION

How much do you need to know about blockchain-based assets to give effective legal advice? Just the basics? Should you understand public-private key cryptography? Byzantine fault tolerance? Hash functions?

On the one hand, lawyers can benefit from understanding the technical details of a client's product. On the other hand, most lawyers likely face challenges in finding time to learn about Merkle roots or SHA-256. In this collection of essays covering key legal topics relevant to blockchain-based assets, we hope to provide an accessible and useful overview that will help practitioners begin to understand one of the most exciting technological developments that is still evolving and that we expect will become a major sector of the global economy.

To set the stage, this chapter describes blockchain-based assets at a high level designed to present key concepts in plain English. Our goal is to provide an introduction to blockchain-based assets that is accessible, practical, and stripped to the bare necessities.

The chapter starts by discussing a few aspects of more traditional digital assets, such as money. You might be surprised to see that these common assets are not quite what you thought. This exploration of traditional digital assets will prepare you to understand the impetus for and basic mechanics of blockchain. The chapter then introduces a classification scheme for common types of blockchain-based assets, including cryptocurrencies, stablecoins, utility tokens, and tokenized equity and debt. It concludes with a brief description of the blockchain industry and other potential uses for blockchain technology.

TRADITIONAL DIGITAL ASSETS

To understand blockchain, first consider more "traditional" digital assets. They permeate our modern world so regularly, intimately, and seamlessly that we do not typically stop to think about them.

Money is one of the most basic digital assets. Today, money is largely digital, more so every day. Some may find this counterintuitive. Many of us still pay in paper and coin, and you might picture bank vaults as containing stacks of $100 bills. But consider the following.

Consumers use cash in only a minority of transactions.[1] The Cash Product Office of the Federal Reserve System conducts a yearly study of several thousand individuals, tracking their payments and transactions over three consecutive days.[2] In 2019, consumers used cash in just 26 percent of transactions, consistent with 2018 and down from 30 percent in 2017.[3] The percentage of dollars exchanged in cash as a total of the amount of money transferred was even smaller; cash was used for only 7 percent of payments $100 and higher.[4] As expected, there is a trend toward using cash less frequently.[5]

Like consumers, banks largely transact without actual cash. As of late 2020, US banks hold only about $100B in hard currency in their vaults at any given moment, about $300 per person.[6] Banks are also transacting largely in the digital world, without movement of actual cash or coin. As a practical matter, many of us already live in a world virtually devoid of paper or metal currency.

As another example of a digital asset, consider ownership slices of a company, called *shares* or *stock*. There was a time when each share was represented by a physical, paper stock certificate. Today company ownership is tracked digitally, and paper certificates are a relic. Disney made

---

1. *See* Laura Kim, Raynil Kumar & Shaun O'Brien, *2020 Findings from the Diary of Consumer Payment Choice* (July 31, 2020), https://www.frbsf.org/cash/files/2020-findings-from-the-diary-of-consumer-payment-choice-july2020.pdf.

2. *Id.*

3. *Id.* at 3.

4. *Id.* at 6.

5. *Id.* at 5.

6. *See* The Fed. Rsrv. Bank of St. Louis, *How Much Cash Do Banks Keep in the Vault?*, THE FRED BLOG (Dec. 10, 2018), https://fredblog.stlouisfed.org/2018/12/how-much-cash-do-banks-keep-in-the-vault/.

headlines in 2013 when it announced it would stop printing stock certificates, which had become a collectors' item.[7]

As a final example, consider airline rewards points. Without question, there is no such thing as a physical airline point. They are an example of a purely digital asset.

Note the different ways in which these assets have value. Money has value only to the extent that another party agrees to accept it in exchange for goods and services. The owner of a share of stock may have certain specific rights defined by law and the corporation's documents, such as the right to elect corporate directors.[8] Airline rewards points may be exchanged for various services, such as airline tickets or upgrades, but these may be subject to change. As you will see, different blockchain-based assets also derive value from various sources.

DIGITAL ASSET ECOSYSTEMS

Traditional digital assets live on ecosystems. A digital asset ecosystem typically does at least the following two things. *First*, it records how much of the asset each participant in the system has. For example, a bank will track how many dollars each customer has in their account. A company will track how much stock is held by each registered owner. Or, an airline may track how many rewards points each of its customers has in their account. *Second*, a digital asset ecosystem will facilitate the transfer of assets between accounts. For example, a bank will allow a customer to transfer dollars to the account of someone else. Companies have transfer agents to facilitate the transfer of stock between one registered owner and another. Or, an airline will allow a customer to exchange reward points for various goods or services (e.g., flights, upgrades, etc.).

A digital asset ecosystem must do these things securely and reliably. The bank must ensure that only the correct amount is transferred and that only you can direct transfers from your account. The airline must ensure that today you have the same number of rewards points you had

7. *See* Anders Bylund, *Disney Stock Certificates Go Out of Style*, The Motley Fool (Oct. 10, 2013), https://www.fool.com/investing/general/2013/10/10/Disney-stock-certificates-go-out-of-style.aspx.

8. *See* 12B Fletcher, *Fletcher Cyclopedia of the Law of Corporations* § 5717 (West rev. ed. 2018).

yesterday (assuming you did not redeem any) and that the points can be redeemed only by you and not, say, a hacker.

Importantly, a digital asset ecosystem does not need an actual asset. Digital asset ecosystems do not necessarily require an underlying physical asset, such as a paper dollar or physical stock certificate. Similarly, digital asset ecosystems do not require an actual digital asset. Bank servers do not contain a digital dollar in the sense of code that can be copied or transferred to another drive, like a music or picture file. Instead, your bank merely keeps track of how many dollars you have in your account. Digital asset ecosystems comprise a ledger documenting account balances and transfers but often do not include any digital representations of the asset beyond this. Put another way, they simply track how much you have of an asset, which itself does not actually physically exist.

THE PROBLEM OF TRUSTED THIRD PARTIES

All of this raises a potential concern that has been referred to as the "problem of trusted third parties."[9] Notice that all of the digital assets mentioned earlier require trust in centralized third parties to track account balances and facilitate transfers. In the case of money, we entrust this function to banks, a few in particular: over half of all bank assets in the United States are now held by just five banks.[10] And the Federal Reserve plays a central role in all of this.[11] In the case of stocks, we entrust these functions to a complex web of parties, including brokers,

---

9. *See* Nick Szabo, *Trusted Third Parties Are Security Holes*, Satoshi Nakamoto Institute (originally published in 2001), https://nakamotoinstitute.org/trusted-third-parties/.

10. Wallace Turbeville, *The Bank Oligopoly Sucks Away Economic Value*, U.S. News & World Report (July 17, 2013), https://www.usnews.com/debate-club/should-big-banks-be-broken-up/banking-has-become-too-concentrated.

11. *See* Board of Governors of the Federal Reserve, *Fostering Payment and Settlement System Safety and Efficiency*, https://www.federalreserve.gov/aboutthefed/payment-systems-video.htm (last visited Mar. 8, 2021). Richard Gendal Brown, CTO at R3, has published a simple but comprehensive explanation of how money moves around the banking system. *See* Richard Gendal Brown, *A Simple Explanation of How Money Moves Around the Banking System*, https://gendal.me/2013/11/24/a-simple-explanation-of-how-money-moves-around-the-banking-system (last visited Mar. 8, 2021).

custodians, clearing agents, and transfer agents.[12] In the case of airline points, we entrust this function to the airline.

Over the years, some have objected to this reliance on trusted third parties. One concern is that these intermediary third parties tend to multiply, and each one imposes additional transaction costs in the form of fees and delays. Sending money from a bank in country *X* to a bank in country *Y* may require the assistance of several banks in between and can take many days or even weeks.[13] Transferring stock ownership from one individual to another may require brokers for each party, an exchange, a clearinghouse, a transfer agent, a custodian, and even other parties.[14] Each of these entities will impose fees, increasing transaction costs. Another concern is that these third parties require users to provide sensitive personal information, such as a password and address, which may be subject to fraud and theft.[15]

Setting aside whether these criticisms have merit, they do raise a critical question: is there a digital asset ecosystem that reliably records user account information and processes transactions but does not require reliance on any trusted third party?

ENTER THE BLOCKCHAIN

Blockchain technology can provide a solution. To illustrate, consider a case study of the most well-known and used blockchain and its native currency: Bitcoin.

Case Study: Bitcoin

Bitcoin is essentially a currency, not too different in many ways than the dollar. Like the dollar, Bitcoin can be exchanged for goods and services

---

12. Richard Brown has published a highly recommended explanation on this subject as well. *See* Richard Gendal Brown, *A Simple Explanation of How Shares Move Around the Securities Settlement System*, https://gendal.me/2014/01/05/a-simple-explanation-of-how-shares-move-around-the-securities-settlement-system (last visited Mar. 8, 2021).

13. *See* Brown, *supra* note 11.

14. *See* Brown, *supra* note 12; *see also* Szabo, *supra* note 9 (describing costs that the .com domain name registry Verisign charges).

15. *See* Szabo, *supra* note 9.

at rates agreed upon by buyers and sellers. For example, as of October 2020, Overstock will allow a customer to pay for furniture using Bitcoin.[16] Also, like the dollar, and unlike, say, a stock share, Bitcoin does not entitle the holder to anything in particular; a holder can only hope or expect that a merchant, such as Overstock, will accept it as payment. Like the banking system does for dollars, there exists a secure ecosystem that tracks how many Bitcoins (and fractions thereof) are in each Bitcoin holder's account and, at the holder's request, processes transactions from one holder's account to another. Further, like other types of digital assets, there exist no actual tangible or even digital representation of a Bitcoin other than the ledger described earlier. There is only a system for tracking how much Bitcoin each account holder has and for moving amounts between accounts.

The ecosystem that tracks Bitcoin account balances and processes transactions between them is one example of a blockchain (in this case, the Bitcoin blockchain). At its core, it comprises an ever-growing list (or "ledger") of transactions in Bitcoin from one "account" to another.[17] These lists are chunked together in "blocks" of transactions, and successive blocks are linked together cryptographically in a "chain": thus the term *blockchain*.

A typical, simplified Bitcoin blockchain entry would read something like the following:[18]

From	To	Amount	Time
1M82H9x3Q3g DphywVTk 5Lu3u 6bmCb9ZNCv	37cyf2YVJJ3je NJDsyzTRQ6 qzzBHcJ4Ru8	.00535372 BTC	2018-06-26 00:54:14

16. *See How do I pay with Bitcoin?* OVERSTOCK.COM, https://help.overstock.com/help/s/article/Bitcoin (last visited Mar. 8, 2021).

17. Each "account" on the Bitcoin blockchain is uniquely identified by a long alphanumeric string, such as "1M82H9x3Q3gDphywVTk5Lu3u6bmCb9ZNCv," and is more accurately called a *public address*. For various reasons, no one refers to Bitcoin "accounts" but rather to "addresses." Sometimes addresses may be referred to as "wallets," though this is actually a misnomer, as wallets more specifically refer to pieces of software that record addresses and allow access to the Bitcoin blockchain. Blockchain vernacular is generally somewhat inconsistent.

18. This is an actual transaction that can be verified with any Bitcoin blockchain explorer, such as the free one available at https://www.blockchain.com/explorer.

This entry shows that on June 26, 2018, at approximately 12:54 a.m. UTC, the owner or other password holder of account (or "address") 1M82H9x-3Q3gDphywVTk5Lu3u6bmCb9ZNCv transferred.00535372 Bitcoin from that address to address 37cyf2YVJJ3jeNJDsyzTRQ6qzzBHcJ4Ru8. The Bitcoin blockchain comprises an ever-growing list of these kinds of transactions, chunked into linked blocks of 1,000 or so transactions.

What is remarkable about this ecosystem and what distinguishes it from the ecosystems for money, stocks, and airline points, is that it is not run by a single entity (in the way that an airline runs the points ecosystem) or even a small number of entities (in the way that banks run the dollar ecosystem). Rather, the Bitcoin blockchain is run by innumerable, unaffiliated participants who dedicate some computing power to the enterprise. These participants include individuals running Bitcoin software on their personal laptops, huge, enterprise Bitcoin server farms, and everything in between. Right now, you can download and run Bitcoin software and, assuming your computer is online, volunteer your computer to the endeavor. Participants do this at least in part because the Bitcoin blockchain ecosystem will periodically reward them for doing so with Bitcoin, allocated as a practical matter by chance to participants in proportion to the amount of computing power they dedicate to the network.[19]

The participants in this system do not need to be trustworthy. The design of the ecosystem reliably ensures that, like the dollar and stock ecosystems, you will have as much Bitcoin in each account today as you did yesterday (other than any transfers) and that transactions are processed only at your request. The system itself ensures trust.

Also, unlike the ecosystems for many other digital assets, such as stock, you can directly interact with the Bitcoin blockchain. You can download certain Bitcoin software and create a new account and, after receiving Bitcoin from another account, initiate transfers yourself. Compare this to transferring stock, which requires numerous parties and is not practical for the average individual stockholder.

---

19. This receipt of these newly created Bitcoins as a reward for participating in the network is called *mining*. In reality, in 2021 there are so many specialized computers dedicated to the Bitcoin ecosystem that any given individual who dedicates a non-specialized PC to the task would likely have to do so for some time—statistically, many, many years—before the odds of receiving any Bitcoin reward materialize. This statistical system that weights the chance of a Bitcoin reward in proportion to the computing power dedicated to it is called a *proof-of-work* network.

In theory, Bitcoin can function as a currency, and the Bitcoin blockchain can function as a payments system free from some of the concerns that some have with the existing system of dollars. A holder can send Bitcoin from their address to another holder, anywhere in the world, without a central intermediary and practically anonymously.[20]

Without going into technical detail, the Bitcoin blockchain and other similar ecosystems achieve secure and often anonymous transactions through various mechanisms. Transactions are verified on the blockchain through a consensus of the majority of the computers in the ecosystem.

An Interesting Aside on the Unknown Origin of Bitcoin

The mysterious origin of Bitcoin warrants a mention for the sake of intrigue and as an illustration of how its decentralized blockchain developed. As explained earlier, the Bitcoin ecosystem is run by innumerable, independent participants. But who was the first? Who invented this ecosystem and developed the software used to run it? No one knows, and what is known only raises more questions.

While the idea of a virtual currency has been around for many decades, the trail of evidence about Bitcoin's origins begins in the late 2000s. Possibly the earliest known reference to the name *Bitcoin* is from August 18, 2008, when an unknown individual registered the domain name "bitcoin.org."[21] Two months later, on October 31, 2008, an individual going by the name Satoshi Nakamoto sent an email from satoshi@vistomail.com to the public mailing list Cryptography on the website https://www.metzdowd.com.[22] In the email, the possibly pseudonymous Nakamoto informed recipients that they were "working on a new electronic cash system that's fully peer-to-peer, with no trusted

20. Subsequent chapters discuss various exceptions to this anonymity feature, which can pose challenges for compliance with anti–money laundering and other laws.

21. *See* ICANN/Lookup, *Domain Name Registration Data Lookup*, https://lookup.icann.org/lookup (last visited Mar. 8, 2021).

22. *See* Posting of Satoshi Nakamoto, satoshi@vistomail.com, Bitcoin P2P e-cash paper (Oct. 31, 2008, 14:10 EDT), https://www.metzdowd.com/pipermail/cryptography/2008-October/014810.html (last visited Mar. 8, 2021). As of late 2020, the Cryptography mailing list at https://www.metzdowd.com appears active. *See* https://www.metzdowd.com/mailman/listinfo/cryptography (last visited Mar. 8, 2021).

third party" and included a link to a paper entitled "Bitcoin: A Peer-to-Peer Electronic Cash System," which described the Bitcoin ecosystem.[23] In January 2009, Nakamoto sent another message to the metzdowd Cryptography mailing list with a link to download software to "run a node and generate blocks" (i.e., participate in the ecosystem).[24] On January 3, 2009, the first "block" of transactions (the "genesis block") was created.[25]

In 2010, the first known commercial Bitcoin transaction occurred.[26] Florida software programmer Laszlo Hanyecz had been mining Bitcoins on his computer and persuaded someone to accept the new virtual currency in exchange for two pizzas. The price: 10,000 Bitcoins—worth roughly $120 million as of October 2020.[27]

Satoshi Nakamoto's identity remains unknown. No individual, by that name or otherwise, has presented credible evidence that they are the Satoshi Nakamoto who circulated the October 2008 email. Media outlets from the *New Yorker* to *Newsweek* to *Wired* have attempted to investigate and uncover Nakamoto's true identity, but efforts so far are inconclusive.[28]

Other Blockchains

Bitcoin's blockchain is the most well known, but there are many others, usually each with its own native currency, and the blockchain universe continues to grow. After Bitcoin, the next most well-known and used blockchain is Ethereum, which hosts a native asset called Ether

---

23. *See* Satoshi Nakamoto, *Bitcoin: A Peer-to-Peer Electronic Cash System*, https://bitcoin.org/bitcoin.pdf (last visited Mar. 8, 2021).

24. *See* Posting of Satoshi Nakamoto, Bitcoin v0.1 released (Jan. 9, 2009, 17:05), https://www.mail-archive.com/cryptography@metzdowd.com/msg10142.html (last visited Mar. 8, 2021).

25. *See Genesis Block*, WIKIPEDIA, https://en.bitcoin.it/wiki/Genesis_block (last visited Mar. 8, 2021).

26. *See* Nick Bilton, *Disruptions: Betting on a Coin with No Realm*, N.Y. TIMES (Dec. 22, 2013).

27. *Id.*

28. Andy Greenberg & Gwern Branwen, *Is Bitcoin's Creator This Unknown Australian Genius? Probably Not*, WIRED (Dec. 12, 2015).

(or "ETH").[29] There are innumerable other blockchain or blockchain-like ecosystems, including Cardano, EOS, and Tezos. Many of these, most notably the Ethereum blockchain, allow for the creation of new assets, which can be securely tracked and transferred on the same blockchain.[30] For example, the Ethereum blockchain now hosts not just ETH but also innumerable other blockchain-based assets, often referred to as "tokens."[31] Just like the native ETH, the Ethereum blockchain securely records how much of each new token is held in various accounts (or "addresses") and processes transfers between accounts.

COMMON TYPES OF BLOCKCHAIN ASSETS

Today, blockchain assets are practically infinite in variation. There exists no uniformly recognized categorization, taxonomy, or nomenclature of blockchain assets (though some have tried).[32] Nonetheless, as discussed, there are blockchain assets with common features. This categorization and nomenclature is by no means standard, accepted, or flawless but is helpful in understanding how blockchain assets are typically used and regulated.

Cryptocurrencies

The blockchain assets discussed so far, including Bitcoin and Ether, are often referred to as *cryptocurrencies*. The holder of a Bitcoin or Ethereum address and the associated Bitcoin and Ether do not have any particular rights, other than the ability to transfer them to another address.

---

29. Many refer to this cryptocurrency also as Ethereum, though purists may claim that Ethereum is the name of the blockchain and ecosystem, while the native currency is properly called Ether or ETH.

30. New assets built on an existing blockchain typically differ in the underlying technology and may be referred to as "tokens" or something else, rather than cryptocurrency, though here too the nomenclature is inconsistent.

31. Many of these are created pursuant to certain technical standards, such as the popular ERC-20 standard.

32. *See, e.g.*, Paolo Tasca & Claudio J. Tessone, *A Taxonomy of Blockchain Technologies: Principles of Identification and Classification*, LEDGER J. 4 (2019), http://ledgerjournal.org/ojs/ledger/article/view/140/118 (last visited Mar. 8, 2021).

That is not to say that cryptocurrencies are without value. Quite the contrary. Cryptocurrencies may be exchanged for goods, services, or other currencies (crypto or fiat[33])—to the extent that such a market exists. For example, as previously mentioned, some retailers allow payment for goods in cryptocurrencies. Also, there exist numerous cryptocurrency "exchanges": electronic marketplaces where participants, including individuals, can trade cryptocurrencies for each other or for fiat currencies such as dollars.[34] As of late 2021, a Bitcoin could be bought or sold for approximately $50,000, and an Ether could be bought or sold for approximately $4,000.[35]

A common question is why an asset, such as Bitcoin, has any value such that it can be bought or sold for thousands of dollars on an exchange. One answer, admittedly a bit circular, is that certain assets are perceived by society as "stores of value," that is, assets that maintain their market value.[36] Modern stores of value include not only dollars and other currencies but also metals, such as gold and silver, the market value of which cannot be justified by intrinsic value alone. Stores of value are typically durable, divisible, transferable, and, most importantly, commonly accepted. Any asset may be considered a store of value under the right circumstances when a base level of demand is believed to exist.[37] In short, Bitcoin is worth $50,000 because buyers believe they will be able to resell it tomorrow for that amount (or more).

There are many reasons one might want to hold a store of value, such as gold or Bitcoin.[38] The asset may be seen, perhaps based on history, as something likely to rise with the cost of living and thus act as a

---

33. In this context, "fiat" means standard money such as dollars, euros, etc.

34. *See* Coinbase, https://www.coinbase.com (last visited Mar. 8, 2021); Gemini, https://www.gemini.com (last visited Mar. 8, 2021).

35. *See, e.g., Bitcoin (BTC)*, CoinDesk, https://www.coindesk.com/price/bitcoin (last visited Mar. 8, 2021); *Ethereum (ETH)*, CoinDesk, https://www.coindesk.com/price/ethereum (last visited Mar. 8, 2021).

36. *See* John P. Kelleher, *Why Do Bitcoins Have Value?*, Investopedia, https://www.investopedia.com/ask/answers/100314/why-do-bitcoins-have-value.asp; Lucas Downey, *Store of Value Definition*, Investopedia, https://www.investopedia.com/terms/s/storeofvalue.asp (last visited Mar. 8, 2021).

37. Downey, *supra*, note 36.

38. *See* Tony Daltorio, *8 Good Reasons to Own Gold*, Investopedia, https://available at www.investopedia.com/articles/basics/08/reasons-to-own-gold.asp (last visited Mar. 8, 2021).

hedge against inflation.[39] It may be seen, again perhaps based on history, as an asset that holds value among geopolitical uncertainty.[40] Or it may be seen as simply a good investment.[41]

Note, however, that stores of value do not always make usable currencies. Gold may be a good store of value, but you cannot use it to buy gum. One barrier to using stores of value as currency is price volatility. Like gold, Bitcoin and Ether have varied significantly in price over the past several years.[42] Bitcoin and Ethereum have increased in price more than fiftyfold over the past several years, with intermittent peaks and declines.[43] This volatility poses a number of practical barriers to the use of these assets as currency, particularly when measured against the dollar, which is widely accepted and holds a very stable value.

This leads to a discussion about another type of digital asset: stablecoins.

Stablecoins

Stablecoins are blockchain-based assets that are generally similar in design to cryptocurrencies but instead hold a steady exchange rate with some other asset, such as the dollar. Some stablecoins maintain a roughly 1:1 exchange rate with the dollar, most notably Tether, USD Coin, HUSD, and Gemini Dollar.[44] There are a variety of ways that stablecoins achieve price stability. For example, the issuer of USD Coin, a type of Ethereum token, sells each USD Coin for $1, which the issuer keeps in reserve for redemptions of USD Coin back to dollars, again at a 1:1 ratio.[45] The issuer is always willing to buy a USD Coin or sell a new one for $1. As a result, the

---

39. *See id.*

40. *See id.*

41. *See id.*

42. *See, e.g.*, *Bitcoin (BTC)*, CoinDesk, https://www.coindesk.com/price/bitcoin (last visited Mar. 8, 2021); *Ethereum (ETH)*, CoinDesk, https://www.coindesk.com/price/ethereum (last visited Mar. 8, 2021).

43. *See, e.g.*, *id.*

44. *See, e.g.*, https://www.cryptoslate.com/cryptos/stablecoin (displaying market price quotations for various stablecoins) (last visited Mar. 8, 2021).

45. *See Introducing USD Coin (USDC)–Stablecoin by Coinbase*, Coinbase, https://www.coinbase.com/usdc (last visited Mar. 8, 2021).

market price for USD Coin does not materially fluctuate from $1.[46] Other stablecoins, such as Dai (another Ethereum token), achieve stability in more complex ways.[47] Some stablecoins maintain price stability not with respect to the dollar but with respect to some other asset. For example, the stablecoin issuer Tether, which issues a $1 stablecoin called "Tether," also issues a token called "Tether Gold," each of which is backed by and thus retains price stability with respect to a troy ounce of gold.[48]

Stablecoins may deliver the price stability required to function as a replacement currency, including on the trading platforms that issue them. On many exchanges, they function as currency, and traders exchange assets for stablecoins rather than fiat currency.

Utility Tokens[49]

Another class of blockchain digital assets provides some "utility" or usefulness associated with the token. The utility may come from components on or off the blockchain. For example, Handshake is the native token of a blockchain and ecosystem also called Handshake.[50] A holder can use Handshake tokens on the Handshake blockchain to purchase certain top-level domain names, such as .firstbit, .http2, or .cantina, that can then be used for website domain names.[51] The purchaser of such a Handshake top-level domain, say .cantina, can use the Handshake blockchain to direct certain web browsers looking for a website ending in .cantina to the website of its choosing. Handshake essentially provides an alternative to

---

46. *See, e.g.*, *Stablecoin Coins*, https://www.cryptoslate.com/cryptos/stablecoin (displaying market price quotations for various stablecoins) (last visited Mar. 8, 2021).

47. *See, e.g.*, Dai 1.0, MAKER DEVELOPER, https://developer.makerdao.com/dai/1/ (describing a complex blockchain design that keeps the price of Dai at $1) (last visited Mar. 8, 2021).

48. *See* Tether Operations Ltd., *Tether Gold—A Digital Token Backed by Physical Gold* (updated Feb. 2, 2021), https://gold.tether.to/Tether%20Gold%20Whitepaper.pdf (last visited Mar. 8, 2021).

49. From here, the categorization and nomenclature get fuzzier and less standardized. As mentioned earlier, I believe the categorization and nomenclature proposed here are helpful and accurate. But, admittedly, they are by no means unimpeachable.

50. *See* HANDSHAKE, https://www.handshake.org (last visited Mar. 8, 2021).

51. *See* NAMEBASE, https://www.namebase.io (last visited Mar. 8, 2021). Namebase offers a platform for buying a domain name outright instead of renting a domain name from large corporations.

the traditional domain naming system maintained by ICANN and its contracting parties (including Verisign), which collectively control the .com, .org, .net, .edu, and other well-known domains. Other examples of such utility tokens include Filecoin, which allows holders of the native cryptocurrency FIL to pay blockchain miners for file storage,[52] and Helium, a blockchain ecosystem that rewards owners and other operators of "Helium Hotspots" (a type of last-mile wireless internet hardware device) with HNT tokens.[53] The Basic Attention Token can be used to obtain a variety of advertising services on the web browser Brave.[54]

Rights-Based Tokens

Some tokens confer upon the owner some legal right, usually defined by contract. For example, in 2020 Overstock issued "digitally enhanced" Series A-1 preferred shares, the transfer agent share registry which is duplicated on a blockchain.[55] The venture capital firm Blockchain Capital issued a BCAP token, which represents an interest in a fund: Blockchain Capital Digital Liquid Venture Fund, LP.[56] The tokens grant holders a portion of the profits earned by the fund.[57] Similar tokens representing debt securities have also been issued.[58]

Non-Fungible Tokens (NFTs)

NFTs have taken the blockchain world by storm in 2021. From a purely technological standpoint, NFTs are simply blockchain-based assets that, unlike many cryptocurrencies, such as Bitcoin, are not fungible or

---

52. *See What Is Filecoin?*, FILECOIN, https://docs.filecoin.io/about-filecoin/what-is-filecoin/ (last visited Mar. 8, 2021).

53. *See Get Involved*, HELIUM, https://www.helium.com/store (last visited Mar. 8, 2021).

54. *See* BASIC ATTENTION TOKEN, https://www.basicattentiontoken.org (last visited Mar. 8, 2021).

55. *See Overstock Dividend Shareholder Information*, OVERSTOCK.COM, https://www.overstock.com/dividend (last visited Mar. 8, 2021).

56. *See Blockchain Capital*, FORGE, https://www.sharespost.com/blockchain-capital_stock/ (last visited Mar. 8, 2021).

57. *See id.*

58. *See* Helen Partz, *Cadence Launches Blockchain-Based Tokenized Debt Marketplace*, COINTELEGRAPH (July 11, 2019), https://cointelegraph.com/news/cadence-launches-blockchain-based-tokenized-debt-marketplace.

divisible. In other words, each NFT token can be uniquely identified as it moves from address to address on a blockchain. Many companies have used NFTs to document ownership of a unique digital asset.

For example, the popular website NBATopShot.com sells short video clips (called "moments") of NBA players, ownership of which is recorded as an NFT on a blockchain called "Flow." The owner of a moment receives a limited license, the terms of which are set forth in the NBATopShot.com user agreement.[59] These moments are treated as collectible items, which can be traded on a marketplace on the website. When a moment is sold to another user on NBATopShot.com, the transfer in ownership of the underlying NFT is recorded on the Flow blockchain.

The use of and interest in NFTs, particularly as records of digital collectible ownership, have exploded in 2021. NFTs are used, among other things, to record and transfer ownership of virtual plots of land in a digital universe called Decentraland,[60] of digital art pieces called Nifties on a platform called Nifty Gateway,[61] and of digital felines in the blockchain-based game CryptoKitties.[62] In early March 2021, a JPG file created by Mike Winklemann (a digital artist known as "Beeple") was sold as an NFT at Christie's in an online auction for $69.3 million.[63]

THE BLOCKCHAIN INDUSTRY

While at the core of this industry are the decentralized miners and users, there are many centralized players. We already touched on two: issuers, meaning those who create blockchains and blockchain-based assets, and exchanges. But there are many others. "Custodians" hold blockchain-based assets for individuals and entities who want or have to keep their holdings with a secure third party. Prime brokers provide bespoke services, typically to larger, wealthier holders of cryptocurrency, such as helping

59. *See Terms of Use*, Top Shot, https://nbatopshot.com/terms (last visited April 16, 2021).

60. *See What Are NFTs?*, Decentraland, https://decentraland.org/blog/technology/what-are-nfts/ (last visited April 16, 2021).

61. *See* Nifty Gateway, https://niftygateway.com (last visited April 16, 2021).

62. *See* CryptoKitties, https:///www.cryptokitties.co (last visited April 16, 2021).

63. Scott Reyburn, *JPG File Sells for $69 Million, as 'NFT Mania' Gathers Pace*, N.Y. Times (Mar. 11, 2021, updated Mar. 25, 2021), https://www.nytimes.com/2021/03/11/arts/design/nft-auction-christies-beeple.html.

them sell large amounts off exchange. And of course, there are consulting firms, accounting firms, law firms, and a whole collection of other professional service firms that offer expertise in blockchain technology.

OTHER POTENTIAL USES FOR BLOCKCHAIN

There have been myriad proposed uses for blockchains outside of the digital asset space. At their core, blockchains are lists of data that, through their distributed nature, are resistant or immune to corruption. Proposed uses for blockchains (other than as digital asset ledgers) include as databases for medical records,[64] intellectual property rights,[65] and land titles.[66] There are many other proposed uses.

For several reasons, we do not discuss these in any more detail in this book. For one thing, in comparison to the digital assets described earlier, many of these blockchain uses are in their infancy or simply theoretical. For another, unlike digital assets, which implicate a common set of laws, these other blockchain uses may implicate an infinite variety of legal and regulatory regimes. These examples would implicate medical record regulations such as the Health Insurance Portability and Accountability Act (healthcare privacy regulations), intellectual property laws, and state and local land registry regulations and protocols. This book does not address these other legal landscapes.

INTRODUCTION TO BLOCKCHAIN REGULATION

At their core, blockchains are an information medium. The regulations they implicate have to do more with their application than their nature. For example, a blockchain used to store medical information may implicate

64. *See* Anuraag A. Vazirani et al., *Blockchain Vehicles for Efficient Medical Record Management*, NPJ DIGIT. MED. 3, 1 (2020), available at www.nature.com/articles/s41746-019-0211-0.

65. *See* Birgit Clark, *Blockchain and IP Law: A Match Made in Crypto Heaven?*, WIPO MAGAZINE (Feb. 2018), https://www.wipo.int/wipo_magazine/en/2018/01/article_0005.html.

66. *See* Qiuyun Shang & Allison Price, *A Blockchain-Based Land Titling Project in the Republic of Georgia*, 12 INNOVATIONS (2019), https://direct.mit.edu/itgg/article/12/3-4/72/9852/A-Blockchain-Based-Land-Titling-Project-in-the.

regulations concerning the privacy of medical records. A blockchain used to track land registries may implicate local real property laws and regulations. And so on.

What follows is a discussion of the regulatory regimes applicable to the most common uses for blockchain-based digital assets. In particular, the application of securities, commodities, tax, banking, payment, money transmission, anti–money laundering, and sanctions compliance laws to blockchain-based assets has generated extensive discussion and in some instances case law, which the following chapters discuss. Also included as a section on select issues in litigation.

2 | Blockchain-Based Assets as Securities

Deborah Meshulam and Michael Fluhr

INTRODUCTION

No area of law has generated more controversy in the blockchain space than US securities law. The high degree of regulation in the securities space combined with skepticism from US securities regulators is viewed by some as limiting innovation while precipitating enforcement actions and even criminal prosecutions. Private lawsuits have followed. But the industry has not given up and may be moving toward a framework for blockchain-based securities.

After a high-level analysis of the relevant securities laws, this chapter addresses the still-debated analysis of when a blockchain-based asset constitutes a security under US law, a crucial question given that classification as a security subjects an asset and those involved in its offer, sale, and promotion to US securities laws related to registration and disclosure, to name a few. This chapter also examines securities regulation as applied to various participants in the securities markets, including broker-dealers, investment companies, investment advisers, and exchanges. Finally, some special regulatory challenges in the issuance and trading of blockchain-based securities are discussed. The chapter does not address every speech or enforcement action but rather highlights key developments to date in the application of US securities laws to blockchain-based assets.

Ultimately, many of the issues discussed in this chapter remain unanswered. Our goal is to familiarize readers with current issues and the framework for their analysis as they existed when this chapter was written.

INTRODUCTION TO SECURITIES AND THEIR REGULATION

What Are Securities?

The question of what constitutes a security is complex and hotly contested in the context of digital assets. While this chapter examines that question in greater detail, US law defines *security* very broadly to encompass virtually any type of instrument that represents some form of financial value.

Company stock is a quintessential security. Investors purchase stock, which represents ownership in a company in common with other stockholders, and hope to profit from the efforts of the company.[1] Bonds are another common example of securities.[2] Stocks and bonds are not the only instruments that fit the definition and thus are not the only types of securities. There are many others.

Not all investments are securities, however. For example, investments made for consumptive purposes such as the purchase of shares in a cooperative apartment in which the purchaser plans to reside are not securities.[3] Precious metals are not securities because their value is intrinsic and does not result from investment in a common enterprise or the efforts of others.[4] The same is true for works of art or rare cars, which are also not securities.

Whether and when a blockchain-based asset constitutes a security is a question with much at stake because application of US securities laws to blockchain assets impacts the manner in which they can be distributed and exchanged. For blockchain-based assets, the key question is whether the asset is a type of security known as an *investment contract*.

---

1. *See* Landreth Timber Co. v. Landreth, 417 U.S. 681 (1985). *But see* United Hous. Found., Inc. v. Forman, 421 U.S. 837 (1975) (holding instruments labeled as "stock" may not constitute securities where they do not possess the significant characteristics typically associated with stock, such as right to receive dividends and capacity for appreciation).

2. *See* 15 U.S. § 77b(a)(1).

3. *See* United Hous. Found., Inc. v. Forman, 421 U.S. 837 (1975).

4. *See* 1 Thomas Lee Hazen, Treatise on the Law of Securities Regulation § 1.48 (7th ed. 2016).

Securities Laws Relevant to Blockchain-Based Securities

The Securities Act of 1933 ("Securities Act" or "1933 act") and the Securities Exchange Act of 1934 ("Exchange Act" or "1934 act") are two principal statutes relevant to blockchain-based assets that are securities.

Securities Act of 1933

The Securities Act is a disclosure-focused law. It requires that investors receive information about securities being offered to the public and prohibits fraud, misrepresentations, and other misconduct in connection with the offer and sale of securities. Its purpose is to enable investors to make informed judgments about whether to purchase a company's securities.[5]

The Securities Act fulfills this purpose in part through Section 5 by requiring that every offer and sale of securities be "registered" with the U.S. Securities and Exchange Commission (SEC) or exempt from such registration under one or more statutory exemptions—all of which contain their own requirements.[6] Registration is time consuming, expensive, and complicated. It requires the issuer to prepare a registration statement containing extensive disclosures and, among other things, audited financial statements.[7] A registration statement offering a security is subject to SEC review and approval before it is declared "effective."[8] A security offered to the public requires an effective registration statement unless there is an exemption.[9]

The Securities Act and implementing SEC regulations provide a number of exemptions from the section 5 registration requirement. The exemptions each have different requirements; two are discussed next.

---

5. *See* Elisabeth Keller & Gregory A. Gehlmann, *Introductory Comment: A Historical Introduction to the Securities Act of 1933 and the Securities Exchange Act of 1934*, 49 Ohio State L.J. 329, 330 (1988).

6. *Id.*; *see* 15 U.S.C. § 77e.

7. *See id.*; *see also* U.S. Securities and Exchange Commission, *What Is a Registration Statement?*, https://www.sec.gov/smallbusiness/goingpublic/registrationstatement (last visited May 13, 2021).

8. *See id.*

9. *See* 15 U.S.C. § 77d(a) (listing exemptions from registration requirement).

One of the most commonly used exemptions to registration is SEC Regulation D, which exempts smaller, private sales of securities to individuals who meet sophistication or wealth requirements or certain institutional investors.[10] Under Regulation D, Rule 506, issuers can sell securities to "accredited" or "sophisticated" investors without registering the sale, so long as they meet certain requirements. Among these, issuers must file what is known as a "Form D" with the SEC after they first sell their securities.[11] Form D is a notice that includes the names and addresses of the company's promoters, executive officers, and directors as well as some details about the offering but contains little other information about the company. Also, the securities issued are "restricted," meaning they cannot be resold absent satisfaction of additional requirements. The Regulation D exemption is often used by small, emerging growth companies (e.g., startups) to issue equity to early investors (e.g., venture capital firms).

Another exception to the section 5 registration requirement is Regulation A, which involves a registration-like but less complex process, sometimes referred to as "registration light."[12] Regulation A imposes a monetary cap on the amount a company can raise, either $20 million or $75 million (depending on which of two subexemptions is used). Under Regulation A, securities may be offered and sold to both accredited and retail investors.[13] Unlike other exemptions, such as Regulation D, securities sold under Regulation A are immediately tradable.[14] Also, issuers may engage in public advertising to market and promote the offering, subject to certain restrictions.[15]

There are other exceptions as well, such as Rule 504 of Regulation D and Regulation Crowdfunding, which are available only for offerings of up to $10 million and $5 million, respectively, and which have additional requirements.[16] Rule 144, in conjunction with Securities Act section 4(a)(1),

---

10. *See* 17 C.F.R. §§ 230.500–508.

11. 17 C.F.R. § 230.506.

12. *See* 17 C.F.R. §§ 230.251–263.

13. *See* U.S. Securities and Exchange Commission, *Overview of Exemptions*, https://www.sec.gov/smallbusiness/exemptofferings/exemptofferingschart (last visited May 14, 2021).

14. *Id.*

15. *Id.*

16. *See* U.S. Securities and Exchange Commission, Overview of Capital-Raising Exemptions, https://www.sec.gov/smallbusiness/exemptofferings/exemptofferingschart (last visited May 14, 2021).

allows resale of restricted securities after they have been held for a specified waiting period. Regulation S disclaims regulatory authority over foreign offerings with little or no connection to the United States.[17] In general, however, there is usually no exemption available to an issuer when securities are publicly offered and sold to retail investors.

Securities Exchange Act of 1934 ("Exchange Act")

The Exchange Act created the SEC and gave it "broad authority over all aspects of the securities industry,"[18] including the "power to register, regulate, and oversee brokerage firms, transfer agents, and clearing agencies as well as the nation's securities self-regulatory organizations (SROs)," such as the Financial Industry Regulatory Authority, the New York Stock Exchange, and NASDAQ.[19] The Exchange Act requires a variety of securities market participants, such as exchanges and brokers, to register with the SEC,[20] although exemptions exist to these registration requirements. Under the Exchange Act, the SEC has also promulgated an array of periodic reporting requirements for companies with publicly traded securities.[21] The Exchange Act also contains anti-fraud provisions related to the purchase and sale of securities.

Other Securities Laws and Regulations

The Investment Company Act of 1940 regulates companies, such as mutual funds, that engage primarily in investing and trading of securities and whose own securities are offered to public investors.[22] The Investment Advisers Act of 1940 regulates firms and individuals who receive compensation for providing advice about investing in securities.[23] The Sarbanes-Oxley Act of 2002 and Dodd-Frank Wall Street Reform and Consumer Protection Act of 2010 enacted a number of additional reforms

---

17. *See* 17 C.F.R. §§ 230.901–905.

18. *See* U.S. Securities and Exchange Commission, *The Laws That Govern the Securities Industry*, https://www.sec.gov/answers/about-lawsshtml.html (last visited May 14, 2021).

19. *See id.*

20. *See id.*

21. *See id.*

22. *See id.*

23. *See id.*

and protections, passed in the wake of the 2000 and 2008 financial crises, respectively.[24]

The scope and breadth of these laws and implementing regulations would occupy an entire treatise. If a blockchain asset is a security, it becomes subject to this broad regulatory regime.

WHAT BLOCKCHAIN ASSETS ARE SECURITIES

Given the pervasive regulation of the securities markets, arguably one of the most important legal issues facing the blockchain industry is whether a particular blockchain-based asset constitutes a security, in particular, a specific type of security called an *investment contract.*

Investment Contracts and *Howey*

The federal securities laws previously described all define the term *security* in a similar way: by list. For example, section 2(a)(1) of the Securities Act states the following:

> The term "security" means any note, stock, treasury stock, security future, security-based swap, bond, debenture, evidence of indebtedness, certificate of interest or participation in any profit-sharing agreement, collateral-trust certificate, preorganization certificate or subscription, transferable share, **investment contract**, voting-trust certificate, certificate of deposit for a security, fractional undivided interest in oil, gas, or other mineral rights, any put, call, straddle, option, or privilege on any security (including any interest therein or based on the value thereof), or any put, call, straddle, option, or privilege entered into on a national securities exchange relating to foreign currency, or, in general, any interest or instrument commonly known as a "security," or any certificate of interest or participation in, temporary or interim certificate for, receipt for, guarantee of, or warrant or right to subscribe to or purchase, any of the foregoing.

Section 3(a)(10) of the Exchange Act also defines security through a list although its list differs slightly from the list contained in the Securities Act. Investment Company Act Section 2(a)(36) defines security through a list as well. This definition by list raises a potential issue. Certain instruments

24. *See id.*

share relevant features of those listed above and arguably require regulation as a security but do not fit neatly into any listed category.

The Supreme Court addressed this issue in the seminal case of *SEC v. W.J. Howey Co.*, in which the court articulated a test to determine if a financial instrument constitutes an investment contract and therefore a security.[25]

Howey involved the sale of certain interests in orange groves. The Howey Company owned land in Florida where it cultivated the groves. To fund new development of the groves, Howey sought outside financing and turned to out-of-state tourists who visited a hotel that adjoined one of its properties. Each prospective purchaser was offered both a land sales contract and a service contract. Under the service contract, a Howey affiliate would manage the land on the purchaser's behalf. Since the offerees were primarily nonresidents with no wherewithal to care for orange groves, most of those who purchased an interest in the groves also accepted the service contract arrangement. Upon payment of the purchase price, the land was conveyed to the purchaser, but individual tracts were not separately fenced and were identified by landmarks intelligible only through a plat book record. The service contract granted Howey a leasehold interest and "full and complete" possession of the land. For a specified fee plus the cost of labor and materials, Howey had full discretion and authority over the cultivation of the groves and the harvest and marketing of the crops. Without Howey's consent, purchasers had no right of entry to market the crops. Instead, Howey allocated a share of net profits to each purchaser after the harvest.

Based on these allegations, the SEC instituted an action against Howey alleging it had engaged in the offer and sale of an unregistered and nonexempt security, in violation of Securities Act § 5(a). The district court found that Howey had not offered or sold a security and denied the SEC's request for an injunction. The Fifth Circuit affirmed.

The Supreme Court reversed. The court began its analysis by considering the historical background against which the federal securities laws were adopted, as well as Congress's intent in enacting the Securities Act and including the concept of an investment contract. The court reasoned that the term *investment contract* "embodies a flexible rather than a static principle, one that is capable of adaptation to meet the countless and variable schemes devised by those who seek the use of the money of

25. SEC v. W.J. Howey Co., 328 U.S. 293 (1946).

others on the promise of profits."[26] In this view, a flexible understanding of what an investment contract is helps ensure that the reach of the federal securities laws is not unduly circumscribed.

The court concluded that the transactions at issue clearly involved investment contracts:

> The respondent companies are offering something more than fee simple interests in land, something different from a farm or orchard coupled with management services. They are offering an opportunity to contribute money and to share in the profits of a large citrus fruit enterprise managed and partly owned by respondents. They are offering this opportunity to persons who reside in distant localities and who lack the equipment and experience requisite to the cultivation, harvesting and marketing of the citrus products. Such persons have no desire to occupy the land or to develop it themselves; they are attracted solely by the prospects of a return on their investment. . . . A common enterprise managed by respondents or third parties with adequate personnel and equipment is therefore essential if the investors are to achieve their paramount aim of a return on their investments. Their respective shares in this enterprise are evidenced by land sales contracts and warranty deeds, which serve as a convenient method of determining the investors' allocable shares of the profits. The resulting transfer of rights in land is purely incidental.[27]

Furthermore, as the court explained, the purchasers did not buy interests in the land so that they could eat the produce that Howey grew. The purchasers' motivation was investment, not consumption.

In short, the purchasers depended on Howey to run an orange business for them. The allocation of responsibility between Howey and the purchasers is similar to the separation of ownership and control that characterizes the corporate form, where there exists a centralized management team and generally passive shareholders.

Over time, the *Howey* test has been formulated in a number of ways, most commonly as a four-part test. Specifically, tracking the *Howey* definition, an instrument constitutes an investment contract if it entails (1) an investment of money, (2) in a common enterprise, (3) with the expectation of profit, and (4) the profit is expected to derive from the

---

26. 328 U.S. at 299.

27. *Id.* at 299.

efforts of others.[28] The common enterprise element may be satisfied with either horizontal or vertical commonality.[29] Horizontal commonality exists when investors' assets are pooled and the fortunes of each investor are tied to those of both other investors and the success of the enterprise.[30] Vertical commonality exists where the fortunes of investors are tied to those of the promoter ("strict" vertical commonality) or when the fortunes of the investors are tied to the efforts of the promoter ("broad" vertical commonality).[31] Regarding the fourth element, *Howey* stated that the expectation of profits should stem "solely" from the efforts of the promoter or third party.[32] But subsequent decisions focused on whether profits were "derived" from efforts of others.[33]

For more than seventy years, courts have applied the *Howey* test to analyze a wide array of financial arrangements, including limited partnership interests, condominiums, sale-leasebacks of payphones, and life settlements, to determine whether they are subject to regulation by the SEC.

What Assets Are Not Securities?

Before applying *Howey* to blockchain-based assets, it is helpful to consider cases in which courts have identified assets that do not constitute securities under the test. For example, in *United Housing Foundation, Inc. v. Forman*, the Supreme Court revisited *Howey* as applied to shares of stock that entitled purchasers to lease an apartment in a state-subsidized and supervised nonprofit housing cooperative.[34]

28. *See, e.g.*, Securities and Exchange Commission v. Telegram Group Inc., 448 F.Supp.3d 352, 367 (S.D.N.Y. 2020).

29. *Id.* at 369.

30. *Id.*

31. *Id.* There is a circuit split over whether broad vertical commonality can satisfy the common enterprise element. *Id.* (Second Circuit holds that broad vertical commonality does not satisfy *Howey*); *see In re* Living Benefits Asset Management, LLC, 916 F.3d 528, 536 (5th Cir. 2019) (Fifth and Eleventh Circuits apply broad vertical commonality).

32. *Telegram*, 448 F.Supp.3d at 375.

33. *Id.*

34. United Hous. Found., Inc. v. Forman, 421 U.S. 837 (1975).

Nonprofit cooperative housing corporation Riverbay was organized to own and operate land and buildings to provide affordable housing.[35] Eligible purchasers could acquire an apartment by buying eighteen shares of Riverbay stock for each room desired.[36] The shares functioned as a recoverable deposit and could not be transferred, pledged, or encumbered, only resold back to Riverbay for the initial price.[37] The majority of the cost of the housing project was to be financed by a loan from the New York Private Housing Finance Agency, with only a small portion raised by the sale of shares to tenants.[38] Tenants would then pay monthly rental charges.[39] These rental charges increased, and fifty-seven residents sued on behalf of all apartment owners, alleging, among other claims, violation of the Securities Act and Exchange Act anti-fraud provisions.[40] The district court dismissed these claims on the ground that the stock sold did not constitute a security, but the Second Circuit reversed, and the Supreme Court granted review.[41] The court immediately rejected the assertion that the shares constituted securities merely because they were called "stock."[42] The court then reversed the Second Circuit and reinstated the district court's dismissal, reasoning that the shares did not constitute securities under *Howey* because "there can be no doubt that investors were attracted solely by the prospect of acquiring a place to live, and not by financial returns on their investments."[43]

In *Noa v. Key Futures, Inc.*, defendant Key Futures offered silver bars for sale and as part of the sale contract guaranteed their purity and promised to store them for the buyer.[44] Buyer Union Bank was dissatisfied and sued for violations of the Securities Act and Exchange Act. On Key Futures's motion for summary judgment, the district court dismissed the bank's claims, and on appeal the Ninth Circuit affirmed, holding that as a matter of law no investment contract had been created.

---

35. *Id.* at 840–41.

36. *Id.* at 842.

37. *Id.*

38. *Id.* at 843.

39. *Id.*

40. *Id.* at 844–45.

41. *Id.* at 845.

42. *Id.* at 848.

43. *Id.* at 853.

44. 638 F.2d 77, 79 (9th Cir. 1980).

The court reasoned that once the purchase was made, the profits of the investor depended not on any managerial efforts of Key Future but on fluctuations in the silver market. Purchase of the silver and free storage did not, in the court's view, amount to "undeniably significant" efforts of others, as required to satisfy *Howey*.

A few years later, the Ninth Circuit reached a similar conclusion with respect to contracts for gold coins in *S.E.C. v. Belmont Reid & Co., Inc.*[45] The SEC filed a complaint against defendant Belmont Reid and several individual defendants, alleging violations of the Securities Act and Exchange Act stemming from Belmont's sale of various types of contracts for the purchase of gold. The contracts were not strictly cash-for-gold but contained various provisions intended to offer protection for the buyers, such as guarantees that if the price of gold fell below $375 per ounce at delivery, purchasers would be paid the difference. On defendants' motion for summary judgment, the district court dismissed several claims, and on appeal the Ninth Circuit affirmed. The court held that the profits did not come "solely" from efforts of others; rather the purchasers had as their primary purpose to profit from the anticipated increase in the world price of gold. Any reliance on the managerial efforts of others was merely as any shown by an ordinary buyer on any ordinary seller.

Application of *Howey* to Blockchain-Based Assets

It is against this legal backdrop that the SEC has evaluated the emergence of blockchain-based assets and assessed whether those assets are securities. The SEC has not acted through direct regulation on this topic. Rather, it has issued an investigative report, pursued enforcement actions, and issued a handful of no-action letters. In addition, various commissioners and staff members have spoken publicly or issued written statements regarding their views as to when a blockchain-based asset is a security. SEC divisions have also issued statements on this topic, including the SEC Division of Investment Management's *Statement on Digital Asset Securities Issuance and Trading*. Finally, the SEC's Strategic Hub for Innovation and Financial Technology (FinHub) published a *Framework for "Investment Contract" Analysis of Digital Assets*. The framework represents the views of SEC staff members and is not a regulation; it is not binding on the SEC.

The SEC began its public evaluation of *Howey's* application to blockchain-based assets in mid-2017 with its *Report of Investigation*

45. S.E.C. v. Belmont Reid & Co., Inc., 794 F.2d 1388 (9th Cir. 1986).

Pursuant to Section 21(a) of the Securities Exchange Act of 1934: The DAO (DAO Report).

The DAO Report

Throughout the 2010s, growing numbers of new blockchain-based assets were created and sold. While some of these assets were issued on new blockchains, it became relatively easy to create and issue new assets on existing blockchains, particularly the Ethereum blockchain. In many cases, creators and sellers did not view the assets as securities and neither registered the assets with the SEC nor took steps to ensure compliance with an exemption from registration (such as limiting sales only to accredited investors, under Regulation D). The initial sales of these assets were often referred to as *initial coin offerings* (ICOs), a play on the term *initial public offering* (IPO), used to refer to a company's first public offering of stock.[46]

On July 25, 2017, the SEC weighed in, reporting on an investigation into the unregistered sale of assets called DAO tokens.[47] In April and May 2016, the creators of the decentralized autonomous organization (DAO) sold over a billion DAO tokens in exchange for approximately 12 million ETH (then valued at roughly $150 million). The assets were sold through a publicly available website through which anyone could purchase DAO tokens, through soliciting media attention, and through almost daily updates on the DAO's status on the website and in online forums. The issuers promised purchasers that DAO tokens would permit them to vote on, participate in, and receive profits from unspecified blockchain-based projects, which would be funded by the invested ETH. Purchasers could also freely trade DAO tokens on secondary markets. The issuers exercised substantial control over the project selection.

After an investigation, the SEC determined that DAO tokens constituted securities and had been offered and sold publicly without a registration statement, in violation of the Securities Act. On these facts,

---

46. While once ubiquitous, the term *initial coin offering* (ICO) has fallen out of vogue as it is poorly defined and sometimes pejoratively associated with illegal or low-value sales of new assets. Particularly given its lack of clear meaning, we avoid using it where possible.

47. U.S. Securities and Exchange Commission, *Report of Investigation Pursuant to Section 21(a) of the Securities Exchange Act of 1934: The DAO* (Release No. 81207, July 25, 2017), https://www.sec.gov/litigation/investreport/34-81207.pdf.

the SEC concluded that DAO token purchasers had invested "money" (which need not take the form of cash) with a reasonable expectation of profits. The SEC also concluded that the expected profit derived from the managerial efforts of others, specifically the issuers. The SEC observed that the issuers marketed their involvement as a selling feature, providing critical expertise and efforts in monitoring the network operation, safeguarding network funds, and determining which projects to pursue. In contrast, DAO token holders had only limited rights to actually participate in these projects, particularly given the dilution of authority across many dispersed holders, rendering them "substantially reliant on the managerial efforts" of the issuers. The SEC analogized these limited rights to those of a voting shareholder in a corporation. While the SEC ultimately decided not to pursue an enforcement action in this matter, it issued the report to advise the blockchain industry "to take appropriate steps to ensure compliance with the U.S. federal securities laws."[48]

Utility Tokens and SAFTs

After the DAO report and as SEC regulatory scrutiny intensified, many blockchain projects continued to issue tokens directly to retail investors. As the SEC began to pursue cases alleging that these issuances were unregistered offers and sales of securities, one solution offered was a product called the Simple Agreement for Future Tokens (SAFT).[49]

The SAFT was described in a paper published on October 2, 2017. According to the paper, tokens that represent a consumptive good, which the paper labeled "utility tokens," do not constitute an investment contract security.[50] The paper reasoned that purchasers may not have a profit motive and that any increase in price in tokens on a mature, decentralized blockchain would come only from market supply and demand, not the efforts of a third party. The paper described utility tokens as those with "intrinsic utility" and gave as an example tokens that "will simply act as

---

48. *Id.* at 2.

49. *See* Juan Batiz-Benet, Jesse Clayburgh, & Marco Santori, *The SAFT Project: Toward a Compliance Token Sale Framework* (Oct. 2, 2017), https://www.cooley.com/-/media/cooley/pdf/reprints/saft-project-whitepaper.ashx.

50. As discussed in Chapter 1, many "utility tokens" have been considered securities under US law suggesting that the purported distinction is not recognized.

cryptographic 'coupons' redeemable for mundane goods and services like bags of ground coffee."[51]

The paper identified a roadblock in the development and sale of utility tokens. Often, token creators sought to presell the tokens, before they had been created, using the proceeds to fund the token development. But sale of tokens prior to functioning of a decentralized blockchain increased the risk of classification of the tokens as securities.

The paper proposed a solution. The blockchain developers would break the transaction into two parts. First, the developers would sell investors a SAFT, which comprised the right to receive tokens on some future date if and when the blockchain launched. Developers would use the funds to build the network. The SAFT would be considered a security but sold only to accredited investors under Regulation D, avoiding the regulatory requirements of a public sale. Second, once the blockchain launched and decentralized, the developers would distribute the tokens to the SAFT purchasers. With the network decentralized, the tokens would not be securities and could be freely sold and traded.

The SAFT depended on the premise that utility tokens on a decentralized blockchain would not constitute securities. The defensibility of this argument and status of the SAFT as a viable solution remain uncertain, as discussed later in this chapter.

Early Enforcement Actions

The market for digital tokens exploded in 2017 and early 2018. While available data is inexact, hundreds of token sales are thought to have raised roughly $20 billion in those two years alone. Total funds raised through token sales increased from 2017 to 2018, while at the same time the average offering size was halved, from an average of $24 million in 2017 to $12 million in 2018.

The growth was global. China had a large presence in this market until it essentially outlawed token sales in late 2017. The United States accounted for much of the market in 2017. The United Kingdom, Singapore, and Eastern European countries also became popular forums.

The SEC and other US authorities took notice and commenced a series of enforcement actions against issuers for the sale of unregistered

51. Juan Batiz-Benet, Jesse Clayburgh, & Marco Santori, *The SAFT Project: Toward a Compliance Token Sale Framework* (Oct. 2, 2017), https://www.cooley.com/-/media/cooley/pdf/reprints/saft-project-whitepaper.ashx. at 2.

securities. They began their campaign with cases alleging fraud in addition to the sale of unregistered securities.

Claimed Fraudulent Sales of Digital Assets: REcoin

One of the earliest US enforcement actions was filed against REcoin Group Foundation, LLC, DRC World, and an individual named Maksim Zaslavskiy.[52] According to an indictment in the Eastern District in New York, in 2017, Zaslavskiy founded REcoin and began advertising it to investors as a new blockchain virtual currency.[53] He promised that REcoin was somehow backed by real estate investments with high potential return.[54] In an accompanying white paper, REcoin boasted of a team comprising experienced brokers, lawyers, and developers.[55] Over 1,000 investors transmitted funds to purchase REcoin tokens, but ultimately REcoin never hired any of the professionals about whom it boasted, and it never purchased any real estate.[56] Zaslavskiy declared the token sale a success but simultaneously offered REcoin investors the option to either obtain a refund or convert their REcoin tokens into Diamond tokens, which Zaslavskiy claimed were tokens "hedged" with actual diamonds.[57] No such Diamond tokens were ever developed, and Zaslavskiy purchased no diamonds.[58]

The SEC filed an enforcement action against Zaslavskiy in the Eastern District of New York, but the action was stayed pending resolution of a parallel criminal case filed against him in the same court.[59] In the criminal case, Zaslavskiy moved to dismiss indictment counts for securities fraud on the grounds that REcoin and Diamond did not involve securities.[60]

---

52. United States v. Zaslavskiy, No. 17-cr-647, 2018 WL 4346339 (E.D.N.Y. Sep. 11, 2018); Securities and Exchange Commission v. REcoin Group Foundation, LLC, No. 17-cv-5725, 2018 WL 10529810 (E.D.N.Y. Jan. 31, 2018).

53. *Zaslavskiy*, 2018 WL 4346339, at *2.

54. *Id.*

55. *Id.*

56. *Id.*

57. *Id.*

58. *Id.*

59. *See REcoin*, 2018 WL 10529810.

60. *Zaslavskiy*, 2018 WL 4346339, at *1.

Judge Raymond Dearie denied the motion, holding that a reasonable jury could conclude that the facts alleged in the indictment satisfied the *Howey* test.[61]

Investment of money: Zaslavskiy argued that there was no "investment of money" since the transactions involved only the exchange of "one medium of currency for another."[62] Judge Dearie disagreed, responding that the indictment alleged that investors gave up money or other assets in exchange for "membership" in the ventures and that an "investment" may include "goods and services" or "some other exchange of value."[63]

Common enterprise: While various courts apply different "commonality" tests, Judge Dearie applied a "horizontal commonality" analysis consistent with Second Circuit precedent.[64] Judge Dearie found that it could "readily be inferred from the facts alleged that the REcoin and Diamond investment strategies depended upon the pooling of investor assets to purchase real estate and diamonds" and that the "[i]ndictment makes clear that REcoin and Diamond profits would be distributed to investors pro-rata."[65]

Expectation of profits from Zaslavskiy's managerial efforts: Judge Dearie concluded that the indictment alleged sufficient facts to allow a finder of fact to "conclude that investors were led to expect profits . . . to be derived solely from the managerial efforts of Zaslavskiy and his co-conspirators."[66] The court pointed to promises made to investors in the white paper, for instance that REcoin is led by an "experienced team" and invests "based on soundest strategies."[67] The court also cited content from Zaslavskiy's emails, including a forecast for growth of 10–15 percent per year.[68] In addition, Judge Dearie noted that

61. *Id.* at *4.

62. *Id.* at *5.

63. *Id.*

64. *Id.* at *5–6.

65. *Id.* at *6.

66. *Id.*

67. *Id.*

68. *Id.*

there was "no indication that investors were to have any control over the management of REcoin or Diamond."[69]

This decision demonstrated that courts will evaluate the offer and sale of digital tokens by assessing the economic reality of how the tokens were promoted rather than the terminology used to describe them. As explained by Judge Dearie, quoting Supreme Court precedent, "form should be disregarded for substance and the emphasis should be on economic reality."[70] This is a standard approach for determining whether an asset constitutes a security and highlights the point that carefully curated language will not insulate digital token sellers from regulatory oversight if the economic realities of their activities amount to the offer or sale of investment contracts.

REcoin is one example of initial cases involving alleged fraud in the offer and sale of digital assets where either a court concluded the token was a security or the SEC took that position in a settled action.[71] Within months, however, the SEC expanded its enforcement activities to include actions against companies offering and selling digital assets where no fraud was alleged. These cases focused on claims that the offer and sale of the digital asset were the offer and sale of security for which registration was required and that failure to register the offer violated the registration requirements of the Securities Act.

Registration Failures

Munchee

On December 11, 2017, the SEC issued a settled cease-and-desist order against token seller Munchee Inc. after finding that the company had conducted unregistered offers and sales of securities in violation of

69. *Id.* at *7.

70. *Id.*

71. *See also* Securities and Exchange Commission v. Plexcorps, No. 17-7007 (E.D.N.Y.) (enforcement action to stop misappropriation of funds raised through the allegedly fraudulent and unregistered offer and sale of securities called "PlexCoin" in an initial coin offering); Securities and Exchange Commission v. Arisebank, No., No. 3:18-cv-00186-M (N.D. Tex.) (January 25, 2018) (enforcement action to halt ongoing "fraudulent, and unregistered offering of securities" against Arisebank, which purported to be the world's first "decentralized" bank and sold tokens called AriseCoin).

section 5 of the Securities Act.[72] The company neither admitted nor denied the SEC's findings.

According to the SEC, Munchee sought to raise $15 million for its food review and social platform by selling digital tokens that could be used to buy and sell goods and services in the future through an iPhone app. At the time of the sale, the Munchee "ecosystem" was not yet functional, but the company planned to develop it with the proceeds raised in the offering. Munchee and others promoting the sale represented to individuals that the tokens could be expected to increase in value as the company implemented improvements to the app, and they said that the company would work to support a secondary market for the tokens. Indeed, according to the settlement order, Munchee and its agent promoted the token to people interested in investing in digital assets, which "primed" investors' profit expectations.

Based on these facts and drawing on the DAO Report, the SEC concluded that the tokens were securities in the form of investment contracts under *Howey*. It observed that token purchasers expected a profit derived from the efforts of Munchee in creating the network. The SEC went further and cautioned that "[e]ven if MUN tokens had a practical use at the time of offering, it would not preclude the token from being a security [because] [d]etermining whether a transaction involves a security does not turn on labelling . . . but instead requires an assessment of 'the economic realities underlying a transaction.'"[73]

At the request of the SEC, Munchee halted its sale and refunded investors' money before any tokens were delivered. Due to Munchee's cooperation and its quick action to end the sale and return funds, the SEC chose not to impose a penalty.

By selecting Munchee for enforcement, the SEC telegraphed that the SEC's efforts to police the token market would not be limited to cases involving material misstatements or omissions of information. This is noteworthy in part because, unlike fraud, violation of section 5 is a strict liability offense.

Airfox and Paragon Coin

In a pair of cases brought on November 16, 2018, the SEC settled charges with two token issuers that had allegedly conducted unregistered

---

72. *See In re Munchee Inc.*, SEC Administrative Proceeding No. 3-18304 (Dec. 11, 2017), https://www.sec.gov/litigation/admin/2017/33-10445.pdf.

73. *Id.* at 9 (quoting *Forman*, 421 U.S. at 849).

securities offerings: CarrierEQ Inc. (Airfox) and Paragon Coin Inc.[74] The SEC found that both issuers sold digital tokens to investors to raise funds without registering their token sales pursuant to the federal securities laws or qualifying for an exemption to the registration requirements.

Airfox, a Boston-based startup, raised approximately $15 million worth of digital assets to finance its development of a token-denominated "ecosystem" starting with a mobile application that would allow users in emerging markets to earn tokens and exchange them for data by interacting with advertisements. Paragon, an online entity, raised approximately $12 million worth of digital assets to develop and implement its business plan to add blockchain technology to the cannabis industry and work toward legalization of cannabis.

The SEC found that purchasers of each issuer's tokens would have had a reasonable expectation of obtaining a future profit based on each company's respective efforts, including building out an "ecosystem" and adding new functionality using the proceeds from the sale. One of the companies also committed to support the value of its tokens by controlling the token supply. The SEC explained that each issuer made efforts to facilitate secondary trading and that their promotional communications indicated the profit potential. Consistent with *Howey* and the DAO Report, the SEC concluded that both companies had offered unregistered securities. Unlike with Munchee, the SEC assessed a $250,000 penalty against each company and required them to compensate investors, register the offerings, and begin filing periodic reports with the SEC under the Exchange Act.

SEC Statement on Digital Asset Securities Issuance and Trading

On November 16, 2018, the SEC Divisions of Corporation Finance, Investment Management, and Trading and Markets issued a *Statement on Digital Asset Securities Issuance and Trading.*[75] The statement highlighted the previous enforcement actions and provided the divisions' views on three issues: (1) initial offers and sales of "digital asset securities," (2) investment

---

74. U.S. Securities and Exchange Commission, *Two ICO Issuers Settle SEC Registration Charges, Agree to Register Tokens as Securities* (Nov. 16, 2018), https://www.sec.gov/news/press-release/2018-264.

75. U.S. Securities and Exchange Commission, *Statement on Digital Asset Securities Issuance and Trading* (Nov. 16, 2018), https://www.sec.gov/news/public-statement/digital-asset-securites-issuuance-and-trading.

vehicles investing in such securities and those who advise others about investing in them, and (3) secondary market trading of such securities.

With respect to initial offers and sales, the statement reiterated that the enforcement actions focused on the questions of when a blockchain-based asset constitutes a security and, if so, what registration requirements apply. The SEC noted that in the AirFox and Paragon settlements, each entity agreed to pay a penalty and register their tokens as securities. In doing so, the SEC stated that "there is a path to compliance with the federal securities laws going forward, even where issuers have conducted an illegal unregistered offering of digital asset securities."[76]

With respect to investment vehicles, advisers, and exchanges, the statement clarified that such entities dealing in blockchain-based securities will be subject to registration and other regulatory requirements, including the Investment Company Act of 1940, the Investment Advisers Act of 1940, and the Exchange Act. These requirements are discussed in more detail in a later section.

April 2019 SEC *Framework for "Investment Contract" Analysis of Digital Assets*

In the wake of the ICO boom and growing numbers of these and other enforcement actions, the industry had been demanding clarity on the *Howey* analysis as applied to blockchain-based assets. The SEC responded.

In April 2019, the SEC's FinHub issued its *Framework for "Investment Contract" Analysis of Digital Assets*, which provided a toolkit for applying the *Howey* test to digital assets.[77] The framework purportedly describes the factors used by SEC staff for assessing whether digital assets are "investment contracts" subject to federal securities laws. While the framework appears to describe the SEC's approach, it does not represent a "rule, regulation or statement of the [SEC]" and is not binding on the agency.

The framework includes little discussion of the "investment of money" and "common enterprise" prongs of the *Howey* test and claims—in a conclusory fashion—that those requirements are typically satisfied in a digital asset sale because the digital asset is typically exchanged for something of

76. *Id.*

77. *See* U.S. Securities and Exchange Commission, *Framework for "Investment Contract" Analysis for Digital Assets* (Apr. 3, 2019), https://www.sec.gov/corpfin/framework-investment-contract-analysis-digital-assets.

value and a common enterprise "typically exists." Instead, the framework focuses on the "reliance of the efforts of others" and "expectation of profit" prongs. The framework states generally that these exist when the digital token issuers or third parties such as promotors or sponsors—referred to in the framework as "active participants" (APs)—provide "essential managerial efforts that affect the success of the enterprise, and investors reasonably expect to derive profit from those efforts."[78] The framework then addressed these two *Howey* prongs at issue in more detail.

Reliance on the Efforts of Others

In assessing whether the "reliance on the efforts of others" and "reasonable expectations of profits" requirements are satisfied, the SEC's staff will focus on the "economic reality" of digital asset transactions including the "terms of the offer, the plan of distribution, and the economic inducements" to encourage sales. The inquiry focuses on two key issues: (1) does the purchaser "reasonably expect to rely" on the efforts of an AP and (2) are these efforts "undeniably significant ones, those managerial efforts which affect the failure or success of the enterprise" and not merely ministerial.

The language describing these key issues arguably suggests two very important clues about how the SEC staff will analyze the *Howey* issue for a given sale. First, it appears to be forward looking, examining the efforts on which the purchaser expects "to rely"—as contrasted, say, with the efforts on which he has already relied. Second, it focuses on the efforts of an AP, not the efforts of just any third party.

The framework then sets forth a list of nondispositive factors, the presence of which each strengthen the likelihood the SEC staff will find that a purchaser is relying on the efforts of others. Notice that a common theme of the factors is AP control. These factors include the following:

Network development/operation/promotion: The AP—rather than a "dispersed community of network users"—is responsible for the development, improvement, enhancement, operation, or promotion of the network for the digital asset, especially if the AP's efforts are "necessary for the network or digital asset to achieve

78. *Id.,* Section II. C. Reasonable Expectation of Profits Derived from Efforts of Others.

or retain its intended purpose or functionality."[79] As noted in the framework, the SEC's staff will evaluate the state of development and functionality of the digital assets and associated network both when the offer and sale occur and over time as the assets and network mature. The less developed/functional the digital assets and network are at the time of the offering or sale, the more likely purchasers are relying on the efforts of others. The framework also notes that SEC's staff will also consider whether an AP, in its messaging to actual or prospective purchasers, has suggested that its future developmental efforts may help the digital asset grow in value.

***Market creation/support*:** The AP creates or supports a market for, or the price of, the digital asset. Examples include control of the creation and issuance of the digital assets as well as continuing actions taken to support a market price of the digital asset, such as by limiting supply or ensuring scarcity through buybacks and destruction (or "burning") of the asset.

***Governance, oversight, and control*:** The AP has a "lead or central role in deciding governance issues, code updates, or how third parties participate in the validation of transactions that occur with respect to the digital asset."[80] Also relevant is whether the AP is responsible for "exercising judgment concerning the network or the characteristics or rights the digital asset represents." Such decisions may include compensation to persons providing services to the network, arrangements for the trading of digital assets on secondary markets, and use of funds raised from digital asset sales.

Financial interest/benefits: The AP has the ability to realize capital appreciation from the value of the digital asset. Considerations include whether the AP retains a stake or interest in the digital asset, distributes the digital asset as compensation to management, ties compensation to the price of the digital asset on the secondary markets, owns/controls the intellectual property rights of the network or digital asset, or monetizes the value of the digital asset, especially in instances where the digital asset has limited functionality.

---

79. *Id.* at Section II.C. 1. Reliance on the Efforts of Others.

80. *Id.*

Reasonable Expectation of Profits

According to the framework, the SEC staff will assess a number of non-exclusive factors to determine whether digital asset purchasers have a reasonable expectation of profits. Some of these factors dovetail with the "reliance on the efforts of others" analysis described earlier. A common theme among these factors is the existence of value-generating activity that exceeds the value provided to those who use the digital asset on its network. The factors that support finding a reasonable expectation of profits include the following:

Capital appreciation and income/profit sharing: The digital asset gives purchasers the right to share in an enterprise's income/profits or to realize a gain from the asset's capital appreciation. The framework suggests that virtually all forms of capital appreciation support this element of the *Howey* test.

Secondary market trading: The digital asset can be traded or transferred on or through a secondary market or platform, or if such opportunities are expected in the future enabling digital asset holders to resell the asset and realize gains.

Offer/purchase volume suggests investment intent: The quantities of digital assets offered or purchased are "significantly greater than any likely user would reasonably need" or there is little apparent correlation between digital asset trading or purchase quantities and "the amount of the underlying goods or services a typical consumer would purchase for use or consumption."[81]

Targeting nonusers: The digital asset is offered to an audience beyond those who are likely to use the goods/services or have a need for the network's functionality and, therefore, presumably buying the digital asset with a view toward capital appreciation.

Promotional/marketing activity suggesting a potential to profit: Promotional and marketing activities—whether direct or indirect—that suggest a reasonable expectation of profits. Some of these activities are obvious, such as marketing the digital asset as an investment, stating that the solicited holders are investors or promoting "the availability of a market for the trading of the digital asset." Other examples overlap the "efforts of other

81. *Id.* at Section II.C. 2. Reasonable Expectation of Profits.

analysis" and include promotion of "the expertise of an AP or its ability to build or grow the value of the network or digital asset," "use of the [sale] proceeds . . . to develop the network or digital asset," and "future (and not present) functionality of the network or digital asset, and the prospect that an AP will deliver that functionality."[82]

Other Relevant Considerations

The framework also outlines a number of nonexclusive factors that, if present, would tend to suggest that purchasers do not have a reasonable expectation of profit derived from the efforts of others and that the asset thus is not a security under *Howey*. Many of these factors focus on whether purchasers are buying the assets for consumptive use rather than as a speculative investment. These factors include the following:

Functionality of the assets/network: The digital assets and associated network are fully developed/operational at the time of offer/sale, and purchasers are "immediately able to use [them] for [their] intended functionality." Evidence shows that the digital assets are designed and implemented to "meet the needs of its users" rather than "feed speculation as to its value or development of its network," and that the assets are "marketed in a manner that emphasizes the functionality of the digital asset, and not the potential for [its] increase in market value."[83]

Low likelihood of appreciation: The digital assets have limited prospects for appreciation. For instance, the digital assets are designed in a way such that their value will likely "remain constant or even degrade over time, and, therefore, a reasonable purchaser would not be expected to hold the digital asset for extended periods as an investment."

Notably, the framework states that APs who help facilitate secondary market activity on a network do not push the digital asset sales further into the "investment contract" classification if the "transfers . . . may only be made by and among users of the platform."

---

82. *Id.*

83. *Id.* at Section II.C.3. Other Relevant Considerations.

Also of interest, in the framework, FinHub suggested that a digital asset "previously sold as a security" could be "revaluated at the time of later offers or sales." This echoes prior statements by SEC personnel that assets originally considered securities might, including by virtue of sufficient decentralization, shed this classification. For example, on May 2, 2018, SEC Commissioner Hester Peirce suggested this possibility at a conference, stating "Designating certain ICOs securities offerings does not end the inquiry once and for all. What, for example, are the coins once the environment is completed? Are they still securities. . . .?"[84] Just over a month later, then SEC Director of the Division of Corporation Finance William Hinman hinted at this same point at another conference, stating that "when the efforts of the third party are no longer a key factor for determining the enterprise's success, material information asymmetries recede" and "[a]s a network becomes truly decentralized, the ability to identify an issuer or promoter to make the requisite disclosures becomes difficult."[85] The question of when a security can shed its classification through decentralization remains open and will be revisited later in discussion of a SAFT.

Overall, the framework indicates that the SEC is open to excluding some blockchain-based digital assets from securities regulations. This marked a shift and suggested SEC's desire to promote innovation or at least not stifle it. Though the framework is helpful, it is not binding and is not an adequate substitute for clear rules upon which market participants can rely. As a result, some market participants view the framework as geared more toward guiding judges' analyses in inevitable litigation than informing creators of blockchain-based assets.

Ultimately, the framework represents the most comprehensive statement to date of the position of the SEC's staff on the regulation of digital assets. It is a regulatory stake in the ground, warning market participants that going forward, they need to assess any potential sale of digital assets as outlined in the framework to determine whether there is an offer or sale of a security.

While the SEC staff's position recognizes that not all digital assets are securities requiring registration or an exemption from registration prior to sale, the instances where the sale of such assets will not be viewed by the

---

84. Hester Peirce, *Beaches and Bitcoin: Remarks before the Medici Conference*, Medici Conference (May 2, 2018), https://www.sec.gov/news/speech/speech-peirce-050218.

85. William Hinman, *Digital Asset Transactions: When Howey Met Gary (Plastic)*, Yahoo Finance All Markets Summit (June 14, 2018), https://www.sec.gov/news/speech/speech-hinman-061418.

staff as the sale of a security to date have been very limited. Also, while the framework offers hope that over time a digital asset may lose its characterization as a security through decentralization of its network, when and how that occurs is a question that remains unanswered.

With SEC leadership changes, questions have arisen regarding the continued influence of the framework. What has not changed, however, is the SEC's regulary interest in digital assets and continued challenges for industry participants.

No-Action Letters

The issue of what blockchain-based assets constitute securities remains in flux. Clues come from a variety of sources, including SEC no-action letters, two major enforcement actions, pronouncements by SEC officials, and the sales and trading of other blockchain assets without any visible objection by the SEC.

Avoiding a Securities Classification: TurnKey

Simultaneously with the publication of the framework, on April 3, 2019, the SEC Division of Corporation Finance issued a "no-action letter" (an affirmation it will not recommend enforcement action under a certain fact scenario) to TurnKey Jet, Inc., concerning its sale of certain tokens.[86] TurnKey Jet provides short-term passenger aircraft leases and issued tokens that could be redeemed by customers for air charter services. The SEC stated that in reaching its position, it noted the following:

Fully developed/operational system: TurnKey Jet undertook to have a "fully developed and operational" platform/network/app "at the time any Tokens are sold" and "not use any funds from Token sales to develop" these technologies.[87]

Immediate use/functionality: TurnKey Jet undertook that when sold, tokens "will be immediately usable for their intended functionality (purchasing air charter services)."[88]

---

86. *See* U.S. Securities and Exchange Commission, *Response of the Division of Corporation Finance to Turnkey Jet, Inc.* (Apr. 3, 2019), https://www.sec.gov/divisions/corpfin/cf-noaction/2019/turnkey-jet-040219-2a1.htm.

87. *Id.*

88. *Id.*

Restrictions on token pricing, transfer, and repurchase: TurnKey Jet undertook to sell its tokens "at a price of one USD per Token throughout the life of the Program, and each Token will represent a TKJ obligation to supply air charter services at a value of one USD per Token."[89] In addition, TurnKey Jet agreed to "restrict transfers of Tokens to TKJ Wallets only, and not to wallets external to the Platform" and, in the event that the company repurchases tokens, to "only do so at a discount to the face value of the Tokens (one USD per Token) that the holder seeks to resell to TKJ, unless a court within the United States orders TKJ to liquidate the Tokens."[90]

Marketing limitations: TurnKey Jet agreed to market tokens "in a manner that emphasizes the functionality of the Token, and not the potential for the increase in the market value of the Token."[91]

The SEC's position on the TurnKey Jet tokens is arguably unremarkable.[92] Purchasers cannot transfer the tokens off of TurnKey's platform, and TurnKey will sell additional tokens at a fixed price of $1, so it would appear that purchasers have no clear opportunity to profit from TurnKey Jet tokens. This alone would arguably end the *Howey* analysis. The facts that Turnkey Jet promised not to use the sale funds to develop the network, which was immediately functional, only bolstered the correctness of this result.

Pocketful of Quarters, Inc.

The SEC issued another no-action letter to Pocketful of Quarters, Inc. (PoQ), a blockchain-based gaming platform that planned to sell blockchain-based tokens called Quarters, which would function as currency for games on the platform.[93] The SEC informed PoQ it would not recommend enforcement

---

89. *Id.*

90. *Id.*

91. *Id.*

92. And, arguably, as Commissioner Peirce later commented, the Turnkey Jet transaction, was clearly not an offer of securities. *See* Commissioner Hester M. Peirce, Speech at the Securities Enforcement Forum (May 9, 2019) https://www.sec.gov/news/speech/peirce-how-we-howey-050919.

93. *See* U.S. Securities and Exchange Commission, *Response of the Division of Corporation Finance to Pocketful of Quarters, Inc.* (July 25, 2019), https://www.sec.gov/corpfin/pocketful-quarters-inc-072519-2a1.

if Quarters were sold without a registration statement, relying on facts similar to those in the TurnKey no-action letter, including the following:

- PoQ will not use the funds from the sale of Quarters to build the platform, which will be completed and operational prior to sale.
- Quarters will be immediately usable for their intended purpose.
- PoQ will prevent transfers of Quarters except in connection with gameplay to approved game developers.
- Only game developers and certain influencers will be able to exchange Quarters for another currency (ETH) and at predetermined exchange rates.
- Quarters will be made continuously available in unlimited quantities at a fixed price.
- Quarters will be marketed and sold only for consumptive use.

As with TurnKey, it would appear that given these limitations, purchasers have no clear opportunity to profit from Quarters, quickly ending the *Howey* analysis. Other guideline factors, such as PoQ's promise that it would not use sale proceeds to build the platform and that Quarters would have an immediate, clear consumptive use again bolstered the conclusion.[94]

Certain 2020 Enforcement Litigation

Telegram

Telegram was one of two high-profile SEC enforcement actions that came to a head in 2020. Prior to its ultimate foray into digital assets, Telegram was well known as the creator of Telegram Messenger, a popular messaging app with over 300 million global users.[95] Despite widespread popularity, however, Telegram Messenger failed to generate revenue.

In 2017, Telegram began work on a new blockchain, called the TON blockchain, and its native token, the Gram. The Gram was to someday

94. *See also* U.S. Securities and Exchange Commission, *Response of the Division of Trading and Markets to Paxos Trust Company, LLC* (Oct. 28, 2019), https://www.sec.gov/divisions/marketreg/mr-noaction/2019/paxos-trust-company-102819-17a.pdf; U.S. Securities and Exchange Commission, *Response of the Division of Corporation Finance to IMVU, Inc.* (Nov. 17, 2020), https://www.sec.gov/corpfin/imvu-111920-2a1.

95. *See* Securities and Exchange Commission v. Telegram Group Inc., 448 F. Supp. 3d 352 (S.D.N.Y. 2020).

serve as a currency on the Telegram Messenger platform. According to a white paper published by Telegram, the supply of Grams would be limited to five billion, which would be held by Telegram. The white paper also provided that the Grams would be sold pursuant to a formula that set a "Reference Price." Should the market price of Grams fall below half the reference price, Telegram had discretion to support the price by repurchasing Grams.

In 2018, Telegram sold "interests in Grams" to 175 entities and high-net-worth individuals. These "Gram Purchase Agreements," essentially SAFTs, entitled the initial purchasers to receive an allotment of Grams upon launch of the TON blockchain. Each purchase agreement contained representations and warranties from the purchaser that they were buying for investment purposes only and did not intend to distribute the Grams. In total, Telegram raised $1.7 billion from the sale of approximately 2.9 billion Grams.

Telegram projected a launch by October 30, 2019. Shortly before launch, the SEC sued Telegram to enjoin the distribution, arguing that Telegram was engaging in an unlawful, unregistered distribution of securities (the Grams) to the public through these 175 purchasers, who were, in the view of the SEC, underwriters. Telegram's distribution of Grams was put on hold while the SEC and Telegram presented their cases to the court.

Southern District of New York Judge P. Kevin Castel granted a motion by the SEC for a preliminary injunction, finding that the SEC was likely to succeed on its claim that Grams constitute securities under a *Howey* analysis. The opinion leaves many open questions about how courts should and will apply *Howey* to blockchain assets.

As an initial matter, Telegram had argued that while the initial Gram purchase agreements constituted securities, the Grams themselves did not. For the purposes of a preliminary injunction analysis, Judge Castel disagreed, holding that the Gram purchase agreements and the future delivery and resale of Grams should be viewed in their totality. The court observed that the "economic reality" of the entire transaction was that initial purchasers provided up-front capital in exchange for future delivery of the Grams, which upon receipt would be resold with the expectation of a profit. In possibly a key phrase, the court added that "[a] reasonable Initial Purchaser understands and expects that they will only profit if the reputation, skill, and involvement of Telegram and its founders **remain behind the enterprise, including through the sale of Grams from the Initial Purchasers into the public market.**"[96]

96. *Id.* at 367.

Judge Castel relatedly rejected Telegram's argument that the sale should be evaluated at the time the blockchain launched, holding instead that *Howey* requires the court to examine the series of understandings, transactions, and undertakings at the time they were made.

He then proceeded through *Howey*'s four-pronged analysis. Judge Castel had little difficulty finding that the SEC had established a likelihood of success on the first three prongs. According to Judge Castel, the exchange of money for future delivery of Grams constituted an investment of money. The SEC had shown horizontal commonality since Telegram pooled investors' money and used it to develop the TON blockchain, the success of which determined whether investors would profit. Judge Castel also found that the SEC had made a substantial showing of vertical commonality because the purchasers' and Telegram's financial returns all depended on Telegram's success in developing and launching the TON blockchain. He found that the expectation of profit prong was met, rejecting Telegram's argument that the purchasers intended to use Grams as a currency and noting the following: the presale prices were discounted from the expected launch price; Telegram had promoted the ability to support the market price for Grams; the purchase amounts suggested investment (not consumptive) intent; certain lockup agreements suggested investment intent; the purchasers were accredited investors (and not obvious Grams consumers); promotional materials highlighted the opportunity for profit; and internal Telegram documents confirmed subjective investment intent by the purchasers.

Judge Castel then held that the SEC had shown a substantial likelihood of success in proving that at the time of the 2018 sales, a reasonable purchaser's expectation of profits was based on the "essential entrepreneurial and managerial efforts of Telegram." The court reasoned that the success of the entire project depended on Telegram's efforts to develop, launch, and support the TON blockchain and Grams. In another potentially important statement, Judge Castel found that "if, immediately after launch, Telegram and its team decamped to the British Virgin Islands, where Telegram is incorporated, and ceased all further efforts to support the TON Blockchain, the TON Blockchain would exist in some form but would likely lack the mass adoption, vibrancy, and utility that would enable the Initial Purchasers to earn their expected huge profits."[97] The court also noted that Telegram's promotion of the TON blockchain and Grams through integration with Messenger created a

97. *Id.* at 375.

reasonable expectation of profits from Telegram's "essential post-launch efforts." Telegram also structured postlaunch financial incentives to ensure that the link between Grams and Messenger was unmistakable, and the purchase agreements required Telegram to use reasonable post-launch efforts in this pursuit.

Based on these facts and findings, Judge Castel granted the SEC's motion to preliminarily enjoin Telegram from distributing Grams. Shortly thereafter, Telegram abandoned the TON blockchain launch and Grams distribution and began working to return investor funds.

Judge Castel's first-of-its-kind opinion on whether a SAFT constitutes a security leaves open questions. Most notably, in what circumstances will the distribution of a blockchain-based asset via a SAFT not constitute a security? On the one hand, portions of Judge Castel's opinion cast doubt on the SAFT's premise that the assets can avoid classification as securities at distribution. In particular, Judge Castel rejected Telegram's assertion that the distribution of Grams should be evaluated separately from the Grams purchase agreements, holding that *Howey* required evaluation of the scheme as a whole. But on the other hand, Judge Castel also focused extensively in several sections on the impact of Telegram's postlaunch role, arguably leaving open the possibility that the SAFT structure remains viable, so long as the issuer's role postlaunch remains sufficiently limited. The viability of the SAFT may turn on resolution of this issue, as we see in the next few case studies.

Kik

Kik came on the heels of *Telegram*.[98] Like Telegram, Kik had also launched a messaging application, Kik Messenger. Also like Telegram, Kik Messenger was not profitable, and Kik also sought to profit through creation and sale of a digital currency, called Kin. Unlike Grams, though, Kin was to be issued not on a new blockchain but on the Ethereum blockchain.

Kik also endeavored to sell Kin through both a private and then public sale. Between June and September 11, 2017, Kik sold $50 million worth of SAFTs for Kin to accredited investors (purportedly under Regulation D), promising to use the proceeds to develop the "Kin Ecosystem." The day after this private sale concluded, on September 12, 2017, Kik commenced a public sale of Kin, raising an additional $50 million (paid in ETH). On September 26, 2017, Kik distributed all Kin (one trillion in all)

98. U.S. Securities and Exchange Commission v. Kik Interactive Inc., No. 19-cv-5244, 2020 WL 5819770 (S.D.N.Y. Sep. 30, 2020).

to the purchasers in the private and public sales. Kik retained an additional three trillion Kin and distributed an additional six trillion Kin to the Kin Foundation, a not-for-profit created and controlled by Kik.

On June 4, 2019, the SEC sued Kik in the Southern District of New York alleging that Kik had offered and sold securities without a registration statement or exemption. The SEC sought an injunction barring Kik from future violations, disgorgement, and monetary penalties.

The parties cross-moved for summary judgment, and on September 30, 2020, Judge Alvin Hellerstein granted the SEC's motion, holding that the undisputed facts showed Kik had offered and sold securities without a registration statement. The analysis focused on the "common enterprise" and "efforts of others" prongs of *Howey*. As in *Telegram*, the court had little difficulty finding that the "common enterprise" prong had been met. Horizontal commonality existed because Kik pooled the purchasers' money and used it to build the Kin Ecosystem, on which the investors' profits depended. The court also held that the investors' profit expectation derived from the entrepreneurial or managerial efforts of Kik. The court rejected Kik's argument that investors could use Kin for consumptive use within the Kin Ecosystem, finding that none of the potential consumptive use existed at the time of distribution and would materialize only if Kik's entrepreneurial and managerial efforts succeeded.

The court also rejected Kik's claim that only the SAFTs constituted securities, holding that the private and public sales were part of a single plan of financing made for the same general purpose: funding Kik's operations and building the ecosystem for Kin. The court added that purchasers received the same class of securities at about the same time.

Kik leaves open the same questions as *Telegram*. In both cases, the postdistribution success of the enterprise and potential profits for investors required continued involvement of the issuer. But what if this were not the case?

Analysis of Particular Blockchain-Based Assets

Bitcoin and Ethereum

As of the writing of this book, we are aware of no case in which a court has evaluated a blockchain asset-based and concluded that it does not constitute a security.[99] But the SEC has announced that there are at least

99. This is likely a function of the facts that courts have addressed the *Howey* question with respect to blockchain assets in only a very few cases and that those cases

two assets it considers to be nonsecurities: Bitcoin and Ethereum. It is worth looking at the SEC's statements and the evolution and nature of each asset to see what we can divine about the reasoning behind the announcements.

As explained in Chapter 1 Bitcoin is the native token for its blockchain and provides no particular set of rights or utility (besides function as a currency). It is a pure digital asset, the transfer and accounting of which depends on a decentralized network of miners and nodes. As discussed in greater detail in Chapter 8, the early history of Bitcoin is somewhat mysterious, but it appears that from the beginning, there was a decentralized network of miners and nodes. Certainly, by the time that the SEC weighed in, the network was quite decentralized.

After numerous hints and informal statements from SEC officials, on October 1, 2019, SEC Associate Director Brent Fields wrote a letter to Cipher Technologies Bitcoin Fund concluding that Bitcoin is not a security.[100] Cipher Technologies had proposed to register a closed-end interval fund as an investment company under the Investment Company Act of 1940, but the SEC rejected the registration statement, responding that Cipher had proposed to invest substantially all assets in Bitcoin, which is not a security.[101] The SEC reasoned that "we do not believe that current purchasers of bitcoin are relying on the essential managerial and entrepreneurial efforts of others to produce a profit."[102] This echoes earlier statements by the then Director of the SEC's Division of Corporation Finance William Hinman that "when I look at Bitcoin today, I do not see a central third party whose efforts are a key determining factor in the enterprise. The network on which Bitcoin functions is operational and appears to have been decentralized for some time, perhaps from inception."[103] Hinman added that "[a]pplying the disclosure regime of

---

were SEC enforcement actions. This should not be taken as an indication of how courts would view other blockchain assets.

100. Letter from Brent Fields to Cipher Technologies on October 1, 2019, https://www.sec.gov/Archives/edgar/data/1776589/999999999719007180/filename1.pdf.

101. *See* 15 U.S.C. § 80a-3 (a)(1) (defining "investment company" as one that, among other things, engages primarily in the business of investing or trading in securities).

102. *See supra* note 100.

103. William Hinman, *Digital Asset Transactions: When Howey Met Gary (Plastic)*, Yahoo Finance All Markets Summit (June 14, 2018), https://www.sec.gov/news/speech/speech-hinman-061418.

the federal securities laws to the offer and resale of Bitcoin would seem to add little value."[104]

Ether is the native token for its blockchain (the Ethereum blockchain), and ownership likewise provides no specific set of rights or particular utility (besides function as a currency and "gas" for other applications in the Ethereum ecosystem). Unlike Bitcoin, Ethereum's history is well documented. After early public discussion of the project, on July 22, 2014, founder Vitalik Buterin published a blog post announcing an upcoming "Genesis Sale" of Ether.[105] Purchasers would not be able to access their Ether until launch of the blockchain. The crowdsale was a success, and the Ethereum team raised just under $20 million (in Bitcoin), which the team used to fund development of the project.[106] Ethereum software for mining and users was released on July 30, 2015, the first Ethereum block was mined, and the number of miners and users grew rapidly.

Around the time that the framework was released, the then SEC Director of the Division of Corporation Finance Hinman commented he did not believe Ether to constitute a security, stating that "based on my understanding of the present state of Ether, the Ethereum network and its decentralized structure, current offers and sales of Ether are not securities transactions."[107] He noted that he was not considering Ethereum's initial fundraising in this analysis.

This suggests a particular focus on the fourth *Howey* prong, profit from the "efforts of others." With respect to both Bitcoin and Ether, it would be hard to ignore that there are individuals who purchase each as an investment, intending to profit and thus satisfying the first two *Howey* prongs. Unlike the court's view of *Kik* or *Telegram*, however, commonality is a bit fuzzier with a truly decentralized network; purchasers are not pooling their money (horizontal commonality), and their fates are not tied to any active promoter (vertical commonality). But more clear, and something that the SEC emphasized in the Cipher Technologies letter, is that with respect to both Bitcoin and Ether, any profits and network functionality come from a decentralized group of miners, nodes, and other similar administrators—not a central entity. This line

---

104. *Id.*

105. Vitalik Buterin, *Launching the Ether Sale*, Ethereum Foundation Blog (July 22, 2014), https://blog.ethereum.org/2014/07/22/launching-the-ether-sale/.

106. *History of Ethereum*, Coinmama, https://www.coinmama.com/guide/history-of-ethereum (last visited May 14, 2021).

107. *See supra* note 103.

becomes all the more important when applying *Howey* to assets that might be referred to as "utility tokens," a few of which we address later.

Filecoin

Filecoin is the native token of the Filecoin blockchain.[108] Filecoin is designed to allow users to store data remotely with a decentralized network of blockchain miners. Users spend Filecoin hiring miners to store and distribute the data. The data are not stored on the blockchain but in secure, encrypted fashion on servers controlled by the miners selected to store a particular user's data.

In the sense described in Chapter 1 Filecoin is thus a utility token. It is designed for holders to use it as currency to buy data storage (the utility) via the network.

But with Filecoin, we see decentralization not just in the blockchain but in the off-chain utility as well. The storage is provided off-chain not by any centralized entity but by one or more of the Filecoin miners participating in the network. This contrasts with the utility in both *Telegram* and *Kik*, which was to come from use in messenger software run centrally by the issuing entity or an affiliate.

Decentraland and MANA

Decentraland and its native token, MANA, provide another example of a token may not be viewed as a security. Decentraland is a platform on which parcels of land in a virtual world can be purchased, and the owner of each parcel can provide a 3D virtual experience in that parcel to any visitors.[109] Ownership of each parcel is tracked on a decentralized blockchain that has a native token called MANA. The 3D virtual experience for each plot of land, including graphics, architecture, foliage, events, and sound, is provided individually by the owner of that plot, not by any centralized third party. Thus, like Filecoin, both the Decentraland blockchain and its off-chain utility are decentralized and do not materially depend on the efforts of a centralized party.

---

108. Protocol Labs, *Filecoin: A Decentralized Storage Network* (July 19, 2017), https://filecoin.io/filecoin.pdf.

109. Decentraland, *Introduction*, https://docs.decentraland.org/decentraland/introduction/ (last visited May 14, 2021).

Stablecoins

Many stablecoins trade publicly in the United States. Recall that stablecoins are assets held at a relatively fixed price by some mechanism. For example, Circle Internet Financial issues a stablecoin called USDC, selling and redeeming each token for $1, thus keeping the market price of USDC on various exchanges at $1 (or extremely close to it).[110] Assuming the stablecoin issuer or other mechanism successfully maintains the price of the asset, there is arguably no "investment" or profit motive or opportunity. Thus, several elements of *Howey*, as well as the central goal of protecting investors from risky assets, do not appear to be present in the case of stablecoins. Perhaps for this reason, the SEC FinHub has stated that they "believe that market participants may structure and sell [a stablecoin] in such a way that it does not constitute a security," though it has cautioned that this requires a facts and circumstances determination.[111]

Since FinHub's statement, SEC Chair Gary Gensler has suggested that stablecoins may be securities and investment companies.[112] When the Presidents Working Group on Financial Markets released its November 2021 Report on Stablecoins (Report),[113] Chair Gensler reiterated his view and highlighted the Report's recognition that "stablecoins, or certain parts of stablecoin arrangements, may be securities, commodities and/or derivatives."[114] The Report also noted that "stablecoin arrangements and activities may implicate the jurisdiction of the SEC and/or CFTC."[115] While the Report generally recommended regulation of stablecoins through Congressional action, it left open the door for regulators such as the SEC to act.

110. Circle homepage, https://www.circle.com/en/ (last visited May 14, 2021).

111. U.S. Securities and Exchange Commission, *SEC FinHub Staff Statement on OCC Interpretation* (Sep. 21, 2020), https://www.sec.gov/news/public-statement/sec-finhub-statement-occ-interpretation.

112. Gensler, Remarks Before the Aspen Security Forum; https://www.sec.gov/news/public-statement/gensler-aspen-security-forum-2021-08-03 (August 3, 2021).

113. https://home.treasury.gov/system/files/136/StableCoinReport_Nov1_508.pdf.

114. https://www.sec.gov/news/statement/gensler-statement-presidents-working-group-report-stablecoins-110121. Quoting the Report at p. 15.

115. *See supra* note 113, at 11.

Non-Fungible Tokens

As discussed in Chapter 1, a non-fungible token (NFT) is a unique digital token. NFTs are often viewed as certificates of authenticity for separate, unique digital assets such as digital artwork. While an NFT may not appear to fit squarely within the *Howey* test's definition of security, recently some NFT purchasers have challenged that perception. In *Friel v. Dapper Labs, Inc. et al.*, a purported class action filed in New York State court, purchasers of NFTs documenting an interest in video clips of NBA basketball games claim that those NFTs are securities. They assert that they (1) invested money to purchase their NFTs; (2) were passive participants in a common enterprise, here a blockchain controlled by defendants; (3) reasonably anticipated profits; and (4) expected profits to be derived from the managerial efforts of the defendants in maintaining the success of the enterprise (including a platform for secondary trading of the NFTs). Consequently, plaintiffs allege that the NFTs are securities that were sold without registration. Plaintiffs are seeking rescission or damages. The case was only filed in May 2021, but it highlights interesting questions related to the sale of NFTs.

Separately, some reports suggest that the SEC is taking a regulatory and enforcement interest in NFTs. One broker-dealer petitioned the SEC in May 2021 for rule-making on NFTs and Commissioner Peirce reportedly agreed in January 2022 that guidance on NFTs is needed.[116]

Other *Howey* Issues as Applied to Blockchain Assets

Application of *Howey* to blockchain assets remains a hot topic in blockchain law. Until additional challenges are adjudicated in court, analysis in this area requires a fair bit of inference and even speculation. But exponential growth in the number of blockchain assets now trading on US nonsecurities exchanges without apparent SEC objection might suggest that regulators and the industry are gradually establishing an

---

116. *See* Robert Anello, *Digital Art May Be Next in the SEC's Crosshairs*, FORBES, (July 15, 2021), https://www.forbes.com/sites/insider/2021/07/15/digital-art-may-be-next-in-the-secs-crosshairs/?sh=7a62de3332df; Letter from Vincent R. Molinari, Chief Executive Officer, President of Sustainable Holdings, to Hon. Vanessa Countryman, Secretary, Securities and Exchange Commission (April 12, 2021) https://www.sec.gov/rules/petitions/2021/petn4-771.pdf (4/21/21); https://rollcall.com/2022/01/25/secs-peirce-says-agency-guidance-on-nonfungible-tokens-needed/ (1/25/22).

implicit, agreed-upon framework. And, at least one SEC commissioner has proposed a regulation to provide clarity.

What Constitutes an Offer or Sale: In re Tomahawk

Section 5 of the Securities Act requires the filing of a registration statement prior to an "offer" or "sale" of securities (unless an exemption applies). When does a distribution not constitute an offer or sale? Specifically, can an issuer avoid the registration requirements by conducting an "airdrop," that is, a free distribution of a token to select addresses?

While courts have yet to provide any definitive guidance on the issue, such an approach was unsuccessfully attempted by oil and gas exploration company Tomahawk Exploration LLC.[117] According to the SEC, Tomahawk sought to raise $5 million to fund oil drilling in California. When it failed to raise any money, the company instead made an airdrop of tokens—called "Tomahawkcoins"—to third parties by means of what it called a "bounty program" in exchange for online promotional and marketing services that targeted potential investors and directed them to the company's offering materials. Those activities included requesting that the tokens be listed on trading platforms and promoting the token on blogs and other online forums. Tomahawk did not register the offer or sale of Tomahawkcoins with the SEC, and it did not meet any exemption to the registration requirement.

The SEC instituted public administrative and cease-and-desist proceedings against Tomahawk and concluded that (1) the tokens were securities and (2) the company's bounty program constituted an unregistered offer and sale of securities because Tomahawk provided tokens in exchange for services designed to advance the company's economic interests and foster a trading market for its securities. Tomahawk resolved the enforcement action by entering into a consent order stipulating to violations of section 5 of the Securities Act, and its founder agreed to pay a civil penalty of $30,000.

The SEC claimed that Tomahawk's distribution of tokens through its bounty program qualified as investment contract securities under the *Howey* test because they constituted an investment of money "or other contributions of value" in a common enterprise with a reasonable expectation of profits, to be derived from the oil exploration and production operations conducted by Tomahawk.

---

117. U.S. Securities and Exchange Commission, *SEC Bars Perpetrator of Initial Coin Offering Fraud* (Aug. 14, 2018), https://www.sec.gov/news/press-release/2018-152.

The SEC reasoned that the lack of monetary consideration for "free" shares did not mean there was not an offer or sale under the federal securities laws. Rather, according to the SEC, a "gift" of a security is a "sale" for securities law purposes when the company receives some real benefit, even if it does not involve the exchange of money.

The SEC found that Tomahawk received value in exchange for the bounty distributions in the form of online marketing, including the promotion of the token on blogs and other online forums. The company also received value in the creation of a public trading market for its securities. Accordingly, the SEC determined that the company issued tokens as part of the bounty program, which in turn benefited the company. Thus, the SEC concluded that a sale had occurred without registration in violation of section 5 of the Securities Act.

This case is reminiscent of the SEC's enforcement actions against several internet companies that distributed "free stock" during the height of the dot-com era twenty years ago. In what have become known to securities lawyers as the free stock cases, investors were typically required to sign up on issuers' websites and disclose personal information in order to obtain "free" shares. Free stock recipients were also offered extra shares for soliciting additional investors or for linking their own websites to those of an issuer or purchasing services offered through an issuer. Due to these activities, the SEC similarly took the position that the issuers received value (and did not make a gift) by creating a public market for their shares, increasing their business prospects, creating publicity, increasing traffic to their websites, and generating possible interest in future securities offerings. Call it an airdrop or call it free stock, the SEC continues to focus on a transaction's substance, not its label.

Thus, while under certain circumstances, a bona fide gift of securities may be deemed not to involve the offer or sale of securities, and under this "no sale" theory the registration requirements of the Securities Act do not apply, the SEC indicated in *Tomahawk* that airdrops in many cases may not receive this favorable treatment. Of note, the SEC has also stated in its *Framework for "Investment Contract" Analysis of Digital Assets* that airdrops of a token are typically issued "to promote its circulation" and that "an airdrop may constitute a sale or distribution of securities."[118]

118. U.S. Securities and Exchange Commission, *Framework for "Investment Contract" Analysis for Digital Assets* (Apr. 3, 2019), https://www.sec.gov/corpfin/framework-investment-contract-analysis-digital-assets.

SEC Commissioner Peirce's Safe Harbor Proposal

While to date the SEC has declined to issue regulations related to blockchain-based assets, on April 13, 2021, SEC Commissioner Peirce issued an update to a token safe harbor proposal she first introduced in 2020.[119] The updated proposal includes a draft of proposed Securities Rule 195 that would provide a time-limited exemption for tokens. The safe harbor would last for three years and only apply if certain conditions are met, including (1) making specified disclosures required by the proposed rule on a freely accessible public website; (2) offering and selling the token for the purpose of providing access to, participation on, or the development of the network; (3) filing a notice of reliance on the exemption with the SEC with certain specified information; and (4) filing an exit report within three years containing specified information regarding network maturity or failure to achieve network maturity. In the latter case, the exit report must acknowledge that the tokens will be registered as securities.

The proposed rule provides two paths to an exit that would allow the company to keep operating without registration of the tokens: network maturity for a decentralized network and network maturity for a functional network. In either case, the company filing the exit report must include in its report an analysis by outside counsel analyzing specified topics designed to demonstrate that the company has either a decentralized or functional network.

During the three-year safe harbor, companies must make semiannual updates to required disclosures regarding their plan of development for their block explorer. Required disclosures also include information about the source code, network transaction history, token economics, initial development team and certain token holders, trading platforms, token sales, related person transactions, and risk warnings.

Commissioner Peirce has urged the SEC, with new Chair Gary Gensler, to consider how to modify existing SEC rules to accommodate new technology. She is seeking public feedback on the updated proposal. Whether the SEC will act remains an open question.

---

119. *See* Commissioner Hester M. Peirce, *Token Safe Harbor Proposal 2.0* (Apr. 13, 2021) (public statement), https://www.sec.gov/news/public-statement/peirce-statement-token-safe-harbor-proposal-2.0; Commissioner Hester M. Peirce, *Running on Empty: A Proposal to Fill the Gap Between Regulation and Decentralization* (Feb. 6, 2020) (speech to the International Blockchain Congress), https://www.sec.gov/news/speech/peirce-remarks-blockress-2020-02-06.

A Note on "Notes," *Reves and Decentralized Finance*

Recently, the SEC has signaled that it may be evaluating as securities certain blockchain activities where users of the blockchain's digital assets are able to earn yield if the user deposits their digital assets on the blockchain in various ways. In an interview with the Wall Street Journal (the Journal), SEC Chair Gensler focused on decentralized finance (DeFi) projects and, as reported by the Journal, commented that projects that reward participants with valuable digital tokens could cross a line into activity that should be regulated, regardless of how decentralized they are.[120] Other SEC Commissioners have expressed similar concerns.[121] From the SEC's perspective such activities might create a relationship analogous to a note where the holder of the digital asset is lending that asset to the platform in exchange for a promise of a payment in the future. Notes are presumed to be securities with certain exceptions or if the note in question bears a "family resemblance" to notes in those excepted categories based on a four-part test established in *Reves v. Ernst & Young*.[122] The four-factor *Reves* test to determine whether a demand note is a security considers:

1. The motivations that prompt the seller and buyer to enter into the transaction: If the seller's purpose is to raise money for general business use or to finance substantial investments and the buyer is interested primarily in the profit the note is expected to generate, the note is likely to be a security. If the note is exchanged to facilitate the purchase and sale of a minor asset or consumer good, to correct for the seller's cash flow difficulties or to advance some other commercial or consumer purpose, the note is less likely to be a security;

120. *Crypto's "DeFi" Projects Aren't Immune to Regulation, SEC's Gensler Says*, Wall Street Journal. (Aug. 19, 2021)

121. *See e.g.*, Statement on DeFi Risks, Regulations, and Opportunities, Commissioner Caroline A. Crenshaw, November 1, 2021, https://www.sec.gov/news/statement/crenshaw-defi-20211109.

122. *See* Reves v. Ernst & Young, 494 U.S. 56, 64-66 (1990); Exchange Act Section 3(a)(10), 15 U.S.C. 78(c)(3)(10), defining security to include "any note" except "any note, draft, bill of exchange, or banker's acceptance which has a maturity at the time of issuance of not exceeding nine months, exclusive of days of frace, or any renewal thereof the maturity of which is likewise limited."

2. The plan of distribution of the instrument: is the instrument one in which there is common trading for speculation or investment;
3. The reasonable expectations of the investing public: investments will be considered securities on the basis of public expectations even where an economic analysis of the circumstances of the particular transaction might suggest that the instruments are not securities as used in that transaction; and
4. The existence of alternate regulatory scheme: if another regulatory scheme significantly reduces the risk of the instrument, rendering the application of the Securities Acts unnecessary, the note may not be a security.[123]

The SEC applied the *Reves* analysis (as well as the *Howey* analysis) to conclude that loans issued by a peer-to-peer on-line lending program were securities and the firm was required to register the loans. The online platform connected individuals who wished to lend money with those who wished to borrow money. The company sold interests in the loans in the form of promissory notes with individual lenders receiving interest as the notes were repaid.[124] In August 2021, the SEC similarly applied *Reves* (as well as *Howey*) in a settled action against a purported DeFi platform. The platform offered two types of digital assets. The first asset accrued interest and the second digital asset gave token holders voting rights, a share of excess profits and the right to profit from token resales in the secondary market. The SEC concluded the first token that offered interest was a note and a security under *Reves* (and also sold as an investment contract). The second token was an investment contract under *Howey*.[125]

More recently, the staff of the SEC issued a Wells Notice to a cryptocurrency exchange indicating that it would recommend that the agency initiate an enforcement action if the exchange went forward with a proposed digital asset lending program that would have allowed customers to earn interest on their digital assets. Reportedly, the SEC was evaluating the program under both *Howey* and *Reves*. Separately, at least five states

---

123. *Id.* at 66–67.

124. *In the Matter of Prosper Marketplace, Inc.*, Admin Proc. File No. 3-13296 (November 24, 2008).

125. *In the Matter of Blockchain Credit Partners d/b/a DeFi Money Market, Gregory Keough and Derek Acree,* Admin. Proc. File No. 3-20453 (August 6, 2021); https://www.sec.gov/litigation/admin/2021/33-10961.pdf.

have acted to block a cryptocurrency platform from offering interest earning accounts claiming that those accounts are securities.

This chapter focuses on the application of *Howey* to digital assets because SEC actions related to digital assets have primarily focused on the *Howey* test. But, as the SEC (and state regulators) increase their focus on decentralized finance platforms that offer users opportunities to earn yields on their digital assets, practitioners should understand *Reves* and its potential application to digital assets and these issues.

Securities Regulation of Other Activities Related to Blockchain-Based Assets

As mentioned early in this chapter, US laws regulate a whole panoply of transactional activities in the securities industry. Those engaged in such activities with respect to blockchain-based securities have, like issuers, been faced with scrutiny and enforcement actions from the SEC and other regulatory organizations.

Unregistered Broker-Dealers

One set of activities are those engaged in by broker-dealers. "Brokers" of securities engage in the business of effecting transactions in securities for the accounts of others.[126] "Dealers" of securities engage in the business of buying and selling securities for their own accounts.[127] Section 15(a)(1) of the Exchange Act makes it unlawful for any broker or dealer to "effect any transactions in . . . any security" or to "induce or attempt to induce the purchase or sale of, any security" unless that broker or dealer is registered with the SEC.[128] The SEC has instituted several enforcement actions against companies alleging that those companies have acted as unregistered broker-dealers in connection with the sale of digital tokens.

Tokenlot, LLC

On September 11, 2018, the SEC announced a series of charges against unregistered broker-dealers for selling digital tokens, including against TokenLot, LLC, and several individuals. According to the SEC's order,

---

126. 15 U.S.C. § 78c(a)(4).

127. 15 U.S.C. § 78c(a)(5).

128. 15 U.S.C. § 78o(a).

the defendants operated a self-described "ICO Superstore" that solicited investors, took thousands of customer orders for digital tokens, processed investor funds, and handled more than two hundred different digital tokens in connection with both the initial token sales and the defendants' own secondary market activities.[129] The defendants also promoted the sale of approximately forty digital tokens in exchange for marketing fees paid by digital token issuers. Because the digital tokens issued in the ICOs and traded by defendants included securities, the SEC concluded that the defendants' activities required broker-dealer registration with the SEC, and failure to do so violated section 15(a) of the Exchange Act and sections 5(a) and (c) of the Securities Act. The SEC instituted several types of sanctions, including an order to cease and desist future violations, a bar on defendants' association with a regulated entity (such as a broker) and prohibition on other securities-related activity (including service as officer, director, or employee of a public company), and monetary disgorgement and penalties.

FINRA Broker-Dealer Enforcement

Also on September 11, 2018, the Financial Industry Regulatory Authority (FINRA), a self-regulatory organization that oversees broker-dealers, announced its first disciplinary action involving cryptocurrencies against a broker-dealer registered representative.[130]

According to FINRA's complaint,[131] respondent Timothy Ayre, who was associated with six FINRA-regulated broker-dealers, attempted to attract investors into a penny stock company he controlled by offering interests in what he advertised as the "the first minable coin backed by marketable securities."[132] FINRA alleged that as the company's business

129. *In re* Tokenlot, LLC, SEC Administrative Proceeding No. 3-18739 (Sept. 11, 2018), https://www.sec.gov/litigation/admin/2018/33-10543.pdf.

130. Complaint, FINRA Dep't of Enf't v. Timothy Tilton Ayre, Disciplinary Proceeding No. 2016049307801 (Sept. 11, 2018), http://www.finra.org/sites/default/files/Ayre_Complaint_091118.pdf. FINRA works under the supervision of the SEC to write and enforce rules governing SEC-registered broker-dealers. FINRA imposes discipline upon registered broker-dealers. In contrast, unregistered broker-dealers are subject only to direct enforcement action by the SEC, as in *In re Tokenlot*.

131. *Department of Enforcement v. Ayre*, Disciplinary Proceeding No. 2016049307801 (Sept. 11, 2018); https://www.finra.org/sites/default/files/Ayre_Complaint_091118.pdf.

132. *Id.* at ¶ 1.

struggled, Ayre acquired the rights to a cryptocurrency named HempCoin and attempted to repackage HempCoin as a security backed by the publicly traded penny stock. Ayre also marketed HempCoin as "the world's first currency to represent equity ownership" in a publicly traded company.[133] FINRA said that investors mined more than 81 million HempCoin through late 2017 and traded the security on two cryptocurrency exchanges. Based on this, FINRA alleged that Ayre had engaged in the unlawful distribution of HempCoin as an unregistered security, made several misrepresentations, and never disclosed these transactions to his broker-dealer employer. Thus, FINRA asserted that Ayre violated not only the federal securities laws but also several FINRA regulations, including one requiring that registered representatives must "observe high standards of commercial honor and just and equitable principles of trade." In a settlement agreement, Ayre agreed to be "barred in all capacities from the securities industry."[134]

Registration of Broker-Dealers for Blockchain-Based Securities

The SEC and FINRA have granted some licenses for broker-dealers to trade in blockchain-based securities. In January 2021, blockchain-based trading platform INX Limited announced that it had reached agreement to acquire Openfinance Securities, LLC, a registered US broker-dealer operating an alternative trading system (an exchange-like trading platform).[135] INX's aim is to allow investors to trade security tokens on the platform. In another development, on May 12, 2021, Figure Securities, a subsidiary of FinTech lending company Figure Technologies, announced it had received regulatory approval for broker-dealer status and registered a blockchain-based trading system for digital securities.[136]

---

133. *Id.* at ¶ 7.

134. FINRA Dep't of Enf't v. Timothy Tilton Ayre, Disciplinary Proceeding No. 2016049307801 (Apr. 23, 2019).

135. INX Limited, *INX Finalizes Openfinance Securities Acquisition Terms*, CISION PR Newswire (Jan. 19, 2021), https://www.prnewswire.com/news-releases/inx-finalizes-openfinance-securities-acquisition-terms-301209833.html.

136. Law360, *Figure Gets Nod for Blockchain-Based Securities Trading* (May 12, 2021), https://www.law360.com/articles/1384205/figure-gets-nod-for-blockchain-based-securities-trading.

The scope of tokens that might be tradable on such platforms and other details are unknown at this point.

Investment Companies and Investment Advisers

Another set of regulated activities in the securities space are those engaged in by investment companies and investment advisers.

Investment companies are issuers of their own securities that engage in the business of investing, reinvesting, owning, holding, or trading in securities of others and that own or propose to acquire investment securities having a value exceeding 40 percent of the value of the issuer's total assets.[137] A mutual fund is a typical investment company; it is set up as a special purpose corporation, trust, or partnership that issues its own shares (or interests) to investors and pools the proceeds to invest in securities of others. Investment companies must register with the SEC and meet nontrivial regulatory requirements (unless they can meet one of several exemptions).[138]

Investment advisers are any person or firm that engages in the business, for compensation, of providing advice to others or issuing reports or analyses regarding securities.[139] Investment advisers must also register with the SEC and meet various regulatory requirements (unless an exemption applies).[140]

On September 11, 2018, the SEC announced charges against Crypto Asset Management, LP (CAM), the managing member of and investment manager to Crypto Asset Fund, LLC (CAF), which was a pooled investment vehicle formed for the purpose of investing in digital assets.[141] It raised over $3.6 million from fourteen investors for this purpose. CAF had never registered with the SEC as an investment company.

The SEC concluded that CAF had engaged in the business of investing, holding, and trading digital assets that were securities and therefore had to register as an investment company under the Investment Company Act. The SEC also concluded that CAM, as an investment

137. *See* 15 U.S.C. § 80a-3(a).

138. *See id.*; 15 U.S.C. § 80a-8.

139. *See* 15 U.S.C. § 80b-2(a)(11).

140. *See* 15 U.S.C. § 80b-3.

141. *See In re* Crypto Asset Mgmt, LP, SEC Administrative Proceeding No. 3-18740 (Sept. 11, 2018), https://www.sec.gov/litigation/admin/2018/33-10544.pdf.

adviser, made material misstatements and omissions in violation of the Investment Advisers Act of 1940, as well as the Securities Act. Respondents in the case agreed to an order to cease and desist future violations and a $200,000 civil monetary penalty.

Most recently, the staff of the SEC's Division of Investment Management issued a statement[142] announcing that it and the SEC's Divisions of Examinations and Economic and Risk Analysis will "closely monitor" the impact of mutual fund investments in Bitcoin futures on "investor protection, capital formation and the fairness and efficiency of markets."[143] The statement made clear that assessing compliance with the Investment Company Act and its rules and regulations in this area is a "top priority" for the SEC staff and also cautioned investors to carefully evaluate the risks of investing in funds with such exposure, particularly in light of the volatility of the Bitcoin and Bitcoin Futures markets, the lack of regulation, and the potential for fraud in those markets.

The statement signals that funds and advisers should expect increased scrutiny, including in areas such as (1) evaluation of the liquidity and depth of the Bitcoin futures market, (2) the ability of a fund to liquidate Bitcoin future positions, (3) risk management, (4) valuation of holdings, (5) compliance with the open-end fund liquidity rule and how funds classify the liquidity of positions in the Bitcoin futures market, (6) the potential for fraud and manipulation, (7) potential issues with ETFs in the Bitcoin futures market, and in particular, (8) concerns that an ETF cannot close to new investors and could become too large or if liquidity in the market starts to decrease.

Exchanges

The final regulated entities discussed here are exchanges. Securities exchanges are organizations that provide a marketplace for bringing together buyers and sellers of securities, such as the New York Stock

---

142. *See* U.S. Securities and Exchange Commission, *Staff Statement on Funds Registered Under the Investment Company Act Investing in the Bitcoin Futures Market* (May 11, 2021), https://www.sec.gov/news/public-statement/staff-statement-investing-bitcoin-futures-market.

143. *Id.*

Exchange.[144] Securities exchanges must register with the SEC or qualify for an exemption.[145]

On November 8, 2018, the SEC announced settled charges against an unlicensed digital token trading platform called EtherDelta.[146] The case is the SEC's first enforcement action based on findings that such a platform operated as an unregistered national securities exchange. According to the SEC's order, EtherDelta provided online secondary market trading of certain tokens, matching up buyers and sellers. The SEC found that almost all of the orders placed through EtherDelta were traded after the SEC issued the DAO Report, which had alerted the public that the federal securities laws provide a functional test that could include a digital asset trading system within the definition of an "exchange" subject to the SEC's jurisdiction.

Regulation of digital asset trading platforms has been an area of increasing SEC regulatory focus. Most recently, on January 26, 2022, the SEC proposed amendments to the definition of "exchange" in Exchange Act Rule 3b-16 and to Regulation ATS based on the proposed definition. As potentially relevant to digital assets, the revised definition would include Communication Protocol Systems (CPSs). CPSs would be required to register as an exchange or operate under the ATS exemption which would require them to register as a broker-dealer, become a member of a self-regulatory organization, and comply with Regulation ATS. Under the proposal, a CPS "would include a system that offers protocols and the use of non-firm trading interest to bring together buyers and sellers of securities." The definition would encompass a CPS that makes available for trading "any type of security."[147] As discussed earlier in this chapter, SEC officials have repeatedly stated that digital assets are securities. The proposed rule is complex and is already generating reaction. It is yet another example of the fast-paced, ever-changing regulatory environment facing digital assets as potential securities.

---

144. *See* 15 U.S.C. § 78c(a)(1).

145. *See* 15 U.S.C. § 78e.

146. *In re* Zachary Coburn, Administrative Proceeding No. 3-1888 (Nov. 8, 2018), https://www.sec.gov/litigation/admin/2018/34-84553.pdf.

147. *See* e.g., https://www.sec.gov/news/press-release/2022-10; https://www.sec.gov/rules/proposed/2022/34-94062.pdf (at n. 5 and p. 10).

SPECIAL PROBLEMS INVOLVING BLOCKCHAIN-BASED SECURITIES

As mentioned in Chapter 1, the current systems for tracking and transferring ownership of securities, such as stocks, are incredibly convoluted and involve myriad parties.[148] In short, publicly held corporations generally do not issue physical stock certificates. Instead, a "transfer agent" maintains a ledger of all stock owners with amounts held. But the list generally does not contain the identities of the actual stockholders but instead only a smaller number of "holders of record."[149] Record holders are typically not the ultimate "beneficial owners;" they are holders of the shares in "fungible bulk" and keep a separate list of those for whom they hold the stock. These entities may be banks or other institutions that, yet again, are not the ultimate beneficial owners but hold their allocation of shares also in fungible bulk and maintain yet another ledger of entities and individuals for whom they hold the stock.

Sale and transfer of stock require still additional parties. When a beneficial owner (such as a retail investor or mutual fund) wants to sell, their broker may find an exchange or similar trading platform to actually match them up with a buyer. When a buyer is found and a sale matched, a new party enters the mix, a clearinghouse, which steps in between the buyer and seller, breaks the sale between them into two separate parts, and takes the place of a counterparty to both.[150] And, of course, completing the transfer may require updating of the various ledgers described earlier.

Many of these procedures and mechanisms exist to meet legal requirements. For example, SEC regulations require broker-dealers that keep customer assets, such as securities, to safeguard them and separate them from firm assets.[151] State corporate and uniform commercial codes

---

148. For a good overview in the context of a case illustrating this complexity, see *In re* Appraisal of Dell Inc., 143 A.3d 20 (Del. Ct. Chancery 2016).

149. *See In re* Dell, 143 A.3d at 21–22.

150. *See* Richard Gendal Brown, *A Simple Explanation of How Shares Move Around the Securities Settlement System* (Jan. 5, 2014), https://gendal.me/2014/01/05/a-simple-explanation-of-how-shares-move-around-the-securities-settlement-system/.

151. *See* U.S. Securities and Exchange Commission, *Joint Staff Statement on Broker-Dealer Custody of Digital Asset Securities, Division of Trading and Markets, U.S. Securities and Exchange Commission Office of General Counsel, Financial Industry Regulatory Authority* (July 8, 2019), https://www.sec.gov/news/public-statement/joint-staff-statement-broker-dealer-custody-digital-assets-securities.

provide still other requirements for issuers of securities to keep ledgers of ownership and transfer.[152]

Exactly how issuers of blockchain securities can comply with these requirements in various circumstances remains uncertain and has stymied the use of blockchain to issue and trade securities. For example, over the past several years, FINRA and the SEC have delayed resolution of applications to register broker-dealers working in the blockchain securities space, expressing concerns about compliance with the custody rules previously discussed.[153] On September 25, 2020, the SEC Division of Trading and Markets issued a "no-action" letter to FINRA, stating that the division will not recommend enforcement action if a broker-dealer operating an alternative trading system (ATS; a regulatory alternative to an exchange) for the trading of blockchain-based securities follows a three-step process by which buyers and sellers who trade via the ATS settle directly with each other and the ATS does not take custody of the securities.[154]

In 2020, online retailer Overstock.com issued a "digitally enhanced" dividend to current shareholders in the form of preferred stock shares.[155] The term *digitally enhanced* was used to reflect the use of a private blockchain. But Overstock ultimately clarified that the shares would be traditional securities, the holders of record for which would be documented on the register of traditional transfer agent Computershare, and that a blockchain would be used only as a "courtesy carbon copy." Even then, the dividend had limitations: it could only be sold through a subscriber to an ATS operated by tZERO ATS, LLC (an Overstock subsidiary).

On August 20, 2020, INX Limited filed an amended registration statement with the SEC seeking to offer and sell up to 130,000,000 INX tokens, Ethereum-based security tokens that will entitle the holders to

---

152. Reade Ryan & Mayme Donohue, *Securities on Blockchain*, 73 Bus. Law., 85, 96 (Winter 2017–2018).

153. *See* Joint Staff Statement, *supra*.

154. Letter from SEC Division of Trading and Markets to FINRA, Re: ATS Role in the Settlement of Digital Asset Security Trades (Sept. 25, 2020), https://www.sec.gov/divisions/marketreg/mr-noaction/2020/finra-ats-role-in-settlement-of-digital-asset-security-trades-09252020.pdf.

155. Letter from Overstock.com, Inc., to SEC Division of Corporation Finance (Dec. 16, 2019), https://www.sec.gov/Archives/edgar/data/1130713/000119312519315332/filename1.htm.

certain distributions of the company's net cash flow.[156] In the filing, INX stated that it intends to register an ATS called INX Securities, which will be an order book platform with a matching engine for the trading of security tokens. It also stated that it intends to register a broker-dealer called INX Services. INX envisions that security tokens trading on its platform will be first transferred to wallets controlled by a qualified custodian. When INX customers trade them on the platform, INX will update its internal customer ownership records. When the owner of a token wishes to withdraw it from their account, the custodian will transfer it to the customer's private wallet. INX acknowledged, however, that "there is currently significant uncertainty regarding the application of federal and state laws and regulations to the trading of security tokens, including regulations governing market intermediaries, and this uncertainty may cause significant delay or may prevent us from developing our INX Securities trading platform as currently envisioned."[157] While INX started distributing their tokens in late 2020, INX was not actually tradable on any public US platform.[158] In early May 2021, INX concluded its registered token IPO.

* * *

To date, regulatory uncertainty and scrutiny have limited the issuance and public trading of blockchain-based securities in the United States. But steps forward, including from companies like Overstock and INX, suggest that there are efforts to work through these challenges. Separately, Commissioner Peirce's safe harbor proposal may lead to an SEC effort to provide further clarity. Whether the blockchain securities industry can finally break through these barriers remains the single biggest question in blockchain law.

---

156. *See* Form F-1, INX Limited (Aug. 20, 2020), https://www.sec.gov/Archives/edgar/data/1725882/000121390019016285/ff12019_inxlimited.htm.

157. *Id.*

158. *See* INX token offering, https://token.inx.co (estimating launch of INX Digital within six months of the offering).

3 Commodity Futures Trading Commission Regulation of Blockchain-Based Assets

Daniel Nathan, Jonas Robison, and S. Chris Min

INTRODUCTION

Any discussion of the regulation of blockchain-based assets must address their status as a commodity, their treatment under the Commodity Exchange Act (CEA), and the regulation of commodities and derivatives by the Commodity Futures Trading Commission (CFTC). While the CFTC is commonly understood to have jurisdiction over derivatives—typically futures, options, and swaps—based on commonly understood commodities, its jurisdiction is actually much broader. First, while the traditional understanding of "commodities" includes agricultural, mining, and energy commodities, those are actually a very small part of the universe of commodities whose derivatives are regulated by the CFTC; many of the regulated derivatives products are based on financial commodities, including futures and swaps based on bonds, stock indices, interest rates, and foreign currency exchange rates. Second, the meaning of *derivative*, which is broadly defined as a contract whose value derives from the value of an underlying asset, has dramatically expanded in the more than eighty years since the CEA was enacted, and particularly since the passage of the Dodd-Frank Wall Street Reform and Consumer Protection Act (Dodd-Frank Act) in 2010, beyond conventional futures and options to include the broad category of swaps. And, third, the CFTC's jurisdiction is not limited to derivatives trading but also extends to certain "cash" or "spot" transactions in the physical commodity, including when fraud or manipulation under CEA section 6(c)(1) and CFTC Rule 180.1 is involved.

As discussed in this chapter, virtual currencies and, depending on their characteristics, potentially other types of blockchain-based assets appear to be commodities under the CEA's broad *commodity* definition. Consequently, derivatives based on such assets likely come within the CFTC's jurisdiction. This jurisdiction includes, among other things, the CFTC's enforcement authority over fraud and manipulation; regulation of trading activities; registration and oversight of trading exchanges, intermediaries, and associated persons; and examination and enforcement with respect to market participants.

CFTC'S JURISDICTION OVER BLOCKCHAIN-BASED ASSETS

Types of Blockchain-Based Digital Assets

The CFTC has consistently asserted its jurisdiction over transactions in "virtual currencies" in a variety of contexts over the years, including in statements made by CFTC commissioners, CFTC staff guidance, and positions taken in the CFTC's enforcement actions. In its *Digital Assets Primer* from December 2020,[1] the CFTC distinguished among (1) "virtual currencies," described as coins, native tokens, or intrinsic tokens, the intended purpose of which is to serve as a medium of exchange; (2) "digital tokens" that require "another blockchain network to operate and may serve a variety of functions beyond virtual currency, e.g., utility tokens"; and (3) "digital assets," which encompass "additional applications, including ownership, transaction tracking, identity management, and smart contracts. A digital asset may express characteristics of a commodity or commodity derivative." The *Digital Assets Primer* indicated that virtual currencies are a subset of digital tokens, which are, in turn, a subset of digital assets.

In asserting its jurisdiction, the CFTC has generally referred to "virtual currencies." For example, as discussed in greater detail later in this chapter, in *Coinflip, Inc.*, CFTC No. 15-29 (Sept. 17, 2015) ("*Coinflip*"), the CFTC stated that Bitcoin and other "virtual currencies" were properly

1. Commodity Futures Trading Commission, *Digital Assets Primer* (Dec. 17, 2020), https://www.cftc.gov/PressRoom/PressReleases/8336-20.

defined as commodities. That being said, it may be unclear whether particular types of digital assets other than virtual currencies would be considered commodities. In this regard, the leaders of the CFTC, the US Securities and Exchange Commission (SEC), and the Financial Crimes Enforcement Network of the US Department of the Treasury (FinCEN), in a joint statement on activities involving digital assets issued in October 2019, provided the following reminder:

> [R]egardless of the label or terminology that market participants may use, or the level or type of technology employed, it is the facts and circumstances underlying an asset, activity or service, including its economic reality and use (whether intended or organically developed or repurposed), that determines the general categorization of an asset, the specific regulatory treatment of the activity involving the asset . . . for purposes of the BSA [Bank Secrecy Act].[2]

Similarly, the *Digital Assets Primer* from December 2020 stated: "A digital asset may express characteristics of a commodity or commodity derivative."

The following section provides a detailed discussion of the definition of *commodity* and its applicability to virtual currencies and potentially other types of digital assets.

The Commodity Exchange Act Definition of *Commodity*

The CFTC's jurisdiction over transactions involving one or more blockchain-based assets frequently depends on whether the blockchain-based asset falls within the CEA's *commodity* definition.[3] The term *commodity* is defined in CEA section 1a(9) to include (i) any one of a large identified group of agricultural or other products as well as

2. CFTC, *Leaders of CFTC, FinCEN, and SEC Issue Joint Statement on Activities Involving Digital Assets* (Oct. 11, 2019), https://www.cftc.gov/PressRoom/Speeches Testimony/cftcfincensecjointstatement101119.

3. However, the definition of *swap* in the CEA and the regulations thereunder appear not to be limited to products that have a commodity as the underlying instrument. *See* 7 U.S.C. § 1a(47)(A). The CFTC requirements applicable to swaps are discussed later in this chapter.

(ii) "all services, rights, and interests . . . in which contracts for future delivery are presently or in the future dealt in."[4]

While this definition does not have an express reference to blockchain-based assets, it is quite broad. Category (ii) was added in 1974 to grant expansive authority to the CFTC and enable the CFTC, through the flexible language in category (ii), to determine the scope of its own authority through its interpretation of the CEA without requiring congressional action. Such expansive authority granted to the CFTC, however, resulted in some interpretive ambiguities on the scope of that authority. Whether the CFTC has jurisdiction over blockchain-based assets depends on whether the second broad category in the commodity definition can be interpreted to include such blockchain-based assets.[5]

A narrow interpretation of the second category of the commodity definition takes the position that only goods, articles, services, rights, and interests on which a futures contract currently exists are "commodities" under the CEA. Thus, for example, a particular type of blockchain-based asset could be considered a commodity over which the CFTC has jurisdiction only if corresponding futures trading exists. Under this interpretation, congressional action would be required for any transaction involving a new or emerging blockchain-based asset to fall within the CFTC's jurisdiction under the CEA.

A broad interpretation of the second category of the *commodity* definition, by contrast, takes the position that the term *commodity* under the CEA includes all goods, articles, services, rights, and interests as long as they could, in the future, be a subject of futures trading. This reading would not require the existence of a futures market for the CFTC to have jurisdiction over a commodity, but rather simply the

---

4. Specifically, wheat, cotton, rice, corn, oats, barley, rye, flaxseed, grain sorghums, mill feeds, butter, eggs, *Solanum tuberosum* (Irish potatoes), wool, wool tops, fats and oils (including lard, tallow, cottonseed oil, peanut oil, soybean oil, and all other fats and oils), cottonseed meal, cottonseed, peanuts, soybeans, soybean meal, livestock, livestock products, and frozen concentrated orange juice, and all other goods and articles, except onions . . . and motion picture box office receipts (or any index, measure, value, or data related to such receipts). 7 U.S.C. § 1a(9).

5. As discussed later, in *Commodity Futures Trading Comm'n v. McDonnell,* the U.S. District Court for the Eastern District of New York held that virtual currencies fall within the common definition of *commodity* as well as the CEA's broad definition of the term *commodity*, which includes "all other goods and articles . . . and all services, rights, and interests . . . in which contracts for future delivery are presently or in the future dealt in."

possibility of such a market existing in the future. This interpretation would allow the CFTC to regulate transactions involving new or emerging blockchain-based assets as long as it is conceivable that a futures market could develop for them. Such a broad approach may, however, run afoul of the original public interest justification for the CFTC's regulation of the futures market, which was based on the interrelationship between futures markets and underlying cash markets.

An example of this broad interpretation may be found in *Coinflip*, supra, in which the CFTC first stated that Bitcoin and other virtual currencies are properly defined as commodities. Subsequently, in granting preliminary injunctive relief to the CFTC in a fraud action, *Commodity Futures Trading Commission v. McDonnell*,[6] Judge Jack B. Weinstein of the US District Court for the Eastern District of New York (EDNY) held that virtual currencies are commodities under the CEA because they "fall well-within" the common definition of *commodity* as well as the CEA's broad definition of the term *commodity*, which includes "all other goods and articles . . . and all services, rights, and interests . . . in which contracts for future delivery are presently or in the future dealt in." The court included in the definition virtual currencies for which no futures contract is available. The court also found that the absence of futures trading was not an obstacle to the CFTC's jurisdiction, in view of the CEA's anti-manipulation and anti-fraud provisions under section 6(c)(i) and CFTC Regulation 180.1, which prohibit fraudulent and manipulative schemes in connection with "a contract of sale of any commodity in interstate commerce." Multiple federal courts have since held that virtual currencies are commodities under the CEA.

Yet another interpretation of the *commodity* definition that falls somewhere between the narrow and broad interpretations discussed earlier takes the position that the existence of a futures trading on a specific commodity is not required for the CFTC to have jurisdiction over such commodity so long as there is a futures trading in another commodity in the same category of commodity. For example, when it ruled against the defendant in a case involving a digital currency, *CFTC v. My Big Coin Pay, Inc.*, the US District Court in Massachusetts observed that the CEA defines *commodity* by category rather than by "type, grade,

---

6. CFTC v. McDonnell, No. 1:18-cv-00361-JBW-RLM, slip op. (E.D.N.Y. Mar. 6, 2018) (Mem. and Order), http://www.cftc.gov/idc/groups/public/@lrenforcement actions/documents/legalpleading/enfcoindroporder030618.pdf.

quality, brand, producer, manufacturer, or form."[7] The court adopted the CFTC's argument that the CEA only requires the existence of futures trading within a certain class in order for all items within that class to be considered commodities. According to the court, the term *commodity* "includes a host of specifically enumerated agricultural products as well as 'all other goods and articles . . . and all services rights and interests . . . in which contracts for future delivery are presently or in the future dealt in.'" The court specifically agreed with the CFTC that "Congress' approach to defining 'commodity' signals an intent that courts focus on categories—not specific items."[8] This approach avoids some of the problems that are present in the narrow and broad interpretations but presents the question of how to determine the appropriate characteristics to define different categories of commodities. Virtual currencies and blockchain-based assets are quickly evolving and ever diversifying. There are certain blockchain-based assets with characteristics of various categories of tokens, such as payment tokens, utility tokens, and asset tokens. Therefore, the proper categorization of commodities becomes crucial under this interpretation.

Even once it is established that a blockchain-based asset is a commodity, it is important to understand what type of commodity it is. The CEA makes distinctions based on the type or classification of a commodity and refers to foreign currencies, nonfinancial commodities, agricultural commodities, excluded commodities, and exempt commodities. If, for example, a virtual currency could be categorized as a foreign currency, the CEA contains special provisions in CEA section 2(c)(2)(B) and in CEA section 2(c)(2)(C) for permitting and regulating retail transactions involving foreign currency, which are considered more permissive than the provisions governing other types of commodity. In *Coinflip*, supra,

7. CFTC v. My Big Coin Pay, Inc., 334 F. Supp. 3d 492, 497 (D. Mass. 2018).

8. The district court compared this case to a series of cases involving natural gas, in which courts repeatedly rejected arguments that a particular type of natural gas was not a commodity because that specific type was not the subject of a futures contract. Those cases held that because natural gas is "fungible" and may move freely throughout a national pipeline system, this was sufficient to show that natural gas, including the types at issue in these cases, was a commodity. *See* United States v. Brooks, 681 F.3d 678 (5th Cir. 2012); United States v. Futch, 278 F. App'x 387, 395 (5th Cir. 2008); United States v. Valencia, No. CR.A. H-03-024, 2003 WL 23174749, at *8 (S.D. Tex. Aug. 25, 2003), *vacated in part on reconsideration*, No. CRIM.A. H-03-024, 2003 WL 23675402 (S.D. Tex. Nov. 13, 2003), *rev'd and remanded on other grounds*, 394 F.3d 352 (5th Cir. 2004).

however, the CFTC characterized virtual currency as not being "real" currency, which makes it unlikely that virtual currency would be considered foreign currency.[9]

The CEA also makes a distinction between excluded and exempt commodities, which functions as a proxy for distinguishing between financial commodities and nonfinancial commodities. The term *excluded commodity* generally refers to any financial instrument such as a security, currency, interest rate, debt instrument, or credit rating; any economic or commercial index other than a narrow-based commodity index; or any other value that is out of the control of participants and is associated with an economic consequence. The term *exempt commodity* refers to a commodity that is not an excluded commodity or an agricultural commodity, functioning as a catchall category that includes energy commodities and metal. Exempt commodities and agricultural commodities are considered nonfinancial commodities.

Significantly, as discussed in greater detail later in this chapter, if blockchain-based assets are determined to be excluded commodities, both the forward contract exclusion and the trade option exemption would be unavailable, because they are limited to nonfinancial commodities.

The Divide Between CFTC's and SEC's Jurisdiction

Once a blockchain-based asset is determined to fall within the meaning of *commodity* under the CEA, then the question becomes whether such an asset is also a *security* under the securities regulations.[10] The CFTC largely yields its jurisdictional and regulatory claim over securities to the SEC. However, the continued proliferation and variety of blockchain-based assets mean that it may become increasingly difficult

---

9. The CFTC has found that Bitcoin and other virtual currencies, which do not have legal tender status, are distinct from "real currencies." Coinflip, Inc., CFTC No. 15-29 (Sept. 17, 2015).

10. With respect to these questions, former CFTC Chairman Heath Tarbert said in an interview that "[W]e are waiting on the SEC, in many instances, to make that initial threshold determination as to whether it is a security. Basically, the critical question is: Is it a security. If the answer is no . . . then pretty much it is likely to be, if it's a financial contract, a commodity." "The Challenge of Defining Digital Assets," discussion between Terry Duffy and Heath Tarbert on the Global Financial Leadership Conference in Naples, Florida on November 18, 2019, https://www.gflc.com/highlights.html.

to have a clear jurisdictional divide between securities over which the SEC has primary jurisdiction and commodity interests subject to the CFTC's jurisdiction.[11] Based on SEC enforcement actions and other pronouncements, the SEC appears to classify blockchain-based assets by their apparent purpose. Broadly speaking, if the digital asset constitutes an investment for profit in a common enterprise with any profits expected from the efforts of others, then such digital assets are likely to be securities.[12] On the other hand, if the digital asset is used as a medium of exchange to facilitate the purchase and sale of other assets, then it is likely a commodity. While such a distinction appears simple, its application may be murky, as many digital assets have multiple purposes, and the facts may not always point to any one predominant purpose.

While the SEC has taken a somewhat cautious approach in its regulation of blockchain-based assets, the CFTC appears to have been more permissive and open minded about cryptocurrencies. This open-minded approach has been demonstrated by the various forms of guidance it has issued over the last several years, as well as its establishment of LabCFTC (discussed later), and its approval of interests on blockchain-based assets to be traded on designated contract markets.

Position Taken by CFTC to Date

The CFTC has indicated a generally friendly approach to innovation in blockchain-based assets. One example is its creation in May 2017 of LabCFTC, which serves as a platform to inform the industry of the CFTC's understanding of new technologies and as "an information source for the Commission and CFTC staff on responsible innovation that may influence policy development."[13] According to the CFTC, LabCFTC is

---

11. The SEC's approach to whether a blockchain-based asset is a security derives from its application of the test set forth in SEC v. W. J. Howey Co. (the "Howey Test"), which is discussed elsewhere in this book.

12. *See* Chapter 2 for an analysis of when blockchain-based assets constitute securities. Additionally, the SEC and CFTC may have concurrent jurisdiction over regulation of some digital assets. *See* Commodity Futures Trading Comm'n v. McDonnell, 287 F. Supp. 3d 213, 222 (E.D.N.Y. 2018).

13. CFTC, *LabCFTC Overview*, https://www.cftc.gov/LabCFTC/Overview/index.htm#:~:text=LabCFTC%20is%20the%20focal%20point,Commission's%20understanding%20of%20new%20technologies; https://www.cftc.gov/LabCFTC/index.htm. The CFTC credits LabCFTC with helping inform the CFTC's decisions in its crypto-related guidance and enforcement actions.

designed to be the hub for the agency's engagement with the financial technology (FinTech) innovation community. However, despite such proactive steps taken by the CFTC, because it lacks express statutory authority over the blockchain-based assets market, the CFTC's ability to regulate any virtual currency transaction will depend on whether such a transaction falls within its existing jurisdiction under the CEA.

The CEA grants the CFTC jurisdiction over both exchange-traded instruments—including futures and options on futures on nonsecurity commodities and options on nonsecurity commodities—and off-exchange or over-the-counter instruments—including swaps based on nonsecurity commodities, including options on a nonsecurity commodity, retail-leveraged, margined, or financed transaction in commodities that are not securities or foreign currencies and retail-leveraged, margined, or financed transactions in foreign currencies offered by futures commission merchants or retail foreign exchange dealers.[14] Any of these types of transactions, depending on their characteristics, could be based on one or more blockchain-based assets. Accordingly, whether the CFTC can rightly claim its jurisdiction over any such transaction involving a blockchain-based asset frequently depends, as described earlier, on whether that asset falls within the meaning of *commodity* under the CEA. The following provides an overview of those various types of CFTC-regulated transactions.

Application of Commodity Interest Definitions to Virtual Currencies and Other Digital Assets

Commodity Interests Defined

As discussed earlier, with certain exceptions, the CEA gives the CFTC jurisdiction over a broad range of transactions involving commodities. Once it is established that a "commodity" is involved, the CFTC generally has exclusive jurisdiction over transactions involving "commodity interests" based on such a commodity. A "commodity interest" includes (i) commodity futures, (ii) options on future contracts, (iii) swaps, (iv) leveraged retail foreign exchange contracts, and (v) leveraged retail commodity transactions and (vi) certain other leveraged products.[15] The definitions describing the foregoing items (i) through (iii) are provided in the Appendix; the following section discusses leveraged transactions and

14. *See, e.g.*, 7 U.S.C. § 2(a)(1).

15. *See* 17 C.F.R. § 1.3.

in particular, item (v). If no exclusions or exemptions apply, the CFTC has a basis for claiming jurisdiction over such commodity interests. Therefore, once a blockchain-based asset is determined to be a commodity, then the CFTC has jurisdiction to regulate commodity interests based on such a blockchain-based asset.[16] In *Coinflip*, supra, for example, the CFTC found that the defendant, Coinflip, Inc., unlawfully offered commodity options operating a facility for the trading of such options without being registered as a designated contract market or a swap execution facility. Because Coinflip, Inc., offered commodity options, which are derivatives, the CFTC had a clear basis to assert jurisdiction once it determined that Bitcoin is a commodity.

Discussion of Leveraged Retail Commodity Transactions

Jurisdiction under the Dodd-Frank Act

Generally, the CFTC is not authorized to regulate "spot" transactions, which involve immediate delivery and payment of products within a few days of the trade date. However, the CFTC has jurisdictional reach over certain spot transactions through its regulation of "retail commodity transactions." The CFTC's jurisdiction over leveraged retail transactions remained uncertain until passage of the Dodd-Frank Act in 2010, where Congress extended certain provisions of the CEA to apply to all other "retail commodity transactions" pursuant to CEA section 2(c)(2)(D)(iii). CEA section 2(c)(2)(D) applies to any agreement, contract, or transaction in any commodity that is entered into with, or offered to (even if not entered into with), (i) a retail person (i.e., generally, a person who is not an "eligible contract participant"), and (ii) on a leveraged or margined basis, or financed by the offeror, the counterparty, or a person acting in concert with the offeror or counterparty on a similar basis. The definition of *eligible contract participant* is discussed later in this chapter. CEA section 2(c)(2)(D) provides that such an agreement, contract, or transaction is subject to CEA sections 4(a), 4(b), and 4b "as if the agreement, contract, or transactions was a contract of sale of a commodity for future delivery" (i.e., a futures contract).

One important exception to the CFTC's jurisdiction over leveraged retail commodity transaction is for a contract of sale that "results in

---

16. However, as noted in n.2 *supra*, the definition of "swap" in the CEA and the regulations thereunder appear not to be limited to products that have a commodity as the underlying. *See* 7 U.S.C. § 1a(47)(A).

actual delivery within 28 days or such other longer period as the CFTC may determine by rule or regulation based upon the typical commercial practice in cash or spot markets for the commodity involved."[17] The determinative factor as to whether a transaction in virtual currency is subject to regulation by the CFTC then is whether actual delivery occurs within 28 days of trade execution.[18] Under interpretive guidance issued in March 2020 (the "Actual Delivery Guidance"),[19] the CFTC interpreted "actual delivery" in the context of blockchain-based assets as taking place when (a) a customer (i) secures possession and control of the entire quantity of the commodity—whether it was purchased on margin, or using leverage, or any other financing arrangement—and (ii) has ability to use the entire quantity of the commodity freely in commerce, no later than 28 days from the date of the transaction; and (b) the offeror and counterparty seller do not retain any interest in, legal right, or control over any of the purchased commodity after 28 days from the date of the transaction. While this interpretation is carefully drafted to avoid permitting any "sham delivery" to qualify, the Actual Delivery Guidance states that the simplest definition of actual delivery is the ability of a purchaser to use the virtual currency immediately as a unit of exchange. And while the 28-day period is provided as the outside time limit to constitute actual delivery, as a practical matter, it typically takes much fewer than 28 days for a virtual currency transfer to complete. To determine whether the seller no longer retains any interest in the virtual currency, the CFTC may look to whether the seller retains any ability to access or withdraw any quantity of the virtual currency from the purchaser's account or virtual wallet. The Actual Delivery Guidance essentially reaffirms guidance that the CFTC provided in 2013, in a non-virtual currency context, as to the "functional approach" that the CFTC would apply in determining whether actual delivery had occurred.

---

17. 7 U.S.C. § 2(c)(2)(D)(ii)(III)(aa).

18. In the CFTC's enforcement action against Bitfinex, for example, the CFTC stated that the virtual currency platform violated CEA sections 4(a) and 4d because the unregistered entity "did not actually deliver bitcoins purchased from them." Rather, the entity "held the purchased bitcoins in bitcoin deposit wallets that it owned and controlled."

19. Retail Commodity Transactions Involving Certain Digital Assets, 85 Fed. Reg. 37, 734-01 (June 24, 2020).

Independent Exchanges and Self-Regulatory Organization Regulation of Trading in Commodity Interests

Approval of Trading Futures on Bitcoin

In its December 2020 *Digital Assets Primer*, LabCFTC staff explained the approval process for digital assets derivatives that are traded on exchange. The *Primer* points out that such derivatives offer a variety of benefits, including hedging and speculative trading; providing a means to exchange value among different digital assets; and providing a way to obtain price exposure to virtual currencies without taking ownership, since they are cash-settled. The markets for digital assets derivatives are developing; Bitcoin derivatives have been listed for trading, as has a futures contract based on Ether. The CFTC has sought to provide transparency on the product certification and review process, including issuing guidance in 2018 for listing or clearing currency derivative products.[20] This includes guidance to designated contract markets (DCMs) and swap execution facilities (SEFs) about how to either self-certify a blockchain-based asset derivative or submit the proposed contract to the CFTC for approval. As part of such guidance, the *Primer* sets out the issues that the CFTC considers in reviewing both cash-settled and physically settled digital asset derivatives, such as the reliability of contract settlement prices and physical transfer and storage protocols.

In recent years, various exchanges such as the Chicago Mercantile Exchange have listed Bitcoin futures, options on Bitcoin futures, and Bitcoin swaps.[21]

CME, CBOT, NYMEX, and COMEX Rulebooks

CME, CBOT, NYMEX, and COMEX are separate DCMs, CFTC-registered exchanges, that are subject to CFTC regulation and oversight pursuant to section 5 of the CEA. DCMs can provide all types of traders, including retail customers, access to virtual currency derivative products.

---

20. CFTC Staff Advisory No. 18–14: Advisory with Respect to Virtual Currency Derivative Product Listings (May 21, 2018), https://www.cftc.gov/sites/default/files/idc/groups/public/%40lrlettergeneral/documents/letter/2018-05/18-14_0.pdf.

21. The CFTC has provided a list of approved and self-certified listed products at *Contracts and Products*, https://www.cftc.gov/IndustryOversight/ContractsProducts/index.htm.

The CFTC's rule allowing DCMs to "self-certify" new products for listing has led to a number of virtual currency derivative products becoming available. For example, as previously discussed, CME self-certified new contracts for Bitcoin futures products in December 2017 and began listing options on Bitcoin futures in January 2020. Additionally, CME announced the launch of Ether futures on February 8, 2021.[22]

Each DCM has self-regulatory responsibilities and maintains its own set of rules (the rulebooks) that are intended to ensure fair and orderly trading, financial controls, and the efficient dissemination of trade price information. Each rulebook includes access requirements, terms and conditions of any contracts to be traded, and rules prohibiting abusive trade practices. For the Bitcoin futures, for example, the CME Rulebook specifies the characteristics of the subject futures contracts and the various requirements for trading, such as the trading schedule, units and pricing, among others.[23] Any traders participating on any exchanges are required to be aware of and abide by all rules in the rulebooks. Any virtual currency derivative products that are, or will be, listed on DCMs are therefore subject to the applicable rulebook.

National Futures Association

The National Futures Association (NFA) is the industry-wide, self-regulatory organization for the US derivatives industry. The CEA authorized the CFTC to establish registered futures associations with the authority to regulate the practices of its members, and the CFTC oversees the NFA's operation and reviews and approves all of the NFA's most significant actions.

The NFA issued Interpretive Notice 9073 in 2018, in which it implemented new disclosure requirements for NFA members transacting in virtual currency. Among other things, the NFA required futures commission merchants (FCSs) and introducing brokers (IBs) (each as discussed below) to provide an NFA Investor Advisory regarding the risk of virtual currency trading to any customer that engages in trading in a virtual currency derivative transaction with or through the FCM or IB. In addition, the

---

22. Press Release, CME Group, CME Group Announced Launch of Ether Futures on February 8, 2021 (Feb. 8, 2021), https://www.cmegroup.com/media-room/press-releases/2021/2/08/cme_group_announceslaunchofetherfutures.html.

23. Chicago Mercantile Exchange, *CME Rulebook: Chapter 350: Bitcoin Futures* https://www.cmegroup.com/content/dam/cmegroup/rulebook/CME/IV/350/350.pdf.

NFA required commodity pool operators (CPOs) and commodity trading advisors (CTAs) (each as discussed below) that offer pools or trading programs that trade virtual currencies or virtual currency derivatives to follow NFA guidelines designed to ensure that CPOs and CTAs provide robust disclosures related to the risks of such instruments. The NFA also requires all such NFA members to provide prescribed disclosure language to inform customers and counterparties that the NFA does not have regulatory oversight authority over spot virtual currency products or transactions or virtual currency exchanges, custodians, or markets.

OVERVIEW OF VARIOUS CFR CFTC REQUIREMENTS

Certain Categories of Market Participants

The following provides a discussion of certain categories of regulated market participants followed by a discussion of certain CFTC requirements applicable to all participants in the over-the-counter swap markets.

Swap Dealer

Entities that engage in dealing activity in swaps based on blockchain-based assets may become subject to swap dealer regulation if a de minimis threshold is exceeded. A *swap dealer* is generally defined as any person who engages in swap "dealing activity" by (i) holding itself out as a dealer in swaps; (ii) making a market in swaps; (iii) regularly entering into swaps with counterparties as an ordinary course of business for its own account; or (iv) engaging in any activity causing the person to be commonly known in the trade as a dealer or market maker in swaps. Significantly, an exemption from the swap dealer category is provided for entities that engage in only "de minimis" swap dealing activity, which the CFTC has set at $8 billion. This cap looks to the aggregate gross notional amount of swaps that a person combined with its affiliates enters into over the prior twelve months. A host of ongoing requirements apply to registered swap dealers, including business conduct standards and registration and reporting requirements. As of the date of this publication, there are around 100 registered swap dealers.

Because of the relatively high threshold for this exemption, many entities that engage in some amount of swap dealing activity are exempted from swap dealer registration and related requirements. For entities that deal mostly or exclusively in swaps based on blockchain-based assets, the de minimis threshold amount may represent an extraordinarily high amount of dealing activity.

Commodity Pool Operators

A commodity pool operator (CPO) is an individual or organization that operates a commodity pool and solicits funds for that commodity pool. A commodity pool is an enterprise in which funds contributed by a number of persons are combined for the purpose of trading commodity interests (i.e., futures or options on futures, retail off-exchange forex contracts, or swaps) or to invest in another commodity pool. This would include such an enterprise that trades in commodity interests based on blockchain-based assets. CPO registration is required unless the CPO qualifies for one of the exemptions from registration outlined in CFTC Rules 4.5 or 4.13.

Commodity Trading Advisers

A commodity trading advisor (CTA) is an individual or organization that, for compensation or profit, advises others, directly or indirectly, as to the value of or the advisability of trading commodity interests. Again, this would include commodity interests based on blockchain-based assets. All registered CTAs who manage or exercise discretion over customer accounts must be NFA members. CFTC Rule 4.14 sets forth certain requirements for an exemption from CTA registration, including that advice was provided to fifteen or fewer persons during the past twelve months and the entity does not generally hold itself out to the public as a CTA; or entity is CFTC registered and advice is solely incidental to its business or profession; or advice is provided that is not based on knowledge of or tailored to a customer's particular trading account or trading activity.

Certain Requirements Applicable to All OTC Swap Market Participants

Eligible Contract Participants

Only persons who are eligible contract participants (ECPs) may enter into a swap off-exchange (i.e., over-the-counter). There are several ways to qualify as an ECP, but the most common include a corporation or other entity (i) that has total assets exceeding $10,000,000; (ii) that is guaranteed by an ECP (where such guarantor qualifies as an ECP by having total assets exceeding $10,000,000 or under certain other ECP tests); or (iii) that has a net worth exceeding $1,000,000 and enters into the OTC swap for hedging purposes.

The ECP requirement sets a relatively high bar on the types of counterparties that may enter into an off-exchange swap. Accordingly, with respect to swaps based on blockchain-based assets, the ECP requirement may prohibit such swaps if one or both counterparties fails to qualify as an ECP.

Clearing and Exchange-Trading Requirement

A fundamental impact of the Dodd-Frank Act was to require exchange trading and central clearing of certain types of swaps as designated by the CFTC in order to decrease systemic risk. Significantly, certain exceptions to the clearing requirement exist, such as the "end-user exception," which is available if one of the counterparties is using swaps to "hedge or mitigate commercial risk" and satisfies certain other requirements.

Currently, only certain interest rate swaps and credit default swaps are required to be centrally cleared. Accordingly, as of this writing, the clearing requirement does not yet apply to swaps that are based on blockchain-based assets.

Reporting and Recordkeeping

The CEA generally requires certain swap data to be reported to a registered "swap data repository" (SDR). Generally, there are two types of reporting requirements under the act (i) reporting of swap data to an SDR; and (ii) real-time reporting requirements. In SDR reporting, generally one of the counterparties to a swap must be designated as the reporting party and provide certain "creation data and continuation data" to SDR within specified time frames.

Real-Time Reporting. Real-time reporting requires that "swap transaction and pricing information" be reported to an SDR "as soon as technologically possible." The information required to be reported includes, among other information, the time and date of execution, whether the swap is cleared, effective date and end date, price information, and time stamps. SDRs, in turn, are required to anonymize such information and disseminate it to the market in order to enhance price discovery.

Additionally, each swap counterparty must maintain full, complete, and systematic records, together with all pertinent data and memoranda, with respect to each swap in which they are a counterparty. These records must be maintained throughout the life of the swap and for at least five years from the final termination of the swap.

Forward Contract Exclusion

The CFTC has provided a "forward contract exclusion" to the definition of "swap." Subject to certain conditions, this exclusion applies to any sale of a nonfinancial commodity for deferred shipment or delivery, so long as the transaction is intended to be physically settled.[24] "Nonfinancial commodity" refers to "a commodity that can be physically delivered and that is an exempt commodity or an agricultural commodity."[25] Products qualify for this exclusion based on the following factors:

1. The agreement provides for physical settlement, and thereby provides for the transfer of the ownership of each product rather than solely its price risk;
2. The parties intend that the transactions be physically settled; and
3. Both parties are commercial parties and regularly make or take delivery of the products in the ordinary course of business.[26]

As previously discussed, it appears that a blockchain-based asset constitutes an "exempt" commodity as opposed to "excluded" commodity (although some degree of uncertainty remains), in which case the forward contract exclusion should be available for a qualifying transaction. Notably, however, the foregoing test refers to "commercial parties." It is not fully clear how that requirement would apply to a blockchain-based asset.

EXCHANGE-TRADED MARKETS

The exchange-traded markets involve regulated exchanges and certain other categories of regulated institutions and parties, as discussed below.

---

24. 7 U.S.C. § 1a(47)(B).

25. Further Definition of "Swap," "Security-Based Swap," and "Security-Based Swap Agreement"; Mixed Swaps; Security-Based Swap Agreement Recordkeeping, 77 Fed. Reg. 48, 208, at 48, 233 (Aug. 13, 2012).

26. *Id.* at 48, 227–28.

Designated Contract Markets and Swap Execution Facilities

A designated contract market (DCM) is a board of trade or exchange designated by the CFTC to trade futures, options, or swaps. A DCM can allow both institutional and retail participants and can list for trading such contracts on any commodity, provided that each contract is not readily susceptible to manipulation.

A SEF is subject to fewer regulatory requirements than a DCM. To qualify as a SEF, an exchange can only trade certain commodities and generally must exclude retail participants (retail participants may trade on SEFs through futures commission merchants with adjusted net capital of at least $20 million or registered commodity trading advisers that direct trading for accounts containing total assets of at least $25 million).

Derivatives Clearing Organizations

A derivatives clearing organization (DCO) refers to a derivatives clearinghouse or, more specifically, an entity that, in respect to a contract, (1) enables each party to the contract to substitute, through novation or otherwise, the credit of the DCO for the credit of the parties; (2) arranges or provides, on a multilateral basis, for the settlement or netting of obligations resulting from such contracts; or (3) otherwise provides clearing services or arrangements that mutualize or transfer among participants in the DCO the credit risk arising from such contracts.

Futures Commission Merchants, Introducing Brokers, and Associated Persons

A futures commission merchant (FCM) is an entity that solicits or accepts orders to buy or sell futures contracts, options on futures, retail off-exchange forex contracts or swaps, and accepts money or other assets from customers to support such orders.

An introducing broker (IB) is an individual or organization that solicits or accepts orders to buy or sell futures contracts, commodity options, retail off-exchange forex contracts, or swaps but does not accept money or other assets from customers to support these orders. An IB must be registered unless the individual or organization is registered as and acting in the capacity of an associated person; registered as an FCM; registered as a CPO and only operates pools; registered as a CTA and either solely manages accounts under powers of attorney or does not receive per-trade compensation; or is a non-US resident or firm with only non-US customers and the firm submits all trades for clearing to an FCM.

An associated person is an individual who solicits orders, customers, or customer funds (or who supervises persons so engaged) on behalf of an FCM, retail foreign exchange dealer, IB, CTA, or CPO. An associated person is, in effect, anyone who is a salesperson or who supervises salespersons for any of these categories of individuals or firms.

ENFORCEMENT EFFORTS AND LITIGATION

Like many other federal financial regulators, the CFTC dedicates much of its enforcement effort to combatting fraudulent conduct, and its efforts in pursuing violations involving blockchain-based assets have been no different. While other aspects of CFTC regulation, such as registration and trade reporting requirements, serve a valuable function in maintaining fair markets, fraudulent conduct hurts or threatens members of the public most immediately. And in the case of the CFTC's oversight of the derivatives markets, manipulation of the price or volume of products traded in those markets also presents a serious threat to those markets. While the CFTC has not yet brought enforcement actions involving manipulative trading of digital currency, it has been active in prosecuting fraudulent trading schemes involving or purportedly involving such instruments.

The CFTC has joined other regulators in attempts to assert jurisdiction over activities involving blockchain-based assets and to address potential fraud. "The CFTC has been particularly assertive of its enforcement jurisdiction over virtual currencies. It has formed an internal virtual currency enforcement task force to garner and deploy relevant expertise in this evolving asset class. The task force shares information and works cooperatively with counterparts at the SEC with similar virtual currency expertise."[27]

As the cases discussed later demonstrate, the CFTC first entered the virtual currency world through enforcement by bringing cases to establish the agency's jurisdiction over these types of instruments. Two of

27. Written Testimony of J. Christopher Giancarlo, Chairman, CFTC, Before the Senate Banking Committee (Feb. 6, 2018), https://www.banking.senate.gov/imo/media/doc/Giancarlo%20Testimony%202-6-18b.pdf.

the CFTC's first cases, *CoinFlip* in 2015 and *Bitfinex* in 2016, charged the crypto-promoters with engaging in activity in off-exchange options and futures, respectively. In making such findings, in settled administrative proceedings, the CFTC also necessarily found that the commodities underlying the options and futures, principally Bitcoin, were commodities subject to the CEA. After establishing that principle, the CFTC went on to bring enforcement actions addressing fraud in the sale of such commodities and/or related derivatives, as well as various regulatory violations.

In addition to addressing fraudulent and manipulative conduct, the CFTC investigates and brings enforcement actions related to a range of regulatory requirements. Each of the CFTC Enforcement Division's first three annual reports, issued for 2018, 2019, and 2020, described the priorities that guide its enforcement efforts: preserving market integrity, protecting customers, promoting individual accountability, and increasing coordination with other regulators and criminal authorities.[28] The general categories of cases within the CFTC's enforcement program other than fraud or manipulation generally involve the failure to trade a future, option, or swap on a designated exchange or other platform; the failure of an intermediary to register, which would include an exchange or platform, a futures commissions merchant, an IB, a CPO, and a CTA; trading in excess of prescribed position limits; failure to supervise; and various recordkeeping and other compliance obligations.

Enforcement Actions Involving Off-Exchange Trading

Coinflip

In the 2015 *Coinflip* action, the CFTC first found that Bitcoin and other virtual currencies are properly defined as commodities.[29] In that settled action, the CFTC found that Respondents had engaged in activity related

---

28. The Enforcement Division's 2019 and 2020 annual reports state that in pursuit of these goals, the CFTC brought cases involving manipulative conduct and spoofing, commodities fraud, retail fraud, misappropriation of confidential information, trade allocation schemes, mismarking, protection of customer funds, supervision, financial integrity, swap data reporting, illegal off-exchange contracts, failure to register, other trade practices, including wash trades, fictitious trades, position limits, recordkeeping, other reporting, false information to CFTC or self-regulatory organization, and violation of prior orders.

29. *Coinflip*, *supra*.

to commodity option transactions in contravention of the CFTC's requirement that such instruments be traded on a facility that is properly registered. The instruments at issue in that case were put and call options contracts, whose underlying asset was Bitcoin. CME section 4c(b) and Regulation 32.2 require that commodity options be traded in accordance with the CEA or CFTC regulations. Section 5h(a)(1) of the CEA forbids any person from operating "a facility for the trading or processing of swaps unless the facility is registered as a swap execution facility or as a designated contract market. . . .,"[30] and under the act, "swap" includes option contracts. Regulation 37.3(a)(1) similarly requires that trading systems or platforms for trading swaps must be registered as a swap execution facility. Thus, the CFTC found that Coinflip violated section 4c(b) of the act and Commission Regulation 32.2.

Bitfinex

The CFTC again addressed the issue of off-exchange transactions in regulated instruments in 2016, when it brought a settled enforcement action against Bitfinex, which operated an online platform for exchanging and trading blockchain-based assets, mainly Bitcoin. Bitfinex's platform permitted users, including individuals and entities that did not meet the definition of an eligible contract participant or eligible commercial entity, to borrow funds from other users on the platform in order to trade Bitcoins on a leveraged, margined, or financed basis. Bitfinex was not registered with the Commission. The CFTC found that because Bitfinex did not actually deliver Bitcoins purchased on a leveraged, margined, or financed basis to the traders who purchased them but rather held them in Bitcoin deposit wallets that it owned and controlled, the company was engaging in illegal, off-exchange commodity transactions in the United States and failed to register as a futures commission merchant, in violation of sections 4(a) and 4d of the act, 7 U.S.C. §§ 6(a) and 6d.[31]

McDonnell

The first litigated decision finding that virtual currencies are commodities was issued on March 6, 2018, in *Commodity Futures Trading*

30. 7 U.S.C. § 7b-3(a)(1).

31. *In re* BFXNA Inc., CFTC No. 16–19 (June 2, 2016).

Commission v. McDonnell.[32] As discussed supra, the US District Court for the Eastern District of New York (EDNY) granted the CFTC's request for a preliminary injunction against a company alleged to have offered fraudulent trading and investment services related to virtual currency in violation of the CEA, finding that virtual currencies are commodities under the CEA.

1pool Ltd.

In 2018, both the CFTC and the SEC brought civil injunctive actions against 1pool Ltd., a limited liability company located in the Marshall Islands, and its principal, Patrick Brunner of Austria, for operating an online trading platform that solicited customers to trade in contracts for differences (CFDs). The CFTC entered a consent order the following year.[33] A CFD is an agreement to exchange the difference in value of an underlying asset between the time at which the CFD trading position ("position") is established and the time at which it is terminated. The underlying assets of 1pool's CFDs included gold and crude oil ("WTI"). In the consent order settling the action, the court found that because the transactions in commodities were offered to retail customers in the United States on a leveraged or margined basis, they should have been conducted on a designated contract market, exempt board of trade or a bona fide foreign board of trade; therefore, the defendants violated section 4(a) of the CEA, 7 U.S.C. § 6(a). In addition, the court found that 1pool acted as a futures commission merchant by (a) soliciting or accepting orders for retail commodity transactions; (b) acting as a counterparty for these transactions; and (c) in connection with these

---

32. CFTC v. McDonnell, No. 1:18-cv-00361-JBW-RLM, slip op. (E.D.N.Y. Mar. 6, 2018) (Mem. and Order), http://www.cftc.gov/idc/groups/public/@lrenforcement actions/documents/legalpleading/enfcoindroporder030618.pdf.

33. CFTC v. 1Pool Ltd. and Patrick Brunner, No. 1:18-CV-2243-TNM (D.D.C. Mar. 4, 2019). The SEC's complaint in a related action, filed on Sept. 27, 2020, alleged that the CFDs were securities-based swaps, since some of the underlying assets were exchange-listed stocks. The federal securities laws require that offerings in security-based swaps be registered with the SEC and that the transactions be executed on a registered national exchange. In addition, the company, which also called itself 1Broker, acted as a dealer in the CFDs and therefore was required to register with the SEC. The final judgment imposed an injunction for violation of these provisions of the federal securities laws but did not enter any findings. SEC v. 1Pool Ltd. a.k.a. 1Broker and Patrick Brunner, No. 1:18-cv-02244-TNM (D.D.C. Nov. 1, 2018).

activities, accepting money, securities, or property to margin trades or contracts that resulted or may have resulted therefrom. By not registering as an FCM, 1pool violated section 4d(a)(l) of the act, 7 U.S.C. § 6d(a)(l) (2012).[34]

Bitfinex II

In October, 2021, the CFTC filed a settled order against iFinex Inc., BFXNA Inc., and BFXWW Inc. (d/b/a Bitfinex) in connection with their operation of the Bitfinex cryptocurrency trading platform. The order finds Bitfinex engaged in illegal, off-exchange retail commodity transactions in digital assets with US persons on the Bitfinex trading platform and operated as a futures commission merchant (FCM) without registering as required. Specifically, the CFTC found that Bitfinex operated as an FCM by accepting orders for, acting as a counterparty to, and accepting funds or property, including bitcoin and US Dollar tether tokens, in connection with retail commodity transactions. Most of the margin trading was financed through Bitfinex's peer-to-peer funding program through which Bitfinex customers who held fiat or cryptocurrency in their Bitfinex account would "lend" those funds to other Bitfinex customers who would then use those funds to buy, sell, and trade on the Bitfinex platform. The CFTC also found that Bitfinex had violated the 2016 cease-and-desist order entered against it, as discussed earlier.

Actions Involving Fraudulent Conduct

CFTC's General Anti-Fraud and Anti-Manipulation Authority

The CEA makes fraud and manipulation in connection with swaps or commodities illegal. Specifically, CEA section 6(c)(1) provides that is it unlawful "to use or employ, or attempt to use or employ, in connection with any swap, or a contract of sale of any commodity in interstate commerce, or for future delivery on or subject to the rules of any registered entity, any manipulative or deceptive device or contrivance, in contravention of such rules and regulations as the Commission shall promulgate. . . ." CFTC Rule 180.1 states, in part, that it is unlawful, in

34. As discussed later, 1Pool is the first CFTC action that involved any allegations related to anti–money laundering (AML).

connection with any swap, or contract of sale of any commodity in interstate commerce, or contract for future delivery on or subject to the rules of any registered entity, to engage in fraud.[35] The provision was based on the SEC's anti-fraud Rule 10b-5 promulgated under Exchange Act section 10(b), including its description of types of prohibited conduct.

While the CFTC's anti-fraud authority under CEA section 6(c)(1) and Rule 180.1 is similar to the SEC's anti-fraud authority and Rule 10b-5 thereunder, Rule 180.1 differs from the SEC's anti-fraud provisions in several ways. First, it lists a fourth type of fraud, making it illegal to deliver a false or misleading or inaccurate report concerning crop or market information or conditions that affect or tend to affect the price of any commodity in interstate commerce, knowing or acting in reckless disregard of the fact that such report is false, misleading, or inaccurate. Second, it specifically identifies the state of mind for violations of the anti-fraud provisions: acting intentionally or recklessly. And, third, prohibited fraudulent conduct is not limited to acts "in connection with the purchase or sale" of the financial instruments in question but applies more broadly to "all manipulative or deceptive conduct in connection with the purchase, sale, solicitation, execution, pendency, or termination of any swap, or contract

---

35. CFTC Rule 180.1 provides, in part:

Prohibition on the employment, or attempted employment, of manipulative and deceptive devices.

(a) It shall be unlawful for any person, directly or indirectly, in connection with any swap, or contract of sale of any commodity in interstate commerce, or contract for future delivery on or subject to the rules of any registered entity, to intentionally or recklessly:

(1) Use or employ, or attempt to use or employ, any manipulative device, scheme, or artifice to defraud;

(2) Make, or attempt to make, any untrue or misleading statement of a material fact or to omit to state a material fact necessary in order to make the statements made not untrue or misleading;

(3) Engage, or attempt to engage, in any act, practice, or course of business, which operates or would operate as a fraud or deceit upon any person; or,

(4) Deliver or cause to be delivered, or attempt to deliver or cause to be delivered, for transmission through the mails or interstate commerce, by any means of communication whatsoever, a false or misleading or inaccurate report concerning crop or market information or conditions that affect or tend to affect the price of any commodity in interstate commerce, knowing, or acting in reckless disregard of the fact that such report is false, misleading or inaccurate.

of sale of any commodity in interstate commerce, or contract for future delivery on or subject to the rules of any registered entity."[36]

Enforcement Actions Involving Fraudulent Misappropriation

Gelfman Blueprint, Inc.

In September 2017, the CFTC brought its first anti-fraud enforcement action involving virtual currency, charging an individual and his corporation with fraud, misappropriation, and issuing false account statements in connection with operating a Bitcoin Ponzi scheme. The court entered findings by consent in November 2018 that the defendant committed fraud in connection with contracts of sale of Bitcoin, which falls within the definition of a commodity in interstate commerce. The court did not find misconduct in connection with any future or other derivative. Rather, the court found that the fraud included the solicitation of more than $600,000 from at least eighty customers, supposedly for placement in a pooled commodity fund that purportedly employed a high-frequency algorithmic trading strategy executed by defendants' computer trading program. The court found that the strategy was fake, the purported performance reports were false, and supposed profits paid out to customers actually consisted of other customers' misappropriated funds. In addition, defendants issued false performance reports to pool participants, including statements that falsely created the appearance of positive Bitcoin trading gains.[37]

My Big Coin Pay Inc.

The CFTC charged defendants in US District Court in Massachusetts on January 16, 2018, with commodity fraud and misappropriation related to the ongoing solicitation of customers for a virtual currency known as My Big Coin. In a September 26, 2018 order denying defendants' motion to dismiss, the court found that the CFTC had adequately alleged fraud, rejecting the defendants' argument that the CFTC's anti-fraud authority over My Big Coin extended only to fraudulent market manipulation, and holding that the "broad language in the statute" "explicitly prohibit[s]

---

36. CFTC Manipulation Rule, 76 Fed. Reg. at 41, 401.

37. CFTC v. Gelfman Blueprint, Inc., No. 17-cv-7181, 2018 WL 6320653 (S.D.N.Y. Oct. 1, 2018).

fraud even in the absence of market manipulation," and affirming the CFTC's position that all virtual currencies are commodities and subject to CFTC jurisdiction.[38] As discussed earlier, the court here held that the CFTC had sufficiently alleged that the particular virtual currency at issue, My Big Coin, was a commodity under the CEA because the CFTC alleged that My Big Coin "is a virtual currency and it is undisputed that there is futures trading in virtual currencies (specifically involving Bitcoin)."

The Entrepreneurs Headquarters Limited

The CFTC charged the defendants in January 2018 with a fraudulent scheme to solicit Bitcoin from members of the public, misrepresenting that customers' funds would be pooled and invested in products including binary options, making Ponzi-style payments to commodity pool participants from other participants' funds, misappropriating pool participants' funds, and failing to register as a CPO. This action resulted in a default judgment against The Entrepreneurs Headquarters Limited.[39]

Jon Barry Thompson

In September 2019, the CFTC charged an individual in a contested injunctive action with, essentially, stealing $7 million from two customers by falsely representing to them that he was selling to them Bitcoin that he possessed. That action, and a related criminal action brought by the Southern District of New York, could have related to false claims about the sale of any financial instruments, but because they involved fraud related to a spot virtual currency, Bitcoin, the CFTC had jurisdiction and could charge the theft.[40]

Control-Finance Limited

In June 2019, the CFTC charged a purported Bitcoin trading and investment company and its principal with misappropriating $147 million worth of Bitcoin from over 1,000 customers by falsely representing to them that they could earn substantial trading profits on their Bitcoin. In

38. CFTC v. My Big Coin Pay Inc., 334 F. Supp. 3d 492 (Mass. Dist. Ct. 2018).

39. CFTC v. Dean and The Entrepreneurs Limited, No. 18-cv-345, 2018 WL 4573029 (E.D.N.Y. July 9, 2018).

40. CFTC v. Thompson, No. 19-cv-9052, 2020 WL 7122013 (S.D.N.Y. Oct. 1, 2020).

fact, the defendants did not trade the Bitcoin, misappropriated it, and provided false account statements purporting to show trading profits. Again, there is little about this case that is unique to Bitcoin, except for the absence of a regulatory scheme requiring registration of entities that trade cash commodities, that might have brought the defendants within the oversight purview of a regulator like the NFA. In addition, the digital nature of Bitcoin enabled the defendants to move their victims' funds into wallet addresses that were under the defendants' control, through transactions that were designed solely to conceal the misappropriation.[41]

CabbageTech, Corp.

Defendants were charged with fraud and misappropriation in connection with purchases and trading of Bitcoin and Litecoin. As discussed earlier, the district court opinion also interpreted the CEA to find that cryptocurrencies constitute a commodity under the CEA.[42]

Enforcement Action Involving False and Misleading Statements

Tether

In October 2021, the CFTC filed a settled cease-and-desist order imposing a $41 million fine against Tether Holdings Limited, Tether Limited, Tether Operations Limited, and Tether International Limited (d/b/a Tether) for making untrue or misleading statements and omissions of material fact in connection with the US dollar tether token (USDT) stablecoin. The CFTC found that Tether misrepresented that the tether token is a stablecoin with its value pegged to fiat currency and 100 percent backed by corresponding fiat assets, including US dollars and euros. In fact, Tether reserves were not "fully-backed" the majority of the time. The CFTC found that Tether failed to disclose that it included unsecured receivables and non-fiat assets in its reserves, and that Tether falsely represented that it would undergo routine, professional audits to demonstrate that it maintained "100% reserves at all times" even though Tether reserves were not audited.

---

41. CFTC v. Reynolds, No. 19-cv-5631, 2021 WL 796683 (S.D.N.Y. Mar. 2, 2021).

42. CFTC v. McDonnell, No. 18-cv-361 (E.D.N.Y.).

OTHER SIGNIFICANT ACTIONS BROUGHT BY THE CFTC

Offshore Enterprises

The CFTC has brought several cases against unregistered offshore entities that transact in virtual currencies exclusively or as one type of commodity. While the charges might include fraud, the common element to these cases was the failure to register as an FCM or an exchange, and the failure to execute transactions on a designated contract market. Notwithstanding the entities' location outside the United States, the CFTC's jurisdiction is based on transactions by individuals within the United States.

BitMEX

On October 1, 2020, the CFTC filed an action in the US District Court for the Southern District of New York charging executive officers and various affiliates of BitMEX, one of the largest cryptocurrency exchanges in the world, with, among other things, illegally operating the exchange as an unregistered FCM, SEF, and DCM.[43] The complaint alleges a litany of violative conduct against the defendants, including deleting customer identification information, failing to establish rules to minimize conflicts of interest, failing to ensure that contracts offered on BitMEX are not readily susceptible to manipulation, and failing to report market participants who engage in misconduct.[44]

Laino Group Limited d/b/a PaxForex

On September 24, 2020, the CFTC charged the defendant, an offshore entity, with engaging in unlawful retail commodity transactions and failing to register as an FCM. In the action, filed in the US District Court for the Southern District of Texas, the CFTC alleged that for over two years, PaxForex offered or engaged in unlawful retail commodity transactions in Ether, Litecoin, Bitcoin, gold, and silver. The complaint charged that the defendant violated the CEA by failing to conduct these transactions subject to the rules of a board of trade that had been designated or registered by the CFTC as a contract market. The complaint also charged

---

43. As discussed later, this was also the CFTC's first case in which it charged the failure to comply with AML requirements.

44. CFTC v. HDR Global Trading Limited, No.1:20-cv-08132 (S.D.N.Y. Oct. 1, 2020).

that PayForex acted as an FCM without registration by soliciting and accepting orders for retail commodity transactions and by acting as the counterparty for these transactions, and extended credit or accepted money, securities, and property in the form of Bitcoin and other assets in exchange for margin trades or contracts.[45]

Trade Practice Cases

TeraExchange

The CFTC found that an exchange that was provisionally registered with the commission as a SEF failed to enforce its rules against wash trading, and in fact actively arranged a wash trade. As a condition of registration, SEFs are required by section 5h(f)(1) of the act to comply with the SEF core principles, including the core principle that requires SEFs to establish and enforce trading rules that will deter and detect abuses. Among other things, CFTC Regulation 37.203(a) requires SEFs to comply with Core Principle 2 by prohibiting abusive trading practices, including wash trading and prearranged trading.[46] The CFTC found that the firm had facilitated two offsetting transactions in a nondeliverable forward contract based on the relative value of the US dollar and Bitcoin, at the same price and notional amount. These two transactions constituted both wash trading and prearranged trading in violation of the act.[47]

Anti–Money Laundering Cases

The CFTC has had the authority to enforce AML laws, specifically, the Bank Secrecy Act, since 2003, when it enacted Rule 42.2. The regulation requires futures commission merchants and introducing brokers to comply with the applicable provisions of the Bank Secrecy Act and with the regulations requiring that a customer identification program be adopted as part of the entity's Bank Secrecy Act (BSA) compliance program. The CFTC did not exercise that authority, however, until 2020, when it brought three actions against entities for violating that rule, including an action involving a cryptocurrency exchange, BitMEX.

---

45. Complaint, CFTC v. Laino Group Limited d/b/a PaxForex, No. 20-cv-3317 (S.D. Tex. Sept. 24, 2020).

46. 17 C.F.R. § 37.203(a) (2014).

47. *In re* TeraExchange LLC, CFTC No. 15-33 (Sept. 24, 2015).

BitMEX

The CFTC filed its first enforcement action charging a violation of Rule 42.2 on October 1, 2010, when it filed an action in the US District Court for the Southern District of New York against executive officers and various affiliates of BitMEX, one of the largest cryptocurrency exchanges in the world.[48] The action charged the defendants with, among other things, illegally operating the exchange as an unregistered FCM, SEF, and DCM, and failing to implement a BSA-compliant AML program. The complaint alleges a litany of violative conduct against the defendants, including deleting customer identification information, failing to establish rules to minimize conflicts of interest, failing to ensure that contracts offered on BitMEX are not readily susceptible to manipulation, and failing to report market participants who engage in misconduct.[49]

1pool

Other than the BitMEX action, the only other action filed by the CFTC involving money laundering in connection with blockchain-based assets was its action against 1pool, discussed supra, filed two years earlier.[50] In that action, the CFTC did not directly charge a violation of Rule 42.2, but rather alleged, and found in the consent order entered on March 4, 2019, that 1pool failed to supervise in violation of CFTC Rule 166.3 by failing to implement adequate know your customer (KYC)/customer identification procedures (CIP) for reasonably verifying its customers' true identities. The court found that when 1pool customers opened

48. CFTC v. HDR Global Trading Limited, No. 1:20-cv-08132 (S.D.N.Y. Oct. 1, 2020).

49. BitMEX was also the subject of a criminal AML action by the U.S. Attorney for the Southern District of New York, charging BitMEX executives with deliberately failing to implement BSA-compliant AML and KYC programs. The indictment charges that while the defendants began taking affirmative steps to exempt BitMEX from federal AML regulations, including purporting to withdraw BitMEX from the U.S. market and transferring the company's registration to the Seychelles, BitMEX's executives allegedly continued actively targeting—and profiting off—U.S. customers, while purposely failing to implement controls that would identify and block U.S. customers from the platform. The indictment additionally charges the defendants with willfully refusing to adopt AML and KYC programs and failing to file any Suspicious Activity Reports reporting known and suspected illegal use of the platform, including by individuals from sanctioned countries such as Iran.

50. CFTC v. 1pool Ltd., *supra*.

trading accounts, the company only required its customers to provide a username and email address, which the court found was insufficient information to conduct any reasonable inquiry into the true identity of its customers. 1pool did not require that its customers provide their actual name, physical address, or any other identifying information in order to trade.

Liability of Developers, Miners, and Other Parties Involved in a Distributed Ledger Network

Many individuals and companies are involved in creating and supporting digital currency and its trading platforms. Given the highly technological nature of these instruments and platforms, much of the support is from computer programmers and coders. In its 2018 *A Primer on Smart Contracts*,[51] LabCFTC provided a technical explanation of the operation of this form of cryptocurrency and indicated that depending on its structure, operation, and relevant facts and circumstances, a smart contract could be a derivative, such as a commodity, future, or option. The *Primer* also lists prohibited activity involving smart contracts under the CEA:

- perpetrating or effecting fraud or manipulation
- trading on or being processed by a facility that is not appropriately registered
- engaging in disruptive trading practices (e.g., spoofing)
- failing to maintain records or report violations
- failing to be supervised appropriately or to satisfy financial integrity requirements
- being traded or executed by individuals or firms that are required to be registered with the CFTC but are not and do not have an exception or exemption from registration
- violating the Bank Secrecy Act or USA PATRIOT Act

Shortly before LabCFTC published the Smart Contracts primer, on October 16, 2018, Commissioner Brian Quintenz of the CFTC explained

51. LabCFTC, *A Primer on Smart Contracts* (Nov. 27, 2018), https://www.cftc.gov/sites/default/files/2018-11/LabCFTC_PrimerSmartContracts112718_0.pdf.

his belief that smart contract developers can be held liable for aiding and abetting CFTC rule violations if it was reasonably foreseeable that US persons could use the smart contract they created to violate CFTC rules.[52]

PRIVATE RIGHTS OF ACTION UNDER THE CEA

Section 22 of the Commodity Exchange Act, 7 USC section 25, provides a private right of action against anyone who violates the CEA or who willfully aids, abets, counsels, induces, or procures any such violation, on behalf of anyone who received trading advice for a fee, who made a contract of sale of any future, option, or swap through any such person or provided money to such person in connection with any such order, who transacted with or placed an order through such person for the purchase or sale of an option, or who purchased or sold a future, option, or swap, if the defendant employed any manipulative device or contrivance in contravention of CFTC rules, or a manipulation of the price of any such swap or contrivance.

Representative Cases

BDI Capital, LLC v. Bulbul Investments, LLC

The court dismissed a claim by an account holder based on the fact that it was unable to withdraw its Bitcoins stored on a Bitcoin trading platform. The court held that the case did not involve providing trading advice for a fee, that it did not involve a purchase or sale of a future—cash or spot purchasers of physical commodities do not have a claim under section 22—and did not involve an unregulated margin account or leverage contract. The court found that a claim for conversion existed, since Bitcoins are sufficiently identifiable to be considered specific intangible property.[53]

---

52. The CFTC has brought one enforcement action against defendants for their role in writing software that was used to assist someone engaged in manipulative trading, in a case that does not involve blockchain-based assets. Specifically, in CFTC v. Jitesh Thakkar and Edge Financial Technologies, Inc., the CFTC alleged that the defendants aided and abetted the "Flash Crash" spoofer, designing and developing for him the custom trading software application he requested, which included a "Back-of-Book" function that defendants understood that he would use to engage in spoofing.

53. 446 F.Supp.3d 1127 (N.D. Ga. 2020).

Berk v. Coinbase, Inc.

In dismissing an action against Coinbase related to the exchange's launch of Bitcoin Cash trading, the Northern District of California held that the plaintiff does not have a private right of action under the CEA because he did not use the exchange to make a contract of sale for future delivery, only the purchase of Bitcoin Cash. Thus, the court distinguished CFTC enforcement actions, specifically *CFTC v. McDonnell*, supra, which might reach a claim that does not involve a future, from a private action, which only reaches conduct involving a future.[54]

Lagemann v. Spence

The Southern District of New York granted summary judgment to a group of investors who had contributed their cryptocurrency[55]—specifically, Bitcoin, Ether, and Litecoin—to a purported fund manager, who purported to pool the cryptocurrency for trading, but actually misrepresented his activities and the value of the currency as part of a fraudulent scheme. The court upheld all claims related to fraud, including committing commodity pool fraud in violation of sections 4o and 22(a) of the Exchange Act. Specifically, the court found that cryptocurrency is a commodity (citing the decisions in a securities action, *SEC v. Telegram Group Inc.*, No. 19-cv-9439, 2020 WL 1430035, at *1 [S.D.N.Y. March 24, 2020], and the CFTC action, *Gelfman Blueprint,* supra). The court also found that defendant was a CTA and a CPO under the CEA because he, "for compensation or profit, engaged in the business of advising Plaintiffs directly and through electronic media as to the value of or the advisability of trading a commodity." Further, the court found that the defendant acted with scienter, established through his invocation of the Fifth Amendment, among other things.

CONCLUSION

While it is still early in the development of the law regarding the regulation of blockchain-based assets, certain propositions regarding the CFTC's regulation appear unassailable. One is that such assets satisfy the broad

54. Berk v. Coinbase, Inc., No. 18-cv-01364-VC, 2018 U.S. Dist. LEXIS 184284 (N.D. Cal. Oct. 23, 2018).

55. Lagemann v. Spence, No. 18cv-12218 (GBD) (RWL) 2020 WL 5754800 (S.D.N.Y. May 18, 2020).

definition of commodities. Second is that derivative products based on such commodities will be subject to the CFTC's regulatory scheme over futures, options, swaps, and other derivatives, where applicable. Third is that the CFTC's strong customer protection imperative will continue to generate fraud-based actions against the promoters of schemes involving such assets, even where jurisdiction is not completely clear.

In the longer term, additional regulation and guidance might be necessary to clarify the treatment of blockchain-based assets and derivatives based on such assets. In addition, the CFTC and SEC will need to coordinate on regulation of assets that fall within both agencies' jurisdiction. With its technical expertise, experience in regulating innovative financial products, and history in negotiating with the SEC regarding the regulation of securities-based derivatives, the CFTC is well-poised to usher in an era of rational regulation of blockchain-based assets.

APPENDIX

Futures—Futures contracts are "contracts of sale of a commodity for future delivery." CEA section 2(a)(1).

Commodity options—The term *option* is defined as a contract that is "of the character of, or . . . commonly known to the trade as, an 'option', 'privilege', 'indemnity', 'bid', 'offer', 'put', 'call', 'advance guaranty', or 'decline guaranty.'" 7 U.S.C. 1a(36). For a commodity option, the underlying interest is a commodity. Typically, one party (the option buyer) pays a premium for the "exercise right" to purchase from the other party (the option seller) a commodity at a fixed strike price, in the case of a call option, or to sell a commodity to the option seller at a fixed strike price, in the case of a put option. Depending on terms of the option, the option holder typically may exercise the exercise right at any time during the term of the option, during a more narrowly defined time period, or at expiration.

Options on futures—An option on a futures contract gives the option holder the right, but not the obligation, to buy, in the case of a call option, or sell, in the case of a put option, a futures contract at a strike price during the term of the option.

Swaps—In general, the exchange of one asset or liability for a similar asset or liability for the purpose of lengthening or shortening maturities, or otherwise shifting risks. This may entail selling one securities issue and buying another in foreign currency; it may entail buying a currency on the spot market and simultaneously selling it forward. Swaps also may involve exchanging income flows; for example, exchanging the fixed rate coupon stream of a bond for a variable rate payment stream, or vice versa, while not swapping the principal component of the bond. A swap in which the payout to at least one counterparty is based on the price of a commodity or the level of a commodity index. The definition of "swap" is extremely broad and, subject to certain exceptions, includes, inter alia:

- puts, calls, caps, floors, collars or similar options on the value of one or more interest rates or other rates, currencies, commodities, securities (but options on securities are also excluded from the definition), instruments of indebtedness, indices, quantitative measures, or other financial or economic interests or property of any kind.
- contracts for any purchase, sale, payment, or delivery (other than payment of a dividend on an equity security) that are dependent upon the occurrence, nonoccurrence, or extent of occurrence of an event or contingency associated with a potential financial, economic, or commercial consequence (i.e., event contracts or binary options).
- executory contracts for the fixed or contingent exchange of one or more payments based on the value or level of one or more interest rates, other rates, currencies, commodities, securities, instruments of indebtedness, indices, quantitative measures, or other financial or economic interests or property of any kind, or any interest therein or based on the value thereof, and that transfers, as between the parties to the transaction, in whole or in part, the financial risk associated with a future change in any such value or level without also conveying a current or future direct or indirect ownership interest in an asset (including any enterprise or investment pool) or liability that incorporates the financial risk so transferred, including contracts that become commonly known as one of an enumerated list of contracts such as interest rate swaps, currency swaps, agricultural swaps, or energy swaps.
- contracts that are or in the future become commonly known to the trade as swaps.
- security-based swap agreements that meet the definition of "swap agreement" under section 206A of the Gramm-Leach-Bliley Act, a material term of which is based on the price, yield, value, or volatility of any security or any group or index of securities, or any interest therein.
- any combination or permutation of the foregoing types of contracts, including any option thereon.

4 | Federal Taxation of Virtual Currencies

Sarah-Jane Morin and Alexander Reid

The tax treatment of blockchain-based assets, also known as "digital assets," "virtual currencies," or "cryptocurrencies," is at best confusing and at worst, downright illogical. This chapter focuses on the US federal income tax considerations for certain transactions involving blockchain-based assets. As described, the guidance in this area from the US Internal Revenue Service (IRS) and US Department of the Treasury (the Treasury) is helpful but leaves much open to interpretation and debate. The law will continue to evolve rapidly in this area, as Congress recently enacted new reporting requirements on brokers of digital assets as well as new reporting requirements on business transactions over $10,000 involving digital assets occurring after January 1, 2023, which will necessitate significant new regulatory guidance by Treasury and the IRS.

IRS GUIDANCE

IRS Notice 2014-21: *IRS Virtual Currency Guidance*

The IRS first addressed blockchain-based assets in 2014 when it issued Notice 2014-21, *Virtual Currency Guidance*. Notices do not have the full force of law and do not bind a court; however, the IRS will not take positions inconsistent with notices, so taxpayers can rely on notices as authoritative precedent.

Notice 2014-21 addressed how existing general US federal income tax principles apply to transactions involving "convertible" virtual currencies (i.e., those that may be converted into US dollars). Notice 2014-21 provided such guidance in the form of answers to frequently asked questions. It addressed a broad range of tax scenarios but was not comprehensive. Importantly, Notice 2014-21 specifically (and only) referenced Bitcoin as an example of a convertible virtual currency, although it stated that the guidance was meant to apply broadly to any virtual currency that has an equivalent value in real currency or that acts as a "substitute" for real currency. Consequently, all references herein to Notice 2014-21 apply only to these convertible virtual currencies. It is feasible, therefore, that blockchain-based assets that do not meet that definition do not fall under the purview of the guidance in the notice.

In Notice 2014-21, the Treasury and the IRS requested comments from the public regarding other types or tax aspects of cryptocurrency transactions that should be addressed in future guidance. To date, however, the Treasury and the IRS have not released an update to Notice 2014-21 based on these comments, although additional guidance has been issued (as discussed further herein).

Notice 2014-21 states that, in general, the sale or exchange of convertible virtual currency, or the use of convertible virtual currency to pay for goods or services in a "real-world economy transaction" (as opposed to virtual economy transactions such as those occurring in video games), has tax consequences that may result in a real-world tax liability. The key federal tax principles from Notice 2014-21 are as follows. Blockchain-based assets that fall within the purview of Notice 2014-21 are treated as property for US federal income tax purposes.[1] As a result, general tax principles applicable to property transactions apply to transactions using such blockchain-based assets. The conclusion that virtual currency such as Bitcoin is "property" for tax purposes was not necessarily obvious or a given because Bitcoin alternatively might have been viewed as something else entirely, for example, as a prepayment, voucher, or coupon for the services of Bitcoin miners who solve cryptographic problems using computer farms. As discussed later, the treatment of virtual currency as property is helpful because property can be held for investment purposes and receive capital gain treatment, or it can be held as an ordinary asset in the hands of dealers, hedgers, and "miners." That said, Notice 2014-21 is not all good news from a tax perspective. Contrary to what some had believed prior to the release of Notice 2014-21, the notice clarifies that blockchain-based assets are not "foreign currency" for US federal income tax purposes and therefore cannot generate foreign currency gain or loss for US federal tax purposes. Notice 2014-21 further states

1. Notice 2014-21, § 4, Q&A-1.

that transactions involving blockchain-based assets that fall within the purview of the notice must be reported in US dollars.

By way of example of the application of Notice 2014-21, consider a taxpayer who receives blockchain-based assets in exchange for goods or services. In accordance with the guidance in Notice 2014-21, the taxpayer must, in computing gross income, include the fair market value (FMV) of the blockchain-based assets received, measured in US dollars as of the date of receipt.[2] Correspondingly, the taxpayer's basis in the blockchain-based assets is the same FMV amount, measured again in US dollars.

Notice 2014-21 also clarifies the basis of blockchain-based assets. Tax basis is an important concept in assessing tax consequences upon sales, exchanges, or other transactions involving property. Notice 2014-21 states that the basis of blockchain-based assets that a taxpayer receives as payment for goods or services is the FMV of the blockchain-based asset in US dollars as of the date of receipt.[3] This general rule requires that a FMV determination be made. To that end, Notice 2014-21 states that taxpayers are required to determine the FMV of blockchain-based assets in US dollars as of the date of payment or receipt.[4] If blockchain-based assets are listed on an exchange and the exchange rate is established by market supply and demand, the FMV of the blockchain-based assets is determined by converting the blockchain-based assets into US dollars (or into another real currency that in turn can be converted into US dollars) at the exchange rate, in a reasonable manner that is consistently applied.

Applying the same guidance, a taxpayer realizes gain or loss based on the difference in the tax basis of exchanged blockchain-based assets and the FMV of any acquired property.[5] If the FMV of property received in exchange for blockchain-based assets exceeds the taxpayer's adjusted basis of the virtual currency, the taxpayer has taxable gain. The taxpayer has a loss if the FMV of the property received is less than the adjusted basis of the blockchain-based assets. Such gain or loss is capital or ordinary, based on whether the blockchain-based asset is a capital asset in the hands of the taxpayer.[6] Standard tax rules apply to determine

---

2. Notice 2014-21, § 4, Q&A-5.
3. Notice 2014-21, § 4, Q&A-4.
4. Notice 2014-21, § 4, Q&A-5.
5. Notice 2014-21, § 4, Q&A-6.
6. Notice 2014-21, § 4, Q&A-7.

whether such an asset is a capital asset. A taxpayer generally realizes capital gain or loss on the sale or exchange of a blockchain-based asset that is a capital asset in the hands of the taxpayer. For example, stocks, bonds, and other investment property are generally capital assets. A taxpayer generally realizes ordinary gain or loss on the sale or exchange of a blockchain-based asset that is not a capital asset in the hands of the taxpayer. Inventory and other property held mainly for sale to customers in a trade or business are not capital assets.

Notice 2014-21 next applies the foregoing guidance to mining in some detail. Taxpayers who "mine" blockchain-based assets realize gross income upon the receipt of the assets from the mining effort.[7] In effect, miners who successfully mine blockchain-based assets (i.e., discover solutions to cryptographic problems) generate taxable income. Such miners must include in their gross income the value of the blockchain-based assets they are awarded upon receipt. Tax basis is established on that date, which is also when the holding period for the blockchain-based asset starts. If such a miner subsequently sells the mined blockchain-based asset, a second taxable event is triggered. As a result, the miner realizes gain or loss based on the difference in the tax basis of sold blockchain-based assets and the FMV of any property acquired in the transaction (e.g., cash or other property).

Depending on the manner in which the miner engages in the activity (e.g., as a business, as a hobby), the miner may be able to offset any gain with expenses. These general concepts are not dissimilar from those of any activity undertaken as a business or hobby.

Further, if a taxpayer's mining of blockchain-based assets constitutes a trade or business (as opposed to a hobby) and is not undertaken as an employee, the net earnings (generally, gross income derived from carrying on a trade or business less allowable deductions) constitute self-employment income and are subject to self-employment tax.[8] Correspondingly, blockchain-based assets received by an independent contractor for performing services (such as mining) are subject to self-employment tax.[9] Generally, self-employment income includes all gross income derived by an individual from any trade or business carried on by the individual as other than an employee, which may for this purpose include mining. Consequently, the FMV of virtual currency received for services performed as an independent contractor, measured in US dollars

7. Notice 2014-21, § 4, Q&A-8.

8. Notice 2014-21, § 4, Q&A-9.

9. Notice 2014-21, § 4, Q&A-10.

as of the date of receipt, constitutes self-employment income and is subject to the self-employment tax.

Notice 2014-21 also addresses the tax aspects of a payment for services in blockchain-based assets. The notice states that, generally, the medium in which remuneration for services is paid is immaterial to the determination of whether the remuneration constitutes wages for employment-tax purposes.[10] Thus, blockchain-based assets paid by an employer for services performed by an employee constitute "wages" for tax purposes. As in the case of any wages, wages paid in blockchain-based assets are subject to federal income tax withholding, Federal Insurance Contributions Act tax, and Federal Unemployment Tax Act tax, and must be reported on the employee's Form W-2; all are measured based on the FMV of the cryptocurrency when paid to the employee.

Payments using blockchain-based assets are subject to IRS information-reporting requirements and potential withholding, just as they would be in other in-kind payment contexts.[11] For example, per the notice, a person who in the course of a trade or business makes a payment of fixed and determinable income using $600 or more to an independent contractor during any year must report the payment to the payee and to the IRS on Form 1099-MISC.[12] Examples of payments of fixed and determinable income include rent, salaries, wages, premiums, annuities, and compensation. Payments of blockchain-based assets required to be reported on Form 1099-MISC should be reported using the FMV of the virtual currency in US dollars as of the date of payment. According to the notice, the payment recipient may have income even if the recipient does not receive a Form 1099-MISC. Backup withholding rules apply to the same extent as other payments made in property.[13] Therefore, per Notice 2014-21, payers making reportable payments using blockchain-based assets must solicit a taxpayer identification number from the payee and, if the taxpayer identification number is not obtained prior to payment or if the payer receives a notification from the IRS that backup withholding is required, the payer must withhold tax from the payment of the blockchain-based asset. Payments to foreign persons may carry withholding tax consequences applicable to foreign payees.

10. Notice 2014-21, § 4, Q&A-11.

11. Notice 2014-21, § 4, Q&A-12.

12. Notice 2014-21, § 4, Q&A-13.

13. Notice 2014-21, § 4, Q&A-14.

Additional reporting requirements may apply to persons who settle payments made in blockchain-based assets on behalf of merchants that accept such assets from their customers. Notice 2014-21 states that, in general, a third party that contracts with a substantial number of unrelated merchants to settle payments between the merchants and their customers is a third-party settlement organization (TPSO).[14] A TPSO is required to report payments made to a merchant on a Form 1099-K, Payment Card and Third-Party Network Transactions, if, for the calendar year, both (1) the number of transactions settled for the merchant exceeds 200, and (2) the gross amount of payments made to the merchant exceeds $20,000. When completing Boxes 1, 3, and 5a-1 on Form 1099-K, transactions in which the TPSO settles payments made with virtual currency are aggregated with transactions in which the TPSO settles payments made with real currency to determine the total amounts to be reported in those boxes. According to Notice 2014-21, when determining whether the transactions are reportable, the value of the virtual currency is the FMV of the virtual currency in US dollars on the date of payment.

Given that Notice 2014-21 established the IRS's position on numerous legal issues regarding virtual currency without giving taxpayers the benefit of a notice and comment period, the IRS appreciates that taxpayers may well have taken positions on their tax returns prior to the March 25, 2014, effective date of Notice 2014-21 that are contrary to the guidance under Notice 2014-21. Notice 2014-21 addresses this possibility, stating that while taxpayers are subject to penalties for failure to comply with tax laws, penalty relief may be available under certain circumstances.[15] For example, underpayments attributable to virtual currency transactions may be subject to penalties, such as accuracy-related penalties under Code Section 6662.[16] In addition, failure to timely, or correctly, report virtual currency transactions when required to do so may be subject to information-reporting penalties under Code Sections 6721 and 6722. Penalty relief may be available, however, to taxpayers and persons required to file an information return and who are able to establish that the underpayment or failure to properly file information returns is due to reasonable cause. In accordance with Treasury Regulations 1.6662-4, a taxpayer may also obtain penalty relief where the taxpayer discloses items or positions that are not otherwise

---

14. Notice 2014-21, § 4, Q&A-15.

15. Notice 2014-21, § 4, Q&A-16.

16. Unless otherwise stated, references herein to the "Code" are to the U.S. Internal Revenue Code of 1986, as amended.

adequately disclosed on a US federal income tax return by filing an IRS Form 8275 or Form 8275-R with its tax return.

2017 IRS Reminder

On March 23, 2018, the IRS issued a short "reminder" to taxpayers as the April filing deadline for 2017 approached.[17] The IRS stated that virtual currency transactions "are taxable by law just like transactions in any other property." The reminder outlined the guidance set forth in Notice 2014-21 discussed earlier. The IRS further stated that taxpayers who do not properly report the income tax consequences of virtual currency transactions can be audited for those transactions and, where appropriate, can be liable for penalties and interest. The IRS stated that in more extreme situations, taxpayers could be subject to criminal prosecution for failing to properly report the income tax consequences of virtual currency transactions. Criminal charges could include tax evasion and filing a false tax return.

Since the 2017 reminder, the IRS has increased its focus on these issues. For example, in 2019 and again in 2020, the IRS sent warning letters to taxpayers who engaged in virtual currency transactions and who may have not reported their transactions correctly.[18] These letters are discussed later in this chapter.

2019 IRS Frequently Asked Questions

On October 9, 2019, the IRS released additional guidance regarding blockchain-based assets by posting certain frequently asked questions (FAQs) with answers on its website.[19] The FAQs are intended to supplement the guidance provided under Notice 2014-21. While FAQs, as posted

---

17. IR-2018-71: IRS Reminds Taxpayers to Report Virtual Currency Transactions.

18. *See, e.g.,* Kelly Philips Erb, *IRS Sending Warning Letters to More Than 10,000 Taxpayers About Cryptocurrency Reporting*, FORBES (July 26, 2019), https://www.forbes.com/sites/kellyphillipserb/2019/07/26/irs-sending-warning-letters-to-more-than-10000-taxpayers-about-cryptocurrency-reporting/?sh=20d6dbb5d3bf; Shehan Chandrasekera, *Crypto Users Are Receiving IRS Tax Warning Letters, Again*, FORBES (Aug. 25, 2020), https://www.forbes.com/sites/shehanchandrasekera/2020/08/25/crypto-tax-warning-letters-2020/?sh=beeb4d517f77.

19. IRS, *Virtual currency: IRS issues additional guidance on tax treatment and reminds taxpayers of reporting obligations* (IR-2019-167, Oct. 9, 2019), https://www.irs.gov/newsroom/virtual-currency-irs-issues-additional-guidance-on-tax-treatment-and-reminds-taxpayers-of-reporting-obligations.

on a website, generally do not constitute binding legal authority for tax purposes, they are instructive as to how the IRS is likely to regard the subjects the FAQs address. Except as otherwise noted by the IRS on its website, these FAQs apply only to taxpayers who hold virtual currency as a capital asset.

The FAQs clarify that "virtual currency" is a digital representation of value, other than a representation of the US dollar or a foreign currency (real currency), that functions as a unit of account, a store of value, and a medium of exchange.[20] One example of "virtual currency" is "cryptocurrency," which uses cryptography to secure transactions that are digitally recorded on a distributed ledger, such as a blockchain. A transaction involving cryptocurrency that is recorded on a distributed ledger is referred to as an "on-chain" transaction; a transaction that is not recorded on the distributed ledger is referred to as an "off-chain" transaction.[21] Some virtual currencies are convertible, which means that they have an equivalent value in real currency or act as a substitute for real currency. The IRS uses the term *virtual currency* in these FAQs to describe the various types of convertible virtual currency that are used as a medium of exchange, such as digital currency and cryptocurrency. Regardless of the label applied, if a particular asset has the characteristics of virtual currency, it will be treated as virtual currency for federal income tax purposes according to the FAQs.

The IRS confirmed in the FAQs that virtual currency is treated as property, and general tax principles applicable to property transactions apply to transactions using virtual currency.[22] This position is generally consistent with the position the IRS took in Notice 2014-21.

The FAQs clarify that when a taxpayer sells virtual currency **that is treated as a capital asset**, the taxpayer must recognize any capital gain or loss on the sale, subject to any limitations on the deductibility of capital losses.[23] Whether the gain or loss is capital or ordinary will depend on whether the taxpayer is an investor or trader (capital) or a dealer, hedger, or miner (ordinary). Capital gain or loss is short term or long term depending on the holding period (which begins on the day after the blockchain-based asset is acquired and ends on the day the blockchain-based asset is sold or exchanged). If the taxpayer holds the virtual currency for one year

---

20. FAQ Q1.
21. FAQ Q3.
22. FAQ Q2.
23. FAQ Q4.

or less before selling or exchanging the virtual currency, then the taxpayer would have a short-term capital gain or loss; if the taxpayer holds the virtual currency for more than one year before selling or exchanging it, then the taxpayer would have a long-term capital gain or loss.[24] Gain or loss on the sale is derived from the difference between the adjusted basis in the blockchain-based asset and the amount received in exchange, which should be reported on a federal income tax return in US dollars.[25] For this purpose, adjusted basis is the amount spent to acquire the blockchain-based asset, including fees, commissions, and other acquisition costs in US dollars, as increased by certain expenditures and decreased by certain deductions or credits in US dollars.[26]

Hard Forks and Airdrops: Revenue Ruling 2019-24

The IRS released Revenue Ruling 2019-24 on October 9, 2019. The ruling largely addresses the tax aspects of hard forks and airdrops. A revenue ruling is the official interpretation by the IRS setting forth its conclusion on how the law is applied to a specific set of facts. Revenue rulings are published in the *Internal Revenue Bulletin*, and taxpayers can rely on them as legal precedent.

The ruling defines a *hard fork* as occurring "when a cryptocurrency on a distributed ledger undergoes a protocol change resulting in a permanent diversion from the legacy or existing distributed ledger." The ruling states that a hard fork "may result in the creation of a new cryptocurrency on a new distributed ledger in addition to the legacy cryptocurrency on the legacy distributed ledger," and that "[f]ollowing a hard fork, transactions involving the new cryptocurrency are recorded on the new distributed ledger and transactions involving the legacy cryptocurrency continue to be recorded on the legacy distributed ledger." The ruling concludes that a taxpayer does not have gross income under Code Section 61 as a result of a hard fork of a cryptocurrency that the taxpayer owns if the taxpayer does not receive units of a new cryptocurrency.

The ruling defines an *airdrop* as "a means of distributing units of a cryptocurrency to the distributed ledger addresses of multiple taxpayers," and further states that "[a] hard fork followed by an airdrop results in the distribution of units of the new cryptocurrency to addresses

---

24. FAQ Q5.

25. FAQ Q6.

26. FAQ Q7.

containing the legacy cryptocurrency," but that "a hard fork is not always followed by an airdrop." The ruling concludes that a taxpayer has gross income under Code Section 61 that is ordinary in character as a result of an airdrop of a new cryptocurrency following a hard fork if the taxpayer receives units of new cryptocurrency.

BASIS, HOLDING PERIOD, AND CHARACTER CONSIDERATIONS OF BLOCKCHAIN-BASED ASSETS

Each blockchain-based asset subject to Notice 2014-21 and owned by a taxpayer has a unique and separate tax basis. This means that a taxpayer must generally track tax basis on a unit-by-unit basis and cannot use an average basis method to calculate their gains and losses.[27] A taxpayer's "adjusted basis" in property is used to determine taxable gain or loss on the disposition (by trade or sale) of the property. In the case of a blockchain-based asset subject to Notice 2014-21, the taxpayer's adjusted tax basis will generally equal the US dollar value of the cash, property, or services exchanged for the cryptocurrency. The IRS specifically noted in the FAQs that basis is the amount that a taxpayer spends to acquire the virtual currency, including fees, commissions, and other acquisition costs, in US dollars. Adjusted basis is basis increased by certain expenditures and decreased by certain deductions or credits in US dollars.

If, as part of an arm's-length transaction, a taxpayer provides someone with services and in exchange receives a blockchain-based asset subject to Notice 2014-21, the taxpayer's basis in that blockchain-based asset is the FMV of the asset in US dollars when the asset is received.

If, as part of an arm's-length transaction, a taxpayer transferred property to someone and in exchange received a blockchain-based asset subject to Notice 2014-21, the taxpayer's basis in that blockchain-based asset subject to Notice 2014-21 is the FMV of the asset in US dollars when received.

As is the general rule for all property, the period during which the taxpayer holds an asset (known as the holding period) begins on the day after a taxpayer acquires the blockchain-based asset subject to

---

27. The average basis method generally allows electing taxpayers to calculate the value of positions in certain mutual fund stock on an aggregate basis to determine their profit or loss. Such electing taxpayers can determine their tax basis by taking the average basis of all of such positions they own and multiple the average cost by the number of shares they are selling.

Notice 2014-21 and ends on the day that the asset is sold or exchanged. Per the one-year rule of Code Section 1222, short-term capital gain or loss is triggered with respect to the disposition of any capital asset held by the taxpayer for one year or less, whereas long-term capital gain or loss is triggered with respect to the disposition of any capital asset held by the taxpayer for greater than one year. Thus, if a taxpayer holds the blockchain-based asset subject to Notice 2014-21 for one year or less before selling or exchanging the asset, then the taxpayer will have a short-term capital gain or loss (if the blockchain-based asset at issue is a capital asset). If the taxpayer held the asset for more than one year before selling or exchanging it, then the taxpayer will have a long-term capital gain or loss (if the blockchain-based asset at issue is a capital asset). Notice 2014-21 and the FAQs provide taxpayers with two ways to identify the basis of a specific unit of a blockchain-based asset. The first allows taxpayers to document a unique digital identifier, such as a private key, public key, or address. The second allows a taxpayer to record all of the transaction information for the units in a single account, wallet, or address.[28]

Character determinations (e.g., whether the blockchain-based asset is a capital or ordinary asset) are made using the same general rules as would apply for any other property. In other words, character of any gain or loss from the sale or exchange of blockchain-based assets subject to Notice 2014-21 depends on whether the assets are capital assets in the hands of the particular taxpayer. Code Section 1221 provides that the term *capital asset* means property held by a taxpayer, and then excludes a number of categories such as "property held by the taxpayer primarily for sale to customers in the ordinary course of his trade or business and "any hedging transaction which is clearly identified as such." A taxpayer that holds blockchain-based assets as inventory is likely considered a dealer for US federal income tax purposes."

Because a blockchain-based asset is not currently characterized as a security for tax purposes, the default rule for sales of separate assets is specific identification pursuant to Code Section 1012 and the regulations issued thereunder—tracing each sale to a particular coin and calculating gain based on the tax basis associated with such coin. This tracing may be difficult where multiple purchases or acquisitions are made over time. However, tracing may provide greater flexibility in terms of minimizing gains (e.g., a taxpayer may sell high-basis blockchain-based assets

28. FAQ 40.

first) and losses. By way of example, consider the potential to segregate purchases in separate accounts if a taxpayer intends to rely on separate tracing to calculate gains and losses. Treasury regulations section 1.1012-1(c) contains a specific stock rule that defaults to the first in, first out (FIFO) method in which a taxpayer fails to specifically identify shares that are sold. FIFO essentially means that the property from a broader lot of like-kind property in a sale or exchange that will be treated as sold or transferred will be the property that was first acquired by the taxpayer, and such property will in turn determine the basis and holding period for purposes of the sale or exchange. Therefore, unless a taxpayer specifically identifies the lot of blockchain-based assets at issue in the sale or exchange, FIFO will apply by default. As an alternative of applying FIFO, a taxpayer may generally use "last in, first out" or, as noted in the foregoing, a taxpayer may specifically identify which positions or lots they intend to utilize in the sale or exchange.

It is worth pausing to consider the effect, if any, of the wash-sale rules of Code Section 1091. These rules prohibit a taxpayer from claiming a Code Section 165 loss on the sale or exchange of a stock or security when the taxpayer disposes of a stock or security at a loss and then buys a "substantially identical" stock or security thirty days prior to, or thirty days after, the loss, triggering the disposition. For tax years beginning before January 1, 2022, it is not clear whether a blockchain-based asset should be considered a stock or "security" for purposes of Code Section 1091. Certain legislative proposals have been made that would specifically expand the scope of the wash-sale rule to include digital assets such as cryptocurrencies. As of the date of the publication of this treatise, these proposals have not yet been implemented into law. Thus, each taxpayer would need to examine any blockchain-based asset at issue based on analogies to other guidance and court cases to determine whether the wash-sale rule applies.

LIKE-KIND EXCHANGES OF BLOCKCHAIN-BASED ASSETS

Code Section 1031 permits taxpayers to exchange property for "like-kind" property within 180 days without triggering a taxable event. Code Section 1031 was amended in 2018 to provide that like-kind exchanges apply only to certain exchanges of real property. Under current law, like-kind exchanges under Code Section 1031 are not available for exchanges of blockchain-based assets. Prior to January 1, 2018, however, exchanges of one type of blockchain-based asset for a different blockchain-based asset arguably may have qualified as a "like-kind" exchange subject to Code Section 1031 under certain circumstances. For such purposes, the exchanged assets would qualify as properties of like kind if they are of the same nature or character, even if they differ in grade or quality. For example, personal properties of a like class are like-kind properties. To contrast, livestock of different sexes are not like-kind properties. Also, personal property used predominantly in the United States and personal property used predominantly outside the United States are not like-kind properties. Thus, prior to 2018, Code Section 1031 may well have allowed some like-kind exchanges of blockchain-based assets, and such exchanges may have been reported as such on IRS Form 8824. However, a taxpayer should take note of recent guidance in this area in analyzing this possibility. In CCA 202124008, the IRS addressed the application of the like-kind exchange rules to exchanges of BTC, ETC, Litecoin. In such CCA, the IRS held that such convertible virtual currencies are not of a like-kind, thus prior to 2018, an exchange of one for the other did not constitute a like-kind exchange under the facts that the IRS reviewed in such case.

DONATIONS OF BLOCKCHAIN-BASED ASSETS

Most property held for personal or investment purposes is a capital asset.[29] The contribution of a capital asset held by a donor for more than twelve months to a qualifying public charity is generally deductible at the FMV of the asset up to 30 percent of the donor's contribution base, which is the donor's adjusted gross income for the year disregarding any net operating loss carryback to the year.[30] When a donor contributes property that is ordinary-income property (rather than a capital asset), the deduction is

---

29. Code § 1221(a).

30. Code § 170(b)(1)(C). A lower limit of 20% of the donor's contribution base applies to gifts of capital gain property to private nonoperating foundations and gifts "for the use of" the charitable recipient. Special higher limits may apply to qualified contributions to aid relief efforts with respect to certain presidentially declared disasters. *See, e.g.*, section 2205 of the Coronavirus Aid, Relief, and Economic Security Act, P.L. 116-136.

generally limited to the basis in the property, rather than the FMV, but is deductible up to 50 percent of the donor's contribution base.[31]

Deducting charitable donations requires substantiation. A donor can only take a charitable-contribution deduction if the donor receives a contemporaneous written acknowledgment from the charitable organization describing the property and providing that no goods or services were received in exchange for the property.

Applying these rules to donations of blockchain-based assets, it first must be noted that blockchain-based assets are gifts of property and would not be treated as cash donations. Instead, per the guidance provided under Notice 2014-21, the donations would be considered in-kind donations of property, or noncash donations. For most noncash gifts for which a deduction of more than $500 is claimed, the donor must also complete Form 8283 Section A and file it with the return on which the deduction is claimed. Section A of Form 8283 asks for the name and address of the donee, the date of contribution, a description of the property in sufficient detail, the condition of the property (if real or personal property), securities information (for a gift of securities), the FMV on the contribution date and the method used to determine such value, the manner of acquisition of the property by the donor, the cost or other basis of the property, and, in the case of tangible personal property, whether the donee has certified it for a use related to the donee organization's exempt purposes. For most noncash gifts for which a deduction of more than $5,000 is claimed, the donor must complete Form 8283 Section B, have it signed by the donee, file it with the return on which the deduction is claimed, and obtain a qualified appraisal from a qualified appraiser. Section B of Form 8283 asks for similar information as does Section A, as well as additional information about the appraiser, and requires the appraiser's declaration and signature. The qualified appraisal must be attached to the donor's return only for contributions exceeding $500,000.

One important exception to these valuation rules is for a gift of a publicly traded security with readily identifiable market values, for which the donor is entitled to claim a FMV deduction for the contribution and avoid tax on the built-in capital gains.[32] The reason for this favorable treatment is that the charity receiving the publicly traded securities takes

31. Code §§ 170(b)(1)(A), 170(e)(1)(A). A higher limit of 60% of the donor's contribution base applies for gifts of cash.

32. Code § 170(e).

a carried-over basis in the securities from the donor and recognizes the built-in gains when the charity sells the securities, but the charity pays no tax because it is exempt. Under those regulations, market quotations are considered readily available if (1) the security is listed on the New York Stock Exchange, the American Stock Exchange, or any city or regional exchange in which quotations are published on a daily basis, including foreign securities listed on a recognized foreign, national, or regional exchange in which quotations are published daily; (2) the security is regularly traded in the national or regional over-the-counter market, for which published quotations are available; or (3) the security is a share of an open-end investment company (commonly known as a mutual fund) registered under the Investment Company Act of 1940, for which quotations are published on a daily basis in a newspaper of general circulation throughout the United States. For the most part, blockchain-based assets are unlikely to be considered a security for these purposes, with the possible exception of initial coin offerings, as discussed later in this chapter. The IRS has not yet published precedential guidance regarding the treatment of blockchain-based assets, such as tokens, as securities. As a result, it is expected that donations of blockchain-based assets would be treated as gifts of property that require an appraisal in accordance with the rules described earlier.

A complication in contributing blockchain-based assets to charity is that the charity may not have the capacity, sophistication, or desire to hold the asset directly. For example, the transfer of cryptocurrency is often accomplished using third-party "wallet" services (whether online wallets or offline hardware cold-storage wallets) that hold the cryptocurrency and enable it to be converted to US dollars. Fortunately, it is well established that a charity may receive charitable contributions through its agent that does not itself need to be a charitable organization. Whether an agency relationship exists is a matter of state law, typically requiring a contract or other legally binding arrangement. In Revenue Ruling 2002-67, for example, a charitable organization entered into a contractual arrangement with a for-profit company whereby the for-profit company, on behalf of the charity, would (1) solicit donations of used cars; (2) accept, process, and sell the cars; (3) transfer the proceeds of the sales to the charitable organization; and (4) provide each donor with substantiation of the donor's charitable contribution. The IRS held that because the arrangement was a valid agency relationship under state law giving the for-profit company the right to act on the charity's behalf according to the terms of the agency relationship, transfers of cars to the agent were treated as transfers to the charity and thus were deductible as charitable contributions. An agency relationship is generally established when both parties have agreed that one party is acting on behalf of and subject to the control of the other party. The agency arrangement is generally established by an express contract that the agent will act for and on behalf of the principal.

The use of wallets and other third-party agents by charities to accept gifts of blockchain-based assets and convert them to currency raises a tax issue that may well be of concern to the extent that the blockchain-based asset is a security for tax purposes. To gain the benefit of the FMV deduction and avoid built-in gains under Code Section 170(e), the publicly traded security must be donated in a transaction that is separate and distinct from any subsequent transaction whereby the charity sells the security for cash. If the charity never exercises dominion and control over the donated securities prior to receiving cash, there is a risk that the transaction could be viewed as a sale of the securities for cash by the donor, followed by a donation of the cash to charity, in which case the donor would recognize any built-in gains prior to the donation. A best practice is for the wallet provider not to be the same person who buys the cryptocurrency in exchange for fiat currency (e.g. US dollars), thereby ensuring that the charity in fact receives the cryptocurrency first before the charity subsequently sells the cryptocurrency for fiat currency to a third party on an exchange.

A nontax consideration that many charitable organizations consider when accepting blockchain-based assets is whether the gift carries any reputational risk or potential for public relations damage to the charity. Given the reality that blockchain-based assets can be used to transact in illicit activities anonymously, charities often may require donors to certify that the contribution is not derived from any illegal activity prior to accepting the gift.

TAX IMPLICATIONS OF CRYPTOCURRENCY "HARD FORKS"

Hard forks, also known as "chain splits" or "coin splits," may carry tax consequences to those that are party to the hard fork. In essence, a hard fork is a change to the software of a blockchain-based asset that creates two separate versions of the blockchain with a shared history. When a hard fork occurs, a new "branch" splits from the original ledger and thereafter, the two ledgers (original and new) are separately maintained. After a hard fork, the owner of the blockchain-based asset retains ownership of the original coin and obtains the right to separately use the new forked blockchain-based asset. Hard forks might occur for many reasons. One notable hard fork occurred in 2016 when the Ethereum blockchain was split into two, Classic Ethereum and Ethereum, in response to a hacking attack that impacted the original ledger.[33] In another example, in 2017 Bitcoin split into Bitcoin (BTC) and Bitcoin Cash (BCH).[34] Further examples in 2017 include Bitcoin Gold, Bitcoin Diamond, Super Bitcoin, Bitcoin Hot, and Lightning Bitcoin. In these examples and in other hard forks, money did not necessarily change hands, nor were assets necessarily exchanged. It is further feasible that hard forks may occur unbeknownst to the taxpayers' party to the same or that the taxpayers do not as a practical matter have user access or control over the forked blockchain-based asset.

The tax consequences of hard forks are not clear, and analogies to guidance in other areas are often required when examining the tax aspects of a hard fork. A primary issue arises as to whether a hard fork creates a taxable event for the taxpayers that are party to the hard fork. In other words, is a hard fork a realization event? To answer this question, we must ask a second question: do the taxpayers at issue have an accession to wealth attributable to the hard fork that in turn requires a recognition of gross income? US federal tax law generally applies a very broad definition to "gross income." Code Section 61 provides that "gross income" means "all income from whatever source derived." In *Commissioner v. Glenshaw Glass*,[35] the Supreme Court defined *gross income* as "instances of undeniable accessions to wealth, clearly realized, and over which the taxpayers have complete dominion," reflecting Congress's intent to tax all gains except those specifically exempted. The concept of "dominion" may be especially important in reviewing the tax aspects of a hard fork, as it is feasible that the taxpayers at issue do not have dominion or control over the assets created in the chain split. The Supreme Court in *Eisner v. Macomber* addressed whether a pro rata stock dividend paid to the common shareholders of a corporation

33. *See* Alyssa Hertig, *Ethereum's Two Ethereums Explained*, CoinDesk (July 28, 2016), https://www.coindesk.com/markets/2016/07/28/ethereums-two-ethereums-explained/.

34. *See* Amy Castor, *Bitcoin Cash 101: What Users Need to Know Before the Fork*, CoinDesk (July 31, 2017), https://www.coindesk.com/markets/2017/07/31/bitcoin-cash-101-what-users-need-to-know-before-the-fork/.

35. 348 U.S. 426 (1955).

constituted income.[36] Concluding that the stock dividend did not constitute income, the Supreme Court distinguished between (i) "gain derived from capital" and (ii) unrealized "gain accruing to capital or a growth or increment of value in the investment." According to the Supreme Court, the stock dividend at issue was growth in value of the original investment, not a taxable distribution—the shareholder did not receive a distribution out of the corporation's assets, and there was no change in the corporation's assets or liabilities. In short, there was no change in the shareholder's investment, just the receipt of an additional piece of paper reflecting his investment in the company.

This legal precedent establishes two competing theories by which to view forked coins. To the extent that forked coins are similar to the issuance of shares in *Macomber*, the forked coin simply represents an increase in the value of the original ledger and should be treated as unrealized gain rather than an accession to wealth. To the extent that a forked coin is the issuance of a new and independent asset (as evidenced by the creation of a new ledger) that has independent value that was removed and separated from the original ledger, however, the receipt of a forked coin is a realization event for tax purposes and therefore taxable income. However, not all tax advisers agree with this conclusion. There is an argument that the potential for hard forks is inherent in blockchain-based assets, and a buyer acquires that right or attribute of a hard fork when the asset is first sold. Under this theory, the receipt of the hard-forked coin is not a realization event. Instead, it is only the sale of such a coin that triggers a taxable event.

Even if a hard fork results in a realization for tax purposes, the timing of the realization is uncertain. It may be that the timing of realization occurs when the taxpayer has the right to secure the forked blockchain-based asset (in other words, the taxpayer cannot delay realization by failing to take action to download the new forked blockchain-based asset per the doctrine of constructive receipt).[37] The amount realized may be difficult to ascertain, as it would likely be based on FMV. The FMV of the forked blockchain-based asset may not be clear due to lack of an established market.

The basis of the original and forked blockchain-based assets would need to be determined, assuming the fork is a realization event. One option

36. 252 U.S. 189 (1920).

37. *See, e.g.*, American Bar Association Section of Taxation, *Tax Treatment of Cryptocurrency Hard Forks for Taxable Year 2017* (Mar. 19, 2018).

might be to split the basis proportionately based on the relative FMVs of the two assets at the time of the hard fork. This might be difficult if there are not readily ascertainable FMVs ascribed to each asset. Given these challenges, the American Bar Association (ABA) proposed a safe harbor whereby the ABA suggested that the IRS should issue guidance that recognizes that a hard fork is a taxable event for the owner of the original blockchain-based asset.[38] The deemed value of the forked blockchain-based asset at the time of the realization event would be zero, as is the tax basis in the forked blockchain-based asset. The holding period of the forked blockchain-based asset would start on the day of the hard fork. Taxpayers electing the safe-harbor treatment would be required to disclose the position on their tax returns. The IRS will not assert that any taxpayer availing itself of the safe harbor understated its taxes with respect to the hard-fork event (noting that any subsequent sale of the forked coin is not covered by the safe harbor). This safe harbor has not to date been accepted by the IRS or incorporated into binding IRS or Treasury guidance.

As discussed in prior sections, the IRS in 2019 released a revenue ruling addressing the tax aspects of hard forks and airdrops—Revenue Ruling 2019-24.[39] The ruling considers the tax treatment of hard forks and airdrops in two situations: Situation 1 describes a hard fork that does not cause a chain split. In such a case, the IRS ruled that the taxpayer did not have gross income as a result of the hard fork. Situation 2 describes an "airdrop" of cryptocurrency following a hard fork, and the IRS held that the airdropped blockchain-based assets were taxable to the recipients. Neither situation 1 nor situation 2 appears to describe any of the major chain splits, including but not limited to the Bitcoin Cash, Bitcoin Gold, and Ethereum splits described earlier. It is difficult to apply the analysis in Revenue Ruling 2019-24 with more typical fact patterns of chain splits.

INITIAL COIN OFFERINGS

Initial coin offerings (ICOs) had explosive growth in 2017 and 2018 and have continued in recent years. An ICO involves the issuance of a newly generated blockchain-based asset (frequently referred to as a

---

38. *Id.*

39. Rev. Rul. 2019-24, 2019-44 IRB 1004.

"token"). Tokens are typically issued in exchange for a fiat currency (e.g., the US dollar or a euro) or other blockchain-based assets that have an established market. The types of tokens may be utility tokens or security tokens, as described in more detail in earlier chapters.

The taxation of ICOs for the issuing entity is unclear and, until further guidance is issued by the IRS, depends on a facts-and-circumstances analysis in each instance. Each ICO tends to be different, which makes tax generalizations challenging. Pursuant to Notice 2014-21, blockchain-based assets that are convertible virtual currencies are property for tax purposes. The general tax rule is that the receipt of cash or other valuable property in exchange for the sale of property by a taxpayer is taxable, and this rule should apply to tokens issued in an ICO as well. The receipt of ICO proceeds is treated as a sale of property in which the issuer has zero tax basis. All taxable gain is realized in the year of the ICO. Such gain is unlikely to qualify as a capital asset, and such proceeds are likely ordinary income—although the facts of each ICO would need to be reviewed to make this determination.

There is an open question as to whether a security token may be structured to qualify as stock or debt for tax purposes. The answer is unclear and ultimately may well turn on the application of a debt-versus-equity analysis from a tax perspective. In terms of consequences to the issuer, Code Section 1032(a) generally provides that no taxable gain or loss shall be recognized to a corporation on the receipt of money or other property in exchange for stock (including treasury stock) of such corporation. Similarly, the issuance of a debt instrument is not a taxable event. Further, in reviewing tax characterization of tokens, different tax characterizations likely apply to different types of tokens. Utility tokens are unlikely to qualify as equity or debt for tax purposes, and the analysis (presented next) regarding personal seat licenses may instead apply. To contrast, security tokens are more likely (based on the authors' experience) to be characterized as equity or debt for tax purposes, depending on the facts.

Other theories may apply to ICOs, depending on the facts. For example, arguments have been made that a token issuance is analogous to a personal seat license. The IRS has ruled in at least one case on the tax aspects of personal seat licenses.[40] In such ruling, the IRS held that the sale of redeemable personal seat licenses by a professional sports team did not result in immediate income for the team. This result applied because a taxpayer "does not have an accession to wealth, nor complete dominion

40. Priv. Ltr. Rul. 201722004 (June 2, 2017).

over an item, if received subject to a legally enforceable and binding obligation to repay the item." In other words, if a taxpayer "receives money or other property with a legally enforceable and binding obligation to return or repay it, the taxpayer is not enriched by the transaction and, therefore, does not realize gross income therefrom within the meaning of [Code Section 61]." Thus, the fact that the licenses were redeemable is a key part of the ruling's tax analysis. Similarly, one might argue that the blockchain-based asset issued in an ICO is redeemable by the holder and as such does not result in an accession to wealth for the issuer. Whether this argument is reasonable will depend on the facts and circumstances of the ICO and the issued tokens.

Purchasers of tokens issued in ICOs are generally not taxed upon the token purchase, assuming the purchase is made with US dollars. However, the purchase of tokens with another blockchain-based asset is a taxable event, with gain or loss measured based on the purchaser's tax basis (or bases) in the asset used in the exchange. Prior to 2018, a taxpayer may have been able in the right circumstances to treat such purchase as a like-kind exchange under Code Section 1031 (see prior discussion regarding same). Under current law, however, such like-kind exchange treatment is not available. The taxpayer's basis in the newly acquired token will be the purchase price (if fiat currency is used) or the FMV of any property exchanged. The post-ICO use of the token by the purchaser to acquire other property or a service would separately give rise to a taxable event, thus triggering gain or loss based on the adjusted basis of the blockchain-based asset as compared to its FMV.

Some token issuers utilize a "presale" structure for their tokens, referred to as a Simple Agreement for Future Tokens (or Equity) (SAFT). SAFTs have been employed by numerous companies to raise funds prior to a token offering. SAFTs are based on the Y Combinator model Simple Agreement for Future Equity (SAFE).[41] Generally, the intended tax characterization is to defer the recognition of taxable income with respect to the funds paid to the SAFT issuer until the time the tokens are issued (presumably in a different tax year). But deferral is not certain and ultimately depends on the terms of the SAFT. Moreover, due to recent Securities and Exchange Commission actions regarding SAFTs, it is unclear whether issuers will continue to materially rely on SAFTs to raise funds.[42]

---

41. *See* J. Batiz-Benet, *The SAFT Project: Toward a Compliant Token Sale Framework* (Oct. 2, 2017), https://saftproject.com/static/SAFT-Project-Whitepaper.pdf.

42. *See, e.g.*, SEC v. Telegram Grp. Inc., No. 19-cv-9439 (S.D.N.Y. June 26, 2020) (final judgment), https://www.sec.gov/news/press-release/2020-146.

REPORTING BLOCKCHAIN-BASED ASSET TRANSACTIONS

As a general matter, taxpayers must report all sales, exchanges, or other disposition of property, including exchanges of services for property. Given that the IRS has taken the position that blockchain-based assets subject to Notice 2014-21 are treated as property for tax purposes, sales, exchanges, or barter transactions involving the same may be subject to tax reporting. Likewise, for tax years beginning before 2023, exchanges for blockchain-based assets may be subject to information reporting requirements if they qualify as brokers or barter exchanges. A broker or barter exchange requires IRS Form 1099-B to report transactions such as sales and redemptions. In 2019, the IRS stated that by August 2019 it intended to send letters to more than 10,000 taxpayers reminding them of these obligations and of an obligation to file or amend past returns and pay back taxes, interest, and penalties in appropriate cases.[43] The letters were sent, and the IRS sent similar letters in 2020. Samples of the letter are available on the IRS website, and detail various forms that may be applicable to taxpayers engaged in transactions involving blockchain-based assets. Several of the form letters outline the common schedules for reporting virtual currency transactions including Schedules C, D, and E.[44] Each schedule is further described next.

Schedule C may apply to an independent contractor that received payment in virtual currency. Such taxpayer must report it in gross income for the amount of the virtual currency's FMV, measured in US dollars, as of the date and time that such taxpayer received the virtual currency. The letter clarifies that gross income derived by an individual from a trade or business, carried on by the individual as other than an employee, is reported on Schedule C. This constitutes self-employment income and is subject to the self-employment tax.

Schedule D may apply to a taxpayer who sold, exchanged, or disposed of virtual currency (e.g., Bitcoin, Ether) or used it to pay for goods

---

43. *See* Press Release, Internal Revenue Service, IRS has begun sending letters to virtual currency owners advising them to pay back taxes, file amended returns; part of agency's larger efforts (July 26, 2019), https://www.irs.gov/newsroom/irs-has-begun-sending-letters-to-virtual-currency-owners-advising-them-to-pay-back-taxes-file-amended-returns-part-of-agencys-larger-efforts.

44. *See* IRS, *Reporting Virtual Currency Transactions*, Letter 6174 (2019), https://www.irs.gov/pub/notices/letter_6174.pdf; https://www.irs.gov/pub/notices/letter_6174-a.pdf.

or services. Such taxpayer may have engaged in a reportable transaction and may have a tax liability. Per the letter, these transactions may be reportable on Schedule D. A taxpayer should maintain and review all transaction records, including bank, wallet, and exchange reports and statements, to determine tax basis, amount received, and other information needed for reporting on Schedule D.

Schedule E may apply to taxpayers that received supplemental income in the form of virtual currency, including income from rental real estate, royalties, partnerships, S corporations, estates, trusts, and x. Such taxpayers may need to report this on Schedule E. The letter instructs taxpayers to report the virtual currency received at its FMV, measured in US dollars, as of the date and time of the transaction. Taxpayers may also need to file supplemental forms (e.g., Form 8582, Passive Activity Loss Limitations).

Taxpayers must be further mindful of reporting virtual currency transactions on IRS Form 1040. IRS Form 1040 was revised in 2019 to include a specific reporting requirement for transactions involving virtual currency.

The Infrastructure Investment and Jobs Act (the Act) recently expanded reporting requirements for blockchain-based assets by extending reporting requirements for certain transactions involving over $10,000 in cash to transactions involving a digital asset (e.g., a cryptocurrency). In addition, the Act expands existing IRS Form 1099 reporting obligations to digital assets brokers. These new reporting requirements generally take effect in 2024 for the 2023 tax year. It is not yet clear how such requirements will be implemented and more guidance is likely to be provided.

HIGHLIGHTS OF ADDITIONAL FEDERAL GUIDANCE ADDRESSING BLOCKCHAIN-BASED ASSET TAX ISSUES

In addition to the IRS and Treasury guidance discussed earlier, some federal agencies have issued guidance or taken actions that implicate the tax aspects of blockchain-based assets. Recent developments are described next.

2016 Treasury Inspector General for Tax Administration (TIGTA) Guidance

The Treasury Inspector General for Tax Administration (TIGTA) issued a twenty-five-page report in September 2016 addressing the growth of cryptocurrencies and the then-current state of IRS engagement.[45] The report states that although the IRS issued Notice 2014-21 (discussed in the foregoing sections), there has been little coordination between the responsible IRS functions to address potential taxpayer noncompliance. The report further concluded that none of the IRS operating divisions have developed any type of compliance initiatives or guidelines for conducting investigations related to cryptocurrencies. For example, as of the date of the report, third-party methods of reporting taxable transactions to the IRS did not separately identify cryptocurrency transactions. The report recommends that the IRS develop a cryptocurrency strategy with goals and a timeline for implementation, and that the IRS revise third-party information-reporting documents to identify cryptocurrency transactions and the amounts at issue.

2016 Department of Justice Actions

The Department of Justice (DOJ) has already taken actions implicating tax issues of blockchain-based assets. On November 17, 2016, the DOJ petitioned for the issuance of a John Doe summons to examine Coinbase records for information related to any US taxpayers conducting transactions in virtual currency during the years ended December 31, 2013, through December 31, 2015. The DOJ was clear in issuing the summons that it made no allegation that Coinbase has engaged in any wrongdoing in connection with its virtual currency exchange business. Rather, the department intended to use the John Doe summons to obtain information about possible violations of internal revenue laws by individuals whose identities are unknown, and the summons directed Coinbase to produce records identifying US taxpayers who have used its services, along with other documents relating to their virtual currency transactions.[46] In April 2021, the IRS received authorization to serve another

---

45. Treasury Inspector General for Tax Admin., Reference No. 2016-30-083, Final Audit Report, *As the Use of Virtual Currencies in Taxable Transactions Becomes More Common, Additional Actions Are Needed to Ensure Taxpayer Compliance* (Audit # 201530022) (Sept. 21, 2016).

46. *See* Press Release, Office of Public Affairs, Department of Justice, Court Authorizes Service of John Doe Summons Seeking the Identities of U.S. Taxpayers Who Have Used Virtual Currency (Nov. 30, 2016), https://www.justice.gov/opa/pr/court-authorizes-service-john-doe-summons-seeking-identities-us-taxpayers-who-have-used#:~:text=The%20court's%20order%20grants%20the,John%20

John Doe summons on at least one global crypto finance company seeking information about US taxpayers who conducted at least the equivalent of $20,000 in cryptocurrency transactions during 2016 to 2020.[47] Again the summons is not meant to suggest that the company engaged in any wrongdoing. Rather, it is intended to obtain information related to a group or class of persons that the IRS has reasonable basis to believe has failed to comply with US tax laws.

LB&I Compliance Campaigns

On July 2, 2018, the IRS Large Business and International Division (LB&I) announced the approval of a compliance campaign with respect to virtual currency.[48] The announcement declares that US persons are subject to tax on worldwide income from all sources, including transactions involving virtual currency. As described herein, Notice 2014-21 stated that virtual currency is property for federal tax purposes and provides information on the US federal tax implications of convertible virtual currency transactions. The Virtual Currency Compliance campaign addresses noncompliance related to the use of virtual currency through multiple treatment streams including outreach and examinations. The compliance activities will follow the general tax principles applicable to all transactions in property, as outlined in Notice 2014-21. The IRS will continue to consider and solicit taxpayer and practitioner feedback in education efforts, future guidance, and development of practice units. Taxpayers with unreported virtual currency transactions are urged by the IRS to correct their returns as soon as practical. The IRS stated that it is not contemplating a voluntary disclosure program specifically to address tax noncompliance involving virtual currency.

Doe%E2%80%9D%20summons%20on%20Coinbase.&text=This%20John%20Doe%20summons%20directs,to%20their%20virtual%20currency%20transactions.

47. *See* Press Release, Office of Public Affairs, Department of Justice, Court Authorizes Service of John Doe Summons Seeking Identities of U.S. Taxpayers Who Have Used Cryptocurrency (Apr. 1, 2021), https://www.justice.gov/opa/pr/court-authorizes-service-john-doe-summons-seeking-identities-us-taxpayers-who-have-used-0.

48. *See* Internal Revenue Service, *Five Compliance Campaigns* (July 2, 2018), https://www.irs.gov/businesses/irs-lbi-compliance-campaigns-july-2-2018.

2020 Government Accountability Office (GAO) Report

In February 2020, the Government Accountability Office (GAO) issued a report stating, among other things, that it has limited data on tax compliance for virtual currencies. Tax forms, including the information returns filed by third parties such as financial institutions, generally do not require filers to indicate whether the income or transactions they report involve virtual currency.[49] In the report, the GAO recommends that the IRS take steps to increase information reporting and that the Financial Crimes Enforcement Network and IRS address how foreign asset–reporting laws apply to virtual currency.

2021 Financial Crimes Enforcement Network Notice

The Financial Crimes Enforcement Network (FinCEN) stated in Notice 2020-2 that it intends to propose to amend the regulations implementing the Bank Secrecy Act (BSA) regarding reports of foreign financial accounts (FBAR) to include "virtual currency" as a type of reportable account under 31 C.F.R. 1010.350.[50] This regulation currently requires that each person with a financial interest or signatory authority over a financial account in a foreign country file an FBAR.

---

49. *See* U.S. Government Accountability Office, *Virtual Currencies: Additional Information Reporting and Clarified Guidance Could Improve Tax Compliance*, GAO-20-188 (Feb. 2020), https://www.gao.gov/assets/710/704573.pdf.

50. *See* FinCEN, *Report of Foreign Bank and Financial Accounts (FBAR) Filing Requirement for Virtual Currency*, FinCEN Notice 2020-2, https://www.fincen.gov/sites/default/files/shared/Notice-Virtual%20Currency%20Reporting%20on%20the%20FBAR%20123020.pdf.

5 Digital Assets as Payment and Money Transfer Systems

Margo Tank and Andrew W. Grant

Digital assets in the form of virtual currency are used both as a means of payment and a means of transferring value from one location to another. This chapter discusses the federal and state laws applicable to this use of virtual currency. At a high level, transferring money or value from one person or location to another person or location constitutes money transmission. Money transmitters may be subject to both state and federal requirements. Federally, the Financial Crimes Enforcement Network (FinCEN), which is part of the US Department of the Treasury, is the primary regulator for money transmitters, while for states, typically the state's financial institution regulator has primary authority.[1] Furthermore, entities who hold a consumer's virtual currency (e.g., in a virtual currency wallet) may be subject to the Electronic Fund Transfer Act (EFTA) and its implementing regulation, Regulation E, which provides consumers with specific protections related to electronic fund transfers (EFTs).

---

1. As discussed later, FinCEN's primary concern when regulating money transmitters is to prevent money laundering (focus is on societal harms, e.g., that bad actors do not manipulate the system to launder money), while states' primary focus is on consumer protection (focus is on preventing personal harms, e.g., ensuring that the entity the state licenses can "transmit" money from one person to another such that the consumer is not at risk of losing their money in the process).

FinCEN REGULATION OF VIRTUAL CURRENCY MONEY TRANSMISSION

The federal government seeks to regulate virtual currency to promote national security by combating money laundering and terrorism financing. FinCEN carries out this mission. FinCEN's authority arises primarily from the Currency and Foreign Transactions Reporting Act of 1970, which has been amended by Title III of the USA PATRIOT Act of 2001 and the Anti–Money Laundering Act of 2020.[2] These laws are commonly referred to as the Bank Secrecy Act (BSA), or because the BSA is also considered an anti–money laundering law (AML), it is jointly termed *BSA/AML*.[3] The BSA and its implementing regulations require *financial institutions* to protect against financial crime by, in part, establishing robust AML programs,[4] developing know your customer programs, and filing suspicious activity reports.[5]

FinCEN regulates virtual currency money transmission through its regulation of financial institutions. The BSA defines a "financial institution" broadly. In addition to banks, "financial institution" includes "a licensed sender of money or any other person who engages in the transmission of currency, funds, *or value that substitutes for currency*. . . ." (emphasis added).[6] FinCEN regulates such entities under the term *money*

2. The Anti–Money Laundering Act of 2020 was included within the William M. (Mac) Thornberry National Defense Authorization for Fiscal Year 2021, H.R. 6395, 116th Cong. Div. F (2021).

3. For background on FinCEN and the BSA, *see* https://www.fincen.gov/what-we-do and https://www.fincen.gov/resources/statutes-regulations. For the BSA statutes, *see* 31 U.S.C. 5311-5332.

4. *See* FinCEN, *Guidance on Existing AML Program Rule Compliance Obligations for MSB Principals with Respect to Agent Monitoring*, FIN-2016-G001 (Mar. 11, 2016), https://www.fincen.gov/resources/statutes-regulations/guidance/guidance-existing-aml-program-rule-compliance-obligations.

5. On Dec. 23, 2020, FinCEN published a notice of proposed rulemaking that seeks to adopt regulations that would require reporting and recordkeeping requirements regarding convertible virtual currency, including requiring counterparty information on unhosted wallets for certain transactions. 85 Fed. Reg. 83,840. As of November 2021, FinCEN has not issued a final rule, so it is not clear whether any changes will be made from the proposed rule.

6. 31 U.S.C. § 5312(a)(2)(R). "Or value that substitutes for currency" was added as part of the Anti–Money Laundering Act of 2020.

services business (MSB).[7] An MSB includes "money transmitters."[8] A money transmitter is a person that provides *money transmission services*, which means the acceptance of currency, funds, or other value that substitutes for currency from one person and the transmission of currency, funds, or other value that substitutes for currency *to another location or person* by any means.[9] The facts and circumstances surrounding the person's activities determine whether the person is a money transmitter.[10,11]

Not all entities that transmit money are money transmitters. For example, FinCEN exempts (1) payment processors who facilitate the purchase of or payment of a bill through a clearance and settlement system by agreement with the creditor or seller or (2) those who operate a clearance and settlement system or otherwise act as an intermediary solely between BSA-regulated institutions.[12]

---

7. 31 C.F.R. § 1010.100(t). Note that the BSA includes a definition for "money transmitting business" and "money transmitting service"—both of which were also amended by the Anti–Money Laundering Act of 2020 to include "or value that substitutes for currency"—but that FinCEN adopted the term "money services business" to help prevent confusion regarding which entities required registration. Amendment to the Bank Secrecy Act Regulations, 64 Fed. Reg. 45,438, FN1 (Aug. 20, 1999), https://www.govinfo.gov/content/pkg/FR-1999-08-20/pdf/99-21667.pdf.

8. 31 C.F.R. § 1010.100(ff)(5).

9. *Id.* Note that in 2011, FinCEN adopted a final rule that, in part, expanded the definition of "money transmission services" to include the element that value that substitutes for currency is considered money transmission. *See* FinCEN, Bank Secrecy Act Regulations; Definition and Other Regulations Relating to Money Services Businesses, 76 Fed. Reg. 43,585 (July 21, 2011), https://www.govinfo.gov/content/pkg/FR-2011-07-21/pdf/2011-18309.pdf. If there were any doubt about FinCEN's ability to regulate virtual currency activities as part of its authority to regulate money transmission services, the inclusion of "value that substitutes for currency" in the Anti–Money Laundering Act of 2020 clearly establishes such authority.

10. The BSA broadly defines a "person" to include an "individual, a corporation, a partnership, a trust or estate, a joint stock company, an association, a syndicate, joint venture, or other unincorporated organization or group, an Indian Tribe (as that term is defined in the Indian Gaming Regulatory Act), and all entities cognizable as legal personalities." 31 C.F.R. § 1010.100(mm).

11. 31 C.F.R. § 1010.100(ff)(5)(ii).

12. *Id.*

FinCEN's Guidance Addressing Convertible Virtual Currency

In March 2013, FinCEN released its first guidance (2013 Guidance)[13] addressing why it has authority to regulate entities that transmit convertible virtual currency (CVC). The 2013 Guidance created three categories related to CVC—administrators, exchangers, and users—and it describes why FinCEN regulates administrators and exchangers but not users of CVC.

"Real" Currency Versus Convertible Virtual Currency

Consistent with FinCEN's focus on money and money-like assets, FinCEN uses the term *CVC* to describe a category of cryptocurrency assets it regulates that includes many blockchain-based assets.[14] In the March 2013 Guidance, FinCEN contrasted "real" currency from virtual currency as follows:[15] while virtual currency is a medium of exchange that operates like currency in some environments, it does not have all the attributes associated with "real" currency, such as not having legal tender status in any jurisdiction.[16] Despite missing those attributes, because "convertible" virtual currency either has an equivalent value in real currency or acts as a substitute for real currency, FinCEN can regulate its transmission. Transmitting virtual currency that cannot be converted to

---

13. *Application of FinCEN's Regulations to Persons Administering, Exchanging, or Using Virtual Currencies*, FIN-2013-G001 (Mar. 18, 2013), https://www.fincen.gov/sites/default/files/shared/FIN-2013-G001.pdf.

14. Under the taxonomy in Chapter 1, the assets on which FinCEN focuses are probably best categorized as cryptocurrencies (including stablecoins), though they could include other types of blockchain-based assets, such as utility tokens.

15. "Real" currency is the coin and paper money of the United States or of any other country that [i] is designated as legal tender and that [ii] circulates and [iii] is customarily used and accepted as a medium of exchange in the country of issuance. 31 C.F.R. § 1010.100(m).

16. 2013 Guidance, at p. 1. In the 2013 Guidance, FinCEN also distinguished between "centralized virtual currencies" and "de-centralized virtual currencies," which lack a central repository or single administrator. *Id.* at 4–5. The term "de-centralized virtual currencies" refers generally to blockchain-based assets, though it is possible to create a privately administered blockchain, with only a single or small number of miners and nodes, all of which are acting in concert, and also possible to create a decentralized asset that does not use a blockchain.

or sold for "real" currency or other CVC is not money transmission services.[17]

Within the 2013 Guidance as well as in subsequent guidance and enforcement actions, FinCEN expanded on what activities do or do not constitute "money transmission services." Because FinCEN created the categories of "administrator," "exchanger," and "user" in the 2013 Guidance, this chapter first describes those categories and then explains how specific types of entities and persons fall within or outside FinCEN's reach.

What Are an Administrator, an Exchanger, and a User?

The 2013 Guidance defined an *administrator* as "a person engaged as a business in issuing (putting into circulation) a virtual currency, and who has the authority to redeem (to withdraw from circulation) such virtual currency." It defined an *exchanger* as "a person engaged as a business in the exchange of virtual currency for real currency, funds, or other virtual currency." And it defined a *user* as "a person who obtains virtual currency to purchase goods or services."[18] FinCEN notes that the label of *how* a person obtains virtual currency—be it "earning," "mining," "harvesting," etc.—is not material to determining whether the person is a "user."[19]

Additional FinCEN Guidance on Convertible Virtual Currency

As of November 2021, FinCEN released seven additional guidances that address virtual currencies. These guidances typically elaborate on what constitutes an administrator, an exchanger, or a user. The following are the seven guidances:

- *Application of FinCEN's Regulations to Virtual Currency Mining Operations*, FIN-2014-R001 (Jan. 30, 2014) (hereinafter "2014 Guidance on Mining")

17. For example, FinCEN considers freely transferable digital certificates to be commodity-backed virtual currency because "the definition of a money transmitter does not differentiate between real currencies and convertible virtual currencies." FIN-2015-R001, p. 4.

18. 2013 Guidance, p. 2.

19. *Id.*, p. 2, fn. 7; 2019 Guidance on CVC Business Models, ¶ 5.3.

- *Application of FinCEN's Regulations to Virtual Currency Software Development and Certain Investment Activity*, FIN-2014-R002 (Jan. 30, 2014) (hereinafter "2014 Guidance on VC Software Development")
- *Application of Money Services Business Regulations to the Rental of Computer Systems for Mining Virtual Currency*, FIN-2014-R007 (Apr. 29, 2014) (hereinafter "2014 Guidance on Renting VC Mining Systems")
- *Request for Administrative Ruling on the Application of FinCEN's Regulations to a Virtual Currency Trading Platform*, FIN-2014-R011 (Oct. 27, 2014) (hereinafter "2014 Guidance on VC Trading Platform")
- *Request for Administrative Ruling on the Application of FinCEN's Regulations to a Virtual Currency Payment System*, FIN-2014-R012 (hereinafter "2014 Guidance on VC Payment System")
- *Application of FinCEN's Regulations to Persons Issuing Physical or Digital Negotiable Certificates of Ownership of Precious Metals*, FIN-2015-R001 (hereinafter "2015 Guidance on Digital Negotiable Certificates")
- *Application of FinCEN's Regulations to Certain Business Models Involving Convertible Virtual Currencies*, FIN-2019-G001 (hereinafter "2019 Guidance on CVC Business Models")

These, along with the 2013 Guidance, constitute "FinCEN Virtual Currency Guidances."

Persons or Activities That FinCEN Deems to Be Engaged in "Money Transmission Services"

Based on FinCEN Virtual Currency Guidances and particular FinCEN enforcement actions and regulator statements, FinCEN would likely consider the following persons and entities to be engaging in money transmission services. With that said, the following labels will not determine whether the person is acting as an MSB. Each person's facts and circumstances may differ, and these differences may lead to an alternative regulatory conclusion.

- *Centralized virtual currencies*: An administrator of a centralized virtual currency that has a central repository will be a money transmitter if it allows transfers of value (1) between persons or (2) from one location to another. The administrator will be a money transmitter whether the transferred value is denominated in real currency or CVC.[20] Any entity—including an exchange—that uses its access to the CVC services provided by the administrator to accept and transmit the CVC on behalf of others, including transfers intended to pay a third party for virtual goods and services, is an exchanger.[21]

- For centralized virtual currencies, FinCEN understands that an exchanger's activities generally take two forms: one requires the transmission to another location (which FinCEN interprets very broadly)[22] while the other requires the transmission to another person:
    - *To another location*: The first form consists of an exchanger (acting as a "seller" of the CVC) that accepts real currency or its equivalent from a user (e.g., a purchaser) and transmits the value of that real currency to fund the user's CVC account with the administrator. This event constitutes transmission ***to another location***, specifically from the user's account at one place (e.g., a user's real currency account at a bank) to the user's CVC account with the administrator.[23]
    - *To another person*: The second form involves a de facto sale of CVC. The exchanger accepts currency or its equivalent from a user and privately credits the user with an appropriate portion of the exchanger's own CVC held with the administrator (and as noted earlier, these entities can be the same). The exchanger then transmits that internally credited value to third parties at the user's direction. This transaction constitutes transmission ***to another person***, specifically each third party to which transmissions are made at the user's direction.[24]
- *Peer-to-peer (P2P) exchangers*: A peer-to-peer exchanger is a natural person engaged in the business of buying and selling CVC, who typically advertises and markets their services through classified ads, specifically designed web platform websites, online forums,

---

20. 2013 Guidance, p. 4.
21. *Id.*
22. 2019 Guidance on CVC Business Models, p. 12.
23. 2013 Guidance, pp. 4, 5; 2019 Guidance on CVC Business Models, pp. 12–13.
24. 2013 Guidance, pp. 4, 5.

other social media, and word of mouth.[25] A natural person that operates as a P2P exchanger and engages in money transmission services must comply with FinCEN's MSB requirements.

- *CVC wallets*: CVC wallets are interfaces for storing and transferring CVCs. There are numerous types of CVC wallets, including hosted wallets (where a third party controls the user's funds), unhosted wallets (users control their funds), and multiple-signature wallets (require more than one private key for the wallet operator to transact). Whether the CVC wallet provider acts as an intermediary between the owner of the value and the value itself does not depend on the technology used. Instead, the regulatory analysis depends on four criteria: (1) who owns the value, (2) where the value is stored, (3) whether the owner directly interacts with the payment system where the CVC runs, and (4) whether the intermediary has total independent control over the value.[26]
  - For example, hosted wallet providers are money transmitters that receive, store, and transmit CVC on their accountholder's behalf. When applying the previous criteria to a hosted wallet, the value belongs to the CVC owner, the value is stored in the host's wallet, the owner interacts with the host and not the payment system, and the host has total independent control over the value.[27]
  - Multiple-signature wallet providers that combine the services of a multiple-signature wallet provider and a hosted wallet provider will qualify as a money transmitter for the reasons previously listed.[28]
- *Issuer of commodity-backed digital certificates*: If a person or entity issues a freely transferable digital certificate of ownership

25. 2019 Guidance on CVC Business Models, pp. 14–15; *In re matter of: Eric Powers*, Assessment of Civil Money Penalty, No. 2019-01 (Apr. 19, 2019) (FinCEN assessed a civil money penalty against Eric Powers for willfully violating the BSA's MSB requirements, including [a] registering with FinCEN as an MSB; [b] establishing and implementing an effective written AML program; [c] detecting and adequately reporting suspicious transactions; and [d] reporting currency transactions.)

26. 2019 Guidance on CVC Business Models, p. 14, ¶ 4.2.

27. *Id.* at pp. 15–16, ¶ 4.2.1.

28. *Id.* at p. 17, ¶ 4.2.2.

to buyers, that person or entity allows the unrestricted transfer of value from a customer's commodity position to another customer's (or third-party's) position. By doing so, the person or entity acts as a CVC administrator because it no longer limits itself to the type of transmission of funds that is a fundamental element to executing the contract for the purchase or sale of the currency or the other commodity.[29]

- *Brokers and dealers of e-currency and e-precious metals*: An entity that transfers funds between a customer and a third party that is not part of the currency or commodity transaction is a money transmitter. This includes entities that (1) transfer funds between a customer and a third party by permitting a third party to fund a customer's account, (2) transfer value from a customer's currency or commodity position to the account of another customer, or (3) close out of a customer's currency or commodity position and transfer the proceeds to a third party.[30]
- *Investor*: Whether an investor is an "exchanger" is a fact-intensive analysis, whereas, if an investor engaged as a business in exchanging virtual currency against real currency (or even against other CVC), it would be a money transmitter.[31]
- *Trading platforms*: Trading platforms that allow trading of convertible virtual currencies can be "exchangers" even if the platform does not finalize a trade because the precondition set by the platform was not met.[32] Further, an "exchanger" includes maintaining customer accounts that contain real or CVC with a mechanism to match traders seeking to buy/sell from each other, then purchasing from one customer and selling to the other if the platform finds a match.[33] Additionally, from FinCEN's perspective, it does not matter *how* the platform funds itself for the trades it enables. FinCEN will classify the platform as an exchanger—rather than

---

29. 2015 Guidance on Digital Negotiable Certificates, p. 4.

30. 2013 Guidance, p. 3; *Application of the Definition of Money Transmitter to Brokers and Dealers in Currency and Other Commodities*, FIN-2008-G008 (Sep. 10, 2008) (hereinafter "2008 Guidance on Brokers and Dealers in Other Commodities").

31. 2014 Guidance on VC Software Development, p. 4.

32. 2014 Guidance on VC Trading Platform, p. 3.

33. *Id.* at p. 3.

"user"—if the platform acts as a broker (attempting to match parties) or as a dealer (using one's reserves, either real or CVC, to transact).[34]

- *CVC ATMs*: A person who owns and operates a CVC ATM that uses an electronic terminal to accept currency from one person and transmit an equivalent value in CVC (or vice versa) qualifies as a money transmitter.[35]
- *Decentralized (distributed) application* (DApp): DApps are simple applications run by a distributed network, such as a blockchain, designed such that they are not controlled or run by a single person or group of identifiable persons. According to FinCEN, if a DApp accepts and transmits value, it is a money transmitter, even if it does not operate for a profit.[36] That said, as a practical matter, FinCEN's assertion of jurisdiction to regulate DApps as money transmitters is questionable, if for no other reason than there may be no actual entity to regulate. It is not clear how FinCEN would impose regulations or take enforcement action against what is essentially a computer program, particularly since the entities running the program may be a distributed group of numerous and unidentifiable blockchain miners.
- *Payment services*: Payment services companies take many forms. Whether any particular payment system operates as a money transmitter, or is otherwise eligible for an exemption, is a fact-intensive review. For example, a payment services company that accepts real currency and converts that real currency into CVC—whether it acts as a broker or a dealer to do so—and then transmits the CVC to a merchant acts as an "exchanger."[37] FinCEN notes that CVC payment processors are generally unable to satisfy the "payment processor" exemption because they do not operate through clearance and settlement systems that admit *only* BSA-regulated financial institutions.[38]

34. *Id.* at p. 6.

35. 2019 Guidance on CVC Business Models, p. 17, ¶ 4.3.

36. *Id.* at p. 18, ¶ 4.4.

37. 2014 Guidance on VC Payment System, p. 3.

38. 2019 Guidance on CVC Business Models, p. 22, ¶ 4.6.

- *Mixer/tumbler*: Businesses providing anonymizing services (commonly called "mixers" or "tumblers") that seek to conceal the source of the transmission of virtual currency are money transmitters when they accept and transmit CVC.[39]

Persons or Activities That Do Not Constitute Money Transmission

While FinCEN's interpretation of what constitutes "money transmission services" for virtual currency activities is both broad and, at times, vague, FinCEN has provided guidance on specific actions that are outside its regulatory domain. With that said, if the person is engaged in different business models at the same time, the person may be exempt from the BSA under one model while covered by the BSA when operating the other model.[40]

- *Software developer*: Producing and distributing software that facilitates selling virtual currency is not accepting and transmitting value.[41] This exclusion includes anonymizing software, provided the person does not use it to engage as a business in accepting and transmitting value.[42]
- *P2P exchangers*: As noted earlier, if the P2P exchanger engages in money transmission, that natural person must comply with the BSA's MSB requirements, but if the natural person engages in such activity infrequently *and* not for profit or gain, that person would

39. Kenneth A. Blanco, Prepared Remarks at 2018 Chicago-Kent Block (Legal) Tech Conference (Aug. 9, 2018), https://www.fincen.gov/news/speeches/prepared-remarks-fincen-director-kenneth-blanco-delivered-2018-chicago-kent-block; 2019 Guidance on CVC Business Models, p. 19, ¶ 4.5.1(a). Note that FinCEN does not view protecting a consumer's information by providing anonymizing services as being eligible for the "integral" exemption because the business consists exclusively of providing secured money transmission.

40. 2019 Guidance on CVC Business Models, p. 3.

41. 2014 Guidance on VC Software Development, p. 2; *see also* 2019 Guidance on CVC Business Models, p. 3 (noting that a software developer may have BSA obligations if the developer has a separate business model that allows it to use the application to engage as a business in accepting or transmitting CVC).

42. 2019 Guidance on CVC Business Models, p. 20, ¶ 4.5.1(b).

be exempt from the scope of money transmission.[43] To reiterate, the facts and circumstances will determine whether any natural person is acting as a P2P exchanger.

- *Unhosted CVC wallet providers*: Unlike hosted wallets, unhosted wallets are stored on the user's device and allow the user to store and conduct CVC transactions. In these scenarios, the value belongs to the owner and is stored in a wallet while the owner interacts with the payment system directly and has total independent control over the value. So long as the person is using the unhosted wallet to purchase goods or services on that person's own behalf, the person is not a money transmitter.[44]
- *Investors in CVC*: An investor acts as a user when the investor invests in CVC for its account, and sells the CVC when the investor realizes the value of its investment.[45]
- *Renting mining hardware*: Renting computer systems to third parties to enable them to mine virtual currencies administered by other entities is not covered by FinCEN regulations. The regulations exempt a person that only provides the delivery, communication, or network data access services used by a money transmitter to supply money transmission services.[46]
- *Broker/dealer in e-currencies or e-precious metals*: Not all broker/dealer activities in convertible virtual currencies or e-precious metals constitute "money transmission services." A broker or dealer in real currency or other commodities is not a money transmitter if they accept and transmit funds *solely* to effect a bona fide purchase or sale of the real currency or other commodities for or with a customer.[47]
- *CVC trading platform*: If the CVC trading platform only allows buyers and sellers of CVC to post their bids and offers, and the parties settle the exchange through an outside venue, the CVC platform is not a money transmitter.[48]

---

43. 31 C.F.R. § 1010.100(ff)(8)(iii); 2019 Guidance on CVC Business Models, p. 15.
44. 2019 Guidance on CVC Business Models, pp. 15–16, ¶ 4.2.1.
45. *Id.* at p. 4.
46. 2014 Guidance on Renting VC Mining Systems.
47. 2013 Guidance, p. 3; 2008 Guidance on Brokers and Dealers in Other Commodities.
48. 2019 Guidance on CVC Business Models, p. 22, ¶ 5.1.

Status of Decentralized Token or Virtual Currency Developers

While producing and distributing software that facilitates the sale of virtual currency is **not** alone money transmission,[49] whether a token developer who then sells its virtual currency or tokens is an MSB under FinCEN is a more complicated question. FinCEN guidance leads to the conclusion that decentralized virtual currency developers may be money transmitters if they sell from their stock of virtual currency. However, the exact contours of when an entity constitutes a "software provider" and when the entity becomes a money transmitter are not clearly defined.

First, in the 2013 Guidance, FinCEN stated that for decentralized virtual currency, a person that creates units of it and sells those units to another person for real currency or its equivalent is engaged in transmission to another location and is a money transmitter.[50] This conclusion is reinforced in the 2019 Guidance on CVC Business Models, in which FinCEN states that a person that develops a decentralized CVC payment system will become a money transmitter if that person also engages as a business in the acceptance and transmission of value denominated in the CVC it developed, even if mined at an earlier date.[51] Second, FinCEN's first civil enforcement action was against a virtual currency administrator and exchanger, Ripple Labs.[52] Specifically, the Statement of Facts and Violations states that Ripple's currency, XRP, was pre-mined (meaning it was fully generated before distribution) and that Ripple sold XRP for fiat currency while not being registered with FinCEN as an MSB.[53] The enforcement action does not state whether Ripple was an "administrator" or an "exchanger," though it notes that Ripple described itself as an "exchange."

---

49. 2014 Guidance on VC Software Development, p. 2.

50. 2013 Guidance, p. 5.

51. 2019 Guidance on CVC Business Models, p. 21, ¶ 4.5.2.

52. FinCEN, *FinCEN Fines Ripple Labs Inc. in First Civil Enforcement Action Against a Virtual Currency Exchanger* (May 5, 2015), https://www.fincen.gov/news/news-releases/fincen-fines-ripple-labs-inc-first-civil-enforcement-action-against-virtual.

53. Note that FinCEN additionally alleged that Ripple incorporated a subsidiary, XRP Fund II, LLC, to sell and transfer XRP to third parties on a wholesale basis. While XRP registered with FinCEN, FinCEN alleged that it did not meet the compliance requirements.

The Status of Initial Coin Offerings

The US Department of the Treasury and FinCEN have addressed initial coin offerings (ICOs),[54] which are a method that companies use for funding that uses virtual currency, on record only a handful of times. First, the US Department of the Treasury addressed ICOs in a letter to Senator Ron Wyden. In that letter, the US Department of the Treasury stated that "[g]enerally, under existing regulations and interpretations, a developer that sells CVC, including in the form of ICO coins or tokens, in exchange for another type of value that substitutes for currency is a money transmitter."[55] The letter noted, however, that how an ICO is structured varies. Depending on the structure, the entity may be subject to regulation by the Securities and Exchange Commission (SEC) or the Commodity Futures Trading Commission (CFTC) instead. The letter concluded by stating that "Treasury expects businesses involved in ICOs to meet the BSA obligations that apply to them." Director Kenneth A. Blanco echoed this last sentiment in recent public remarks: "FinCEN, and our partners at the SEC and CFTC, expect businesses involved in ICOs to meet all of their AML/CFT obligations."[56]

Second, in the 2019 Guidance on CVC Business Models, FinCEN addressed two forms of ICOs: (1) those conducting a preferential sale of CVC to a select group of buyers, and (2) those raising funds by offering digital debt or equity instruments among a group of lenders or investors to finance a future project. For the first ICO model, the seller is a money transmitter acting as an administrator because the seller is the only person authorized to issue and redeem the CVC.[57] For the second ICO model, the ICO raises funds for a new project, and how the BSA regulations apply will depend on the purpose of the funded project, which can include receiving new CVC, exchanging the token for a DApp coin

54. As mentioned in Chapter 2, the term *ICO* is used less frequently since it is somewhat ambiguous and may be viewed negatively. We use the term here only insofar as FinCEN has, generally to refer to initial sales of a token.

55. Department of the Treasury, Letter to Senator Ron Wyden (Feb. 13, 2018), https://www.coincenter.org/app/uploads/2020/05/fincen-ico-letter-march-2018-coin-center.pdf.

56. Kenneth A. Blanco, Prepared Remarks at 2018 Chicago-Kent Block (Legal) Tech Conference (Aug. 9, 2018), https://www.fincen.gov/news/speeches/prepared-remarks-fincen-director-kenneth-blanco-delivered-2018-chicago-kent-block.

57. 2019 Guidance on CVC Business Models, pp. 24–25, ¶ 5.2.

that unlocks use of the DApp, or receiving some other type of return.[58] Some ICOs may be exempt from FinCEN rules but may still have BSA obligations if the SEC or CFTC regulates them.[59]

FINANCIAL ACTION TASK FORCE APPROACH TO VIRTUAL CURRENCY MONEY TRANSMISSION

The Financial Action Task Force (FATF) is an intergovernmental body that sets standards and promotes the implementation of legal, regulatory, and operational measures to combat money laundering, terrorist financing, and other similar threats to the international financial system.[60] FATF has developed a series of recommendations to help set the international standard for combating money laundering, terrorist financing, and the proliferation of weapons of mass destruction. FATF last issued the recommendations in 2012 but has updated them since.[61]

FATF recently revised the recommendations to better address the risk presented by virtual assets. Specifically, in October 2018, FATF amended Recommendation 15 to clarify how FATF standards apply to activities involving virtual assets and virtual asset service providers (VASPs):

> To manage and mitigate the risks emerging from virtual assets, countries should ensure that virtual asset service providers are regulated for AML/CFT purposes, and licensed or registered and subject to effective systems for monitoring and ensuring compliance with the relevant measures called for in the FATF Recommendations.[62]

FATF realized that to more adequately mitigate the risk of money laundering and terrorist financing, it needed to set out more detailed

---

58. *Id.*

59. *Id.*

60. FATF, *Who We Are*, http://www.fatf-gafi.org/about/whoweare/#d.en.11232.

61. *Id.*

62. FATF. *International Standards on Combating Money Laundering and the Financing of Terrorism and Proliferation: The FATF Recommendations* (2012–2021), http://www.fatf-gafi.org/media/fatf/documents/recommendations/pdfs/FATF%20Recommendations%202012.pdf; *see also* FATF, *Regulation of Virtual Assets* (Oct. 19, 2018), http://www.fatf-gafi.org/publications/fatfrecommendations/documents/regulation-virtual-assets.html.

implementation requirements for regulating and supervising/monitoring VASPs. FATF adopted an Interpretive Note to Recommendation in June 2019, which established requirements for countries to assess and mitigate risks associated with VASPs.[63] In June 2019, FATF also published its Guidance for a Risk-Based Approach to Virtual Assets and Virtual Asset Service Providers (VASP RBA Guidance). This guidance addressed (1) how virtual asset activities and VASPs fall within the scope of the recommendations, (2) how countries should apply the recommendations to virtual assets and VASPS, and (3) how do the recommendations apply to VASPs and other entities, such as banks, that engage in or provide virtual asset covered activities.[64]

In June 2019, FATF also announced that it would conduct a twelve-month review that monitored the implementation of the new requirements by countries and service providers. When released in June 2020, the report found that overall, public and private sectors had made progress implementing the revised FATF standards, but substantial work remained to effectively implement the revised FATF standards. Despite that, FATF found that there was no clear need to amend the revised FATF standards.[65] However, FATF noted that it will continue its monitoring and released a second twelve-month review in July 2021. In this second report, FATF noted that even though jurisdictions had made significant progress in implementing the revised FATF standards on virtual assets and VASPs, less than half of the jurisdictions surveyed had introduced the necessary legislation to implement the revised standards. FATF noted that while progress has been made, there is still not yet sufficient implementation of the revised standards to enable a global AML/CFT regime for virtual assets and VASPs. However, as FATF noted in its first twelve-month review, FATF does not currently see a need to amend the revised FATF standards.

---

63. *See* FATF, *Public Statement on Virtual Assets and Related Providers* (June 21, 2019), https://www.fatf-gafi.org/publications/fatfrecommendations/documents/public-statement-virtual-assets.html.

64. FATF, *Guidance for a Risk-Based Approach to Virtual Assets and Virtual Asset Service Providers* (June 21, 2019), https://www.fatf-gafi.org/publications/fatfrecommendations/documents/guidance-rba-virtual-assets.html.

65. FATF, *12-Month Review of the Revised FATF Standards on Virtual Assets and Virtual Assets Service Providers* (June 2020), https://www.fatf-gafi.org/media/fatf/documents/recommendations/12-Month-Review-Revised-FATF-Standards-Virtual-Assets-VASPS.pdf.

In October 2021, FATF updated its VASP RBA Guidance.[66] The updated VASP RBA Guidance focuses on the six key elements: (1) definitions for virtual assets and VASPs, (2) how FATF standards apply to stablecoins, (3) risks and tools for addressing money laundering and terrorist financing for peer-to-peer transactions, (4) licensing and registration of VASPs, (5) implementation of the "travel rule," and (6) information-sharing and cooperation among VASP supervisors.

STATE REGULATION OF VIRTUAL CURRENCY MONEY TRANSMISSION

All states but Wyoming regulate and require licensure for money transmission. Typically, the state regulator will be the primary source for official and unofficial guidance on the law. But because operating a money transmission business without a license is a crime in many states, courts may also be asked whether a particular person or entity has violated the state's money transmission laws (and sometimes courts may disagree with a regulator, leaving companies even more confused). As states grapple with how—or also whether—to regulate virtual currency money transmission, virtual currency entities looking to operate in a particular state need to consider state laws, state regulator pronouncements, and relevant case law as part of their due diligence before determining whether a license is required to operate in that state.

Two state-specific virtual currency developments are also addressed later in this chapter. First is New York, which is the first state to adopt regulations *solely* addressing virtual currency money transmission, and second is the Uniform Regulation of Virtual Currency Businesses Act (URVCBA), a model law drafted by the Uniform Law Commission (ULC).

General Overview of State Money Transmission Laws

The primary purpose of state money transmission laws is to protect consumers. To protect consumers, most states have adopted broadly similar

---

66. FATF, *Updated Guidance for a Risk-Based Approach to Virtual Assets and Virtual Asset Service Providers* (Oct. 28, 2021), https://www.fatf-gafi.org/publications/fatfrecommendations/documents/guidance-rba-virtual-assets-2021.html.

compliance requirements that reflect this purpose.[67] For example, states typically require money transmitters to be licensed (which subjects owners and other interested parties to certain biographical and financial disclosures), have a minimum net worth (and states vary in how they calculate this requirement), and maintain a surety bond (to help protect against outstanding obligations).

Generally, what constitutes money transmission across the states is broadly similar—selling payment instruments or receiving money for transmission constitutes money transmission. However, whether state laws or regulators deem virtual currency transmission to be money transmission can at times be a difficult question to answer.

General Overview of State Regulation of Virtual Currency Transmission

At a high level, state regulation of virtual currency transmission generally falls into one of three buckets:

1. The state requires a license for any activities that involve virtual currency to fiat to be money transmission (or vice versa) but not for virtual currency–to–virtual currency transmission.
2. The state requires a license for any transmission activities involving virtual currency, regardless of whether fiat currency is involved.
3. The state laws and regulator guidance are silent on whether a license is required for virtual currency transmission (either virtual currency to virtual currency or virtual currency to fiat, and vice versa).

When a state or regulator is silent regarding whether its money transmission laws regulate virtual currency transmission, a close analysis of how states define—or whether they even define—"money," "monetary value," and "payment instrument" can be instructive, but is not, by itself, likely to be determinative. It is recommended that where a state has not clarified its stance on virtual currencies, companies seeking to operate

67. We note that while the categories may be similar, the compliance requirements for each state may differ, and any entity operating in multiple states should be aware of the nuances in compliance requirements.

in that state should confirm with the regulator whether their business model requires licensure.

Following are examples of some states that fit into these categories (though note that for any category, state legislatures or regulators may change the approach after the publication of this chapter).

- Example of a state that requires a money transmission license only for virtual currency transmission activities involving fiat currency
  - *Colorado*: The Colorado Department of Regulatory Agencies issued Interim Regulatory Guidance that addressed the applicability of the Colorado Money Transmitters Act to cryptocurrency.[68] This guidance states that cryptocurrencies are *not* legal tender. Therefore, a license is not required for (1) the direct transmission of cryptocurrencies between two parties or (2) transactions involving third parties where fiat currency is not involved. However, Colorado may require licensure if an exchange allows customers to transfer cryptocurrency within the exchange, and the exchange can transfer fiat currency through the medium of cryptocurrency.[69]
- Example of a state that requires a money transmission license for any transmission activities involving virtual currencies
  - *Alabama*: Alabama revised its Alabama Monetary Transmission Act to expressly include virtual currencies, whether or not redeemable in money, within its definition of "monetary value."[70] Therefore, because "money transmission" means selling or issuing payment instruments (which includes "other means utilized for transmission . . . of . . . monetary value")[71] or receiving monetary value for transmission,[72] Alabama requires a money transmission license for both virtual currency

---

68. Colorado Division of Banking, *Regulatory Guidance, Advisory Bulletins, & Operating Memos*, https://www.colorado.gov/pacific/dora/regulatory-guidance-advisory-bulletins-operating-memos.

69. *Id.*

70. Ala. Code § 8-7A-2(8).

71. *Id.* at § 8-7A-2(11).

72. *Id.* at § 8-7A-2(10).

to fiat transmission *and* virtual currency to virtual currency transmission.[73]

- Example of a state whose laws or guidance are silent on whether a license is required to engage in virtual currency money transmission
    - *Arizona*: Neither Arizona's transmitters of money law nor the relevant regulator,[74] the Department of Financial Institutions, has addressed whether virtual currencies are subject to the law. The law defines money to mean "a medium of exchange that is authorized or adopted by a domestic or foreign government as a part of its currency and that is customarily used and accepted as a medium of exchange in the country of issuance."[75] Even though the definition appears to exclude virtual currencies, individual exchanges and other virtual currency businesses maintain an Arizona Money Transmitters license. This result underscores that just reviewing a state's definitions may not, by itself, answer the question of whether a license is required to engage in virtual currency transmission.

Courts Also Have a Say, and Their Interpretations May Differ from the Primary Regulator

In addition to regulator pronouncements, courts have a voice in determining whether virtual currency activities are subject to a state's money transmission laws. Recently, a Florida court held that selling Bitcoin for fiat currency makes a person an MSB under Florida law. In reaching this conclusion, the court appeared to break from the Florida Office of Financial Regulation's interpretation of its money transmission statute regarding whether a third party was required for the activity to constitute "transmission."

Specifically, in *State v. Espinoza*,[76] the court overruled the trial court's grant of a motion to dismiss and held that selling Bitcoin directly to another person meant that the seller was acting as an MSB because the

---

73. *Id.* at § 8-7A-5.

74. Ariz. Rev. Stat. § 6-1201, *et seq.*

75. Ariz. Rev. Stat. § 6-1201(9).

76. 2019 WL 361893 (Fla. Ct. App., 3d Dist. Jan. 30, 2019).

seller was both a "payment instrument seller" and a "money transmitter." The defendant acknowledged that he was not licensed but argued that the reach of Florida's money services law did not extend to Bitcoin. The court disagreed. First, the court concluded that the defendant acted as a payment instrument seller because Bitcoin constitutes a "payment instrument." A payment instrument is "monetary value," which Florida defines as "a medium of exchange, whether or not redeemable in currency." The court concluded that Bitcoin was a "medium of exchange" and highlighted that local Miami businesses accepted payment via Bitcoin.

Next, the court concluded that the defendant acted as a money transmitter. The defendant argued, in part, that being a money transmitter requires transmission to a third party. The court disagreed, noting that because Florida's law—unlike the federal definition of a money transmitter—clearly does not contain a third-party or middleman requirement, it would not read such a condition into the law. This conclusion may conflict with the Florida Office of Financial Regulation's interpretation of the money transmission statute. In various Petitions for Declaratory Statements related to virtual currency businesses, the regulator concluded that if no third parties are involved, and the company is never receiving "currency, monetary value, or payment instruments for the purpose of transmitting the same," the entity is *not* a money transmitter under Florida law.[77] While this third-party element is not solely related to virtual currency businesses, it highlights that even features common to both traditional and virtual currency businesses may be subject to different interpretations depending on who is deciding the issue. This case highlights the difficulties that virtual currency businesses may experience when trying to determine whether their activities require licensure under the state's money transmission law.

New York BitLicense

New York is the only state as of November 2021 that requires a separate license, a.k.a. a "BitLicense," to engage in "virtual currency business

---

77. *See, e.g.,* Petition for Declaratory Statement, Cryptobase, LLC, Admin. Proc. No. 89596 (June 28, 2018); Petition for Declaratory Statement, SandP Solutions, Inc., Admin. Proc. No. 86936 (Nov. 21, 2017).

activity."[78] Specifically, the following conduct involving virtual currency requires a BitLicense in New York:[79]

- Receiving virtual currency for transmission or transmitting virtual currency, except where the transaction is undertaken for non-financial purposes and does not involve the transfer of more than a nominal amount of virtual currency
- Storing, holding, or maintaining custody or control of virtual currency on behalf of others
- Buying and selling virtual currency as a customer business
- Performing exchange services as a customer business
- Controlling, administering, or issuing a virtual currency[80]

The New York Department of Financial Services (NYDFS) does not require a BitLicense for merchants and consumers that use virtual currency solely to purchase or sell goods or services or for investment purposes.[81] Overall, there appears to be significant—but not complete—overlap between the entities that FinCEN requires to register and those that NYDFS requires to receive a BitLicense.

As with a traditional money transmission license, BitLicense applicants are required to pay an application fee, provide financial statements, and have a registered agent. But NYDFS also requires that companies meet requirements similar to those of FinCEN, such as providing the

---

78. The New York Department of Financial Services (NYDFS) enacted these regulations in 2015. Note that receiving a BitLicense does not exempt an entity from also requiring a money transmission license. Further, New York will allow entities to receive a charter under the state's Banking Law, such as a limited purpose trust company, in lieu of receiving a BitLicense.

79. The NYDFS defines *virtual currency* to mean "any type of digital unit that is used as a medium of exchange or a form of digitally stored value. Virtual currency shall be broadly construed to include digital units of exchange that: have a centralized repository or administrator; are decentralized and have no centralized repository or administrator; or may be created or obtained by computing or manufacturing effort." 23 NYCRR 200.2(p).

80. 23 NYCRR 200.2(q).

81. 23 NYCRR 200.3(c)(2).

company's AML/BSA policy, a risk assessment, and the most recent independent review of its AML/BSA program.[82]

In addition to the AML requirements,[83] NYDFS requires licensees to provide certain disclosures to consumers before entering into the transaction (such as a disclosure of material risks and a disclosure of the general terms and conditions) and disclosures before and after each transaction. Companies must provide these disclosures in writing in English and any other predominant language spoken by the customer.[84]

Overall, as of May 2021, the NYDFS has granted only about twenty BitLicenses to applicants since its enactment in 2015. As of May 2021, NYDFS has granted nine limited purpose trust charters to companies for approval to conduct virtual currency business.[85]

The Uniform Law Commission's Uniform Regulation of Virtual-Currency Businesses Act

As noted earlier, state approaches to regulating virtual currency money transmission are inconsistent. This inconsistency can inhibit and frustrate businesses trying to determine whether their activities require licensure. To help remedy this problem, the ULC drafted the URVCBA based on the assumption that predictable regulations tailored to virtual currency businesses will provide them with assurances that states are regulating them like other financial service providers.[86]

---

82. 23 NYCRR 200.15; *see also* NMLS, *NY Virtual Currency Business Activity License New Application Checklist*, https://nationwidelicensingsystem.org/slr/PublishedStateDocuments/NY_Virtual_Currency_New_Application_Checklist.pdf.

83. 23 NYCRR 200.15.

84. 23 NYCRR 200.19.

85. *See* NYDFS, Virtual Currency/Regulated Entities, https://www.dfs.ny.gov/apps_and_licensing/virtual_currency_businesses/regulated_entities (last updated Mar. 19, 2021).

86. URVCBA, Prefatory Note, https://www.uniformlaws.org/HigherLogic/System/DownloadDocumentFile.ashx?DocumentFileKey=ef45a10b-ac62-ad3d-2f42-588d7eac3e40&forceDialog=0. Note that the ULC also proposed a Uniform Supplemental Commercial Law for the Uniform Regulation of Virtual-Currency Businesses Act (the "Supplemental Act") that characterizes virtual currency held by custodians for customers as "investment property" under Article 9 of the Uniform Commercial Code (UCC) and "financial assets" credited to a "securities account" in the indirect holding system under Article 8 of the UCC.

The URVCBA, which the ULC finalized in 2017, provides a framework to regulate companies engaging in "virtual-currency business activity." The URVCBA defines "virtual-currency business activity" to mean:

> (A) exchanging, transferring, or storing virtual currency or engaging in virtualcurrency administration, whether directly or through an agreement with a virtual-currency control-services vendor; (B) holding electronic precious metals or electronic certificates representing interests in precious metals on behalf of another person or issuing shares or electronic certificates representing interests in precious metals; or (C) exchanging one or more digital representations of value used within one or more online games, game platforms, or family of games for: (i) virtual currency offered by or on behalf of the same publisher from which the original digital representation of value was received; or (ii) legal tender or bank credit outside the online game, game platform, or family of games offered by or on behalf of the same publisher from which the original digital representation of value was received.[87] "Virtual currency" (A) means a digital representation of value that: (i) is used as a medium of exchange, unit of account, or store of value; and (ii) is not legal tender, whether or not denominated in legal tender; and (B) does not include: (i) a transaction in which a merchant grants, as part of an affinity or rewards program, value that cannot be taken from or exchanged with the merchant for legal tender, bank credit, or virtual currency; or (ii) a digital representation of value issued by or on behalf of a publisher and used solely within an online game, game platform, or family of games sold by the same publisher or offered on the same game platform."[88]

The ULC notes that the activities covered by the URVCBA are similar to those activities already regulated by state money transmitter laws whose reach includes virtual currency.[89] The regulations similarly include, but are not limited to, minimum capitalization, recordkeeping, and inspection requirements.

---

87. URVCBA, § 102(25). *See also* ULC, *The Uniform Regulation of Virtual-Currency Businesses Act—A Summary* (hereinafter, "URVCBA Summary"), https://www.uniformlaws.org/HigherLogic/System/DownloadDocumentFile.ashx?DocumentFileKey=5ba1e835-9fc2-215b-a10c-a6c505490184&forceDialog=0.

88. URVCBA, § 102(23).

89. URVCBA, Prefatory Note.

With that said, the URVCBA incorporates novel features that distinguish it from state money transmitter statutes. Among these features are the following:

- A three-tier system to determine who is exempt from the URVCBA. This includes a complete exemption for those persons or entities whose volume of activity is below $5,000 annually and an intermediate registration status that is modeled as a "regulatory sandbox"
- A focus on enabling reciprocal licensure
- More flexible provisions on net worth and reserve requirements[90]

As of November 2021, only Rhode Island has enacted the URVCBA.[91]

THE ELECTRONIC FUND TRANSFER ACT AND DIGITAL ASSETS

Federal law also governs the transfer of electronic funds from a consumer's account. Specifically, the EFTA and its implementing regulation,[92] Regulation E,[93] are designed to provide specific protections to consumers who engage in EFTs.[94] Only recently, however, has the issue emerged of whether the EFTA and Regulation E apply to virtual currencies, including virtual currency wallets.

Specifically, on April 1, 2019, the Consumer Financial Protection Bureau's (CFPB) new rule governing prepaid accounts (the Prepaid Rule) took effect, which extends Regulation E's consumer protections to "prepaid accounts." While much of the focus was on how the new rule impacts traditional prepaid card issuers, the Prepaid Rule is sufficiently broad that it

---

90. *Id.*

91. The main ULC webpage devoted to the URVCBA lists only the states that have enacted the URVCBA, *see* http://uniformlaws.org/committees/community-home?communitykey=e104aaa8-c10f-45a7-a34a-0423c2106778&tab=groupdetails.

92. 15 U.S.C. § 1693, et al.

93. 12 C.F.R. § 1005.1, *et seq.*

94. The definition of EFT is comprehensive and includes *any* transfer of funds initiated through an electronic terminal, telephone, computer, or magnetic tape for the purpose of ordering, instructing, or authorizing a financial institution to debit or credit a consumer's account. 12 C.F.R. § 1005.3(b).

could apply to some virtual currency wallets. When finalizing the Prepaid Rule, the CFPB only stated that the application of the Prepaid Rule to virtual currencies is outside the scope of that particular rulemaking, not that virtual currencies themselves are outside the scope of Regulation E.[95]

Therefore, as a threshold matter, and before analyzing whether any virtual currency wallet constitutes a "prepaid account," the analysis begins with whether the virtual currency wallet accesses an "account." Regulation E defines "account" very broadly to include, in part, a "consumer asset account . . . held directly or indirectly by a financial institution and established primarily for personal, family, or household purposes."[96] "Financial institution" is likewise broadly defined and means any person that directly or indirectly holds an account belonging to a consumer.[97] Therefore, nothing in Regulation E excludes an entity that directly or indirectly holds a consumer account that contains virtual currency. Furthermore, "funds" is not defined, so there is no limitation to fiat currency.

"Prepaid account" includes, among other things, any account that has a primary function of conducting person-to-person transfers (including both consumer-to-consumer and consumer-to-business transfers), so long as it is not a bank checking or demand account and is not subject to an applicable exclusion.[98] Therefore, if a virtual currency wallet can be loaded with funds (which as noted earlier is not defined and could plausibly include at least certain types of virtual currency), its primary purpose is to allow person-to-person transfers, and it is not otherwise exempt, then it may be considered a prepaid account and trigger application of the Prepaid Rule.

The Prepaid Rule includes the following requirements:

- Provide two specific, separate disclosure forms mandated by Regulation E.
- Provide specific transaction information, either via periodic statements or via a combination of available telephone and online services.

---

95. 81 Fed. Reg. 83, 934, 83, 978 (Nov. 22, 2016).

96. 12 C.F.R. § 1005.2(b)(1).

97. *Id.* at § 1005.2(b)(i).

98. *Id.* at § 1005.2(b)(3)(D).

- If the virtual currency wallet provider does not verify or validate the user's identity, the virtual currency wallet provider will need to establish procedures for resolving erroneous and disputed transactions and restore to the user any virtual currency that was redeemed or sent as part of an unauthorized transaction.[99]

Additionally, if the virtual currency wallet provider will provide the required notices electronically, it will need to first obtain the user's consent to electronic delivery of disclosures in compliance with the requirements of the federal ESIGN Act.

CONCLUSION

Looking ahead, both the federal government (whether through Congress or regulators or both) and state governments (again, whether through state legislatures or regulator or both) will continue to focus attention and resources toward the use of digital assets as payment systems and money transfer systems.

As noted earlier, the primary concern at the federal level for money transmitters is AML. Congress, in passing the Anti–Money Laundering Act of 2020, stated that "although the use and trading of virtual currencies are legal practices, some terrorists and criminals, including transnational criminal organizations, seek to exploit vulnerabilities in the global financial system and increasingly rely on substitutes for currency, including emerging payment methods (such as virtual currencies), to move illicit funds."[100] Further, as noted earlier, as November 2021, FinCEN has an outstanding proposed rule that seeks to, at least in its current form, impose greater burdens on money transmitters engaged in transmitting CVC than for cash transactions (e.g., requiring counterparty information on transactions involving self-hosted wallets).

On the state law side, regarding the use of distributed ledger technology and virtual currency as payment systems, the ULC established the Uniform Commercial Code and Emerging Technologies Committee, which is drafting amendments to the Uniform Commercial Code to "accommodate emerging technological developments," specifically seeking to address "distributed ledger technology, virtual currency,

---

99. *Id.* at § 1005.18.

100. H.R. 6395, 116th Cong. Div. F, § 6102(a)(3) (2021).

electronic notes and draft, other digital assets, payments, and bundled transactions."[101] From the money transmission and consumer protection angles, state regulators will likely continue to focus efforts on protecting consumers involved in virtual currency transactions.

In short, the legislative and regulatory state of play for digital assets as payment systems and money transfer systems will continue to be a dynamic area of law in the coming years. This will be especially true as new capabilities, such as decentralized finance, which relies on open, permissionless protocols and DApps to offer financial services that are traditionally offered through centralized institutions,[102] become more popular across society.

101. ULC, Uniform Commercial Code and Emerging Technologies Committee, https://www.uniformlaws.org/committees/community-home?CommunityKey=cb5f9e0b-7185-4a33-9e4c-1f79ba560c71.

102. For an introduction into decentralized finance, *see* Fabian Schär, *Decentralized Finance: On Blockchain- and Smart Contract-Based Financial Markets*, 103 Fed. Res. Bank St. Louis Rev. (2d Q 2021) 153–74. https://doi.org/10.20955/r.103.153-74.

6 Anti–Money Laundering for Digital Assets

Alma Angotti and Elizabeth Sisul

BANK SECRECY ACT/ANTI–MONEY LAUNDERING ACT OVERVIEW

As discussed in Chapter 5, the Financial Recordkeeping and Reporting of Currency and Foreign Transactions Act of 1970, also referred to as the Bank Secrecy Act of 1970 (BSA), requires "financial institutions" to assist in detecting and preventing money laundering by maintaining records of customer relationships and file reports involving currency transactions, creating a paper and audit trail in the event that such documentation is necessary for criminal, tax, or other regulatory investigations.[1] Notwithstanding its name, the provisions of the BSA also apply to nonbank financial institutions offering a variety of financial services. The BSA has an expansive definition of *financial institution* that includes brokers or dealers in securities or commodities and currency exchanges, any business or agency designated by the Secretary of the Treasury that engages in activity that is similar or related to those of financial institutions, and any other business designated by the secretary whose cash transactions have a high degree of usefulness in criminal, tax, or regulatory matters.[2] On January 1, 2021, Congress passed the National Defense Authorization Act (NDAA) for Fiscal Year 2021, which includes the Anti–Money Laundering Act of 2020 (AMLA), which, among other changes, expanded that definition to include a "business engaged in the exchange of currency, funds, or value that substitutes for currency or funds."[3]

---

1. Bank Secrecy Act, 31 U.S.C. § 5312 *et seq.*
2. Bank Secrecy Act, 31 U.S.C. § 5312(a).
3. Anti-Money Laundering Act of 2020, § 6102.

In response to the terrorist attacks of September 11, 2001, Congress enacted the Uniting and Strengthening America by Providing Appropriate Tools Required to Intercept and Obstruct Terrorism Act of 2001 (USA PATRIOT Act), to increase the US's ability to prevent and detect money laundering and terrorist financing and increase scrutiny with respect to particularly risky jurisdictions, institutions, and transactions.[4] Title III of the USA PATRIOT Act, the International Money Laundering Abatement and Anti-Terrorist Financing Act of 2001, includes a number of amendments to the BSA that aim to curtail money launderers' and terrorist financiers' use of the financial system, such as prohibitions on certain types of bank accounts, requirements for more information from certain types of foreign banks, and increased transparency into private banking relationships.[5] Collectively, these requirements are referred to as BSA/anti–money laundering (AML) laws and represent a substantial part of financial crime compliance for banks and other financial institutions.

The emergence of virtual currencies and associated business activities has raised questions regarding the applicability of the BSA to digital asset businesses. In expanding the definition of *financial institution*, the AMLA reinforced previous guidance that businesses involved in virtual currency are subject to the BSA. The significance of this amendment remains to be seen. As the cryptocurrency market continues to grow, the need for a clear regulatory framework becomes more evident. Under the current framework, businesses involved in virtual currency must ensure they understand when they may be deemed a money transmitter or other type of financial institution subject to the BSA and therefore obligated to comply with its minimum requirements. In addition, digital asset businesses should apply reasonable controls to prevent money laundering, fraud, and other types of financial crime as a matter of good risk management, notwithstanding their regulatory status.

Chapter 5 focused on the question of when businesses in the blockchain-based asset space must consider and comply with various BSA and other similar regulations. In this chapter, we address in more depth the scope of those obligations.

---

4. USA PATRIOT Act, Pub. L. No. 107-56, §§ 301–77, 115 Stat. 272, 296–342.

5. USA PATRIOT Act, Pub. L. No. 107-56, §§ 351–66, 115 Stat. 272, 320–36.

AML REQUIREMENTS

Digital assets businesses subject to BSA/AML requirements must take a number of steps to manage money laundering risks.

BSA/AML Program

The development of an AML compliance program is one of the first steps a digital assets business that falls within the scope of the BSA must take. An AML compliance program defines how a business manages financial crime risk, monitors accounts, detects unusual activity, and reports potential financial crimes to the relevant regulatory authorities and law enforcement. An effective compliance program must be tailored to the financial institution's business and so begins with a risk assessment. The financial institution should evaluate the inherent risk and mitigating controls to identify the residual financial crime risks the business faces.

According to the Financial Crimes Enforcement Network (FinCEN), a compliance program must be in writing and risk based, as determined by the risk assessment. At a minimum, the business must (1) designate a person to assure day-to-day compliance with the BSA; (2) incorporate policies, procedures, and internal controls reasonably designed to assure compliance with the BSA; (3) provide education and training to appropriate personnel; (4) provide for an independent review to monitor and maintain an adequate program; and (5) establish certain risk-based, customer due diligence procedures.[6] These minimum requirements are commonly known as the five pillars of a BSA/AML program.

Designation of a BSA/AML Compliance Officer

The institution must designate an AML compliance officer who is responsible for maintaining a culture of compliance at every organizational level. The AML compliance officer manages and oversees the development and implementation of the company's AML compliance program. Designating an experienced, senior compliance officer is often the first step a digital asset business should take to strengthen its compliance program.

6. 31 C.F.R. § 1022.210; 31 C.F.R. § 1010.230.

Internal Controls

Internal controls are written internal policies, procedures, and systems that are specifically designed to mitigate the risks of financial crime and support compliance with AML regulations. Internal controls are what enable a digital asset business to comply with AML requirements. Institutions should make sure that controls aimed at mitigating the potential for cryptocurrency-related financial crime are integrated with any already existing AML compliance controls and adequately reflect the nature of the risk. Doing so will generally require close coordination between those responsible for compliance and those with a sound understanding of the technical aspects of digital assets. Digital asset companies that lack adequate controls or that fail to properly report information derived from controls risk being the subject of an enforcement action. Neither BTC-e nor Eric Powers, for example, ever filed any Suspicious Activity Reports (SARs), despite having processed thousands of transactions that should have been flagged as suspicious.[7]

Ongoing Training for Appropriate Personnel

The business must ensure that employees are familiar with AML rules and requirements, as well as their specific roles and obligations. An ideal AML training program is interactive, occurs regularly, and offers general guidance, as well as instructions tailored to employees' day-to-day jobs. The training program should also assign an advanced level of training to staff with specific AML compliance responsibilities or to those in areas prone to higher AML risk.

Independent Testing of BSA/AML Compliance

The compliance program must undergo review by an independent party, either internal, such as internal audit, or external. The testing should identify whether the program is fit for purpose, properly implemented, and sustainable. The testing should provide the organization with a clear outline of issues requiring attention to manage risk and ensure compliance with applicable regulations. Auditors for businesses involved with digital assets must understand the unique characteristics of the

---

7. BTC-e a.k.a. Canton Business Corporation, No. 2017-03 (Fin. Crimes Enforcement Network July 26, 2017) (assessment of civil money penalty); Eric Powers, No. 2019-01 (Fin. Crimes Enforcement Network Apr. 18, 2019) (assessment of civil money penalty).

technology, the additional risks those characteristics introduce, and the best means to mitigate those risks.

Customer Due Diligence Beneficial Ownership

FinCEN issued its Final Rule for Customer Due Diligence (CDD) on May 11, 2016,[8] making CDD the official fifth pillar of a BSA/AML compliance program. Compliance programs must now include the establishment of certain risk-based CDD procedures. Specifically, the fifth pillar imposes a new standard on financial institutions to identify and verify the identity of beneficial owners, the natural persons behind the legal entity customers.

While money transmitters are not currently subject to the fifth pillar or new beneficial ownership reporting requirements, FinCEN expects money service businesses (MSBs) to have a risk-based approach to knowing their customers, as discussed later in this chapter. In addition, FinCEN imposes minimum requirements on financial institutions that have money transmitters as customers, including confirming that the MSB has registered with FinCEN, obtaining basic information about the MSB (such as types of products and services offered, and locations and markets served), and performing a BSA/AML risk assessment of the MSB.[9] Any money transmitter that has an account with a bank would therefore be indirectly subject to the Final Rule and may have to provide specific information about their own beneficial ownership and control, as well as other general information regarding their risk profile.[10]

Know Your Customer/Customer Due Diligence

CDD refers to the processes, policies, and procedures an institution employs to collect information about its customers and assess the risk they may pose to the business. Financial institutions are required to

---

8. 31 C.F.R. § 1010.230.

9. Financial Crimes Enforcement Network et al., *Interagency Interpretive Guidance on Providing Banking Services to Money Services Businesses Operating in the United States* (Apr. 26, 2005), https://www.fincen.gov/sites/default/files/guidance/guidance04262005.pdf.

10. On January 1, 2021, Congress passed the National Defense Authorization Act, which includes the AMLA, and within the AMLA, the Corporate Transparency Act (CTA). The CTA requires certain businesses to file beneficial ownership information with FinCEN. It explicitly exempts most financial service institutions, however, including money transmitters.

have a customer identification program (CIP)[11] that establishes the procedures for customer identification, which, at a minimum, include the collection and verification of customer identification. CIP requirements vary based on the type of financial institution. For MSBs, FinCEN's requirements apply to currency transactions and monetary instruments at $3,000, although many MSBs set their threshold at $1,000.[12] Although MSBs may not be directly subject to the CDD rule, which applies to banks, broker-dealers, and certain other financial institutions, there is still an expectation that banks will identify potential customers that should be subject to additional due diligence.[13] Digital assets businesses must each define minimum customer requirements based on the type of institution (e.g., a retail versus an institutional cryptocurrency exchange), and, using a risk-based approach, develop appropriate due diligence requirements.

An adequate risk-based BSA/AML program necessarily requires an institution to conduct some level of due diligence on its customers; however, performing comprehensive due diligence when dealing with digital assets can prove difficult due to their anonymity and the ease with which users can obscure identifying information.

Recordkeeping and Reporting

Currency Transaction Reporting

The BSA requires reporting of cash currency transactions totaling more than $10,000 during one business day for any one person, or on behalf of any one person.[14] Currently, virtual currencies and digital assets are

---

11. 31 C.F.R. § 1020.220.

12. The Financial Action Task Force recommends collecting customer information for cross-border transfers of $1,000 or more. *See* https://www.fatf-gafi.org/media/fatf/documents/reports/FATF%20Standards%20-%20IX%20Special%20Recommendations%20and%20IN%20rc.pdf.

13. As previously noted, the New York Department of Financial Services "BitLicense" virtual currency rule requires licensees to have a CIP. New York's CIP requirements under the rule are more stringent than the federal requirements for MSBs. They include requirements to reasonably identify/verify customer identity (including name and physical address), perform enhanced due diligence for non-U.S. licensees and for accounts of non-U.S. persons, and verify identity for customers involved in transactions above $3,000. BitLicense Proposal §§ 200.12(1) and 200.15(d)(1).

14. 31 C.F.R. § 1010.311.

not subject to this requirement unless they accept or disburse cash. On December 23, 2020, however, FinCEN published a notice of proposed rulemaking (NPRM) to seek public comments on a proposal to establish new reporting requirements with respect to convertible virtual currency (CVC) and digital assets with legal tender status (LTDA). The proposed rule would prescribe by regulation that CVC and LTDA are "monetary instruments" for the purposes of the BSA. The proposed rules would impose on banks and MSBs currency transaction reporting, and certain recordkeeping and verification requirements for transactions involving CVC or LTDA held in either (1) unhosted wallets or (2) wallets hosted in a jurisdiction identified on a Foreign Jurisdictions List designated by FinCEN as an "otherwise covered wallet."[15,16]

While CVC and LTDA are not currently subject to reporting requirements under the BSA, the New York Department of Financial Services (NYDFS) in 2015 implemented its own virtual currency regulation requiring all New York residents and companies engaging in any virtual currency business activity to obtain a BitLicense issued by the NYDFS. Businesses that obtain BitLicenses must report to the NYDFS any virtual currency transactions totaling more than $10,000 made during one business day by one person.[17]

Suspicious Activity Reports

Suspicious activity reporting is a cornerstone of the BSA, providing critical financial information used to fight money laundering, financial crime, and terrorist financing.[18] Generally, a financial institution must

15. Requirements for Certain Transactions Involving Convertible Virtual Currency of Digital Assets, 85 Fed. Reg. 83840 (proposed Dec. 23, 2020) (to be codified at 31 C.F.R. pts. 1010, 1020, 1022). https://public-inspection.federalregister.gov/2020-28437.pdf.

16. The comment period for the Proposed Rule published on December 23, 2020, which was extended on January 15, 2021, has been further extended on January 28, 2021, for an additional 60 days, with all comments due by March 29, 2021.

17. Press Release, NYDFS, NY DFS Releases Proposed BitLicense Regulatory Framework for Virtual Currency Firms (July 17, 2014), https://www.dfs.ny.gov/reports_and_publications/press_releases/pr1407171.

18. Federal Financial Institutions Examination Council, *Bank Secrecy Act/Anti–Money Laundering Examination Manual*, Suspicious Activity Reporting—Overview, https://bsaaml.ffiec.gov/manual/AssessingComplianceWithBSARegulatoryRequirements/04.

file a SAR when a transaction meets a certain monetary threshold and the institution knows, suspects, or has reason to suspect that the transaction (or a pattern of transactions of which the transaction is a part):

- Involves funds derived from illegal activity or is intended or conducted to hide or disguise funds or assets derived from illegal activity
- Is designed to evade the requirements of the BSA, whether through structuring or other means
- Serves no business or apparent lawful purpose, and the reporting business knows of no reasonable explanation for the transaction after examining all available facts[19]

Most MSBs must file a SAR when a suspicious transaction of $2,000 or more is conducted by, at, or through the MSB.[20] MSBs may have different SAR reporting requirements, however, depending on the products they offer. For example, businesses that only offer check cashing are exempt from the SAR requirements.

Maintenance of Records

In addition, the BSA has numerous requirements for the maintenance of certain customer and transaction records depending on the type of business, the type of transaction, and the amount of the transaction.[21] For the transmittal of funds, MSBs are required to retain information relating to a transmission of $3,000 or more. There are different requirements for established customers and nonestablished customers, but generally, the requirements are similar to traditional CIP information: name, address, form of identification (e.g., driver's license), and identification number (e.g., social security number).[22] Currency dealers and exchangers must obtain information on customers for whom they open accounts or extend

---

19. *See, e.g.*, 31 C.F.R. § 1020.320.

20. Fin. Crimes Enforcement Network, *Money Services Business (MSB) Suspicious Activity Reporting*, https://www.fincen.gov/money-services-business-msb-suspicious-activity-reporting.

21. 31 C.F.R. § 1010.410.

22. *Id.*

a line of credit. The BSA also requires records of currency dealing or exchanges of more than $1,000.[23]

The "Travel Rule"

As noted earlier, FinCEN's May 9, 2019, guidance entitled the *Application of FinCEN's Regulations to Certain Business Models Involving Convertible Virtual Currencies*,[24] summarized applicable regulations, guidance, and administrative rulings issued since 2011 relating to money transmission. Notably, the guidance discusses the applicability of the Travel Rule, which requires money transmitters to provide certain information regarding transmittals of funds of $3,000 or greater to the receiving financial institution,[25] to transactions involving CVC.[26] According to the guidance, cryptocurrency transactions constitute a transmittal of funds, as they are "a series of . . . instruction[s] to pay . . . 'a fixed or determinable amount of money,'" and are therefore subject to the Travel Rule. The guidance advises that regardless of the money transmitter's system for clearing and settling transactions, it must provide the required information before, or at the time of, the transmittal of value, though it notes that the money transmitter need not use the same system or protocol for the transmission of value and the transmission of the required regulatory information.[27] The Travel Rule may present practical difficulties in circumstances in which the money transmitter is

---

23. The New York Department of Financial Services "BitLicense" virtual currency rule requirements for recordkeeping and reporting are similar to the federal requirements; however, licensees only need to file SARs or CTRs if they are not otherwise federally reportable. 23 NYCRR §§ 200.12(1), 200.15(d)(1).

24. Application of FinCEN's Regulations to Certain Business Models Involving Convertible Virtual Currencies, Financial Enforcement Crime Network, FIN-2019-G001, May 9, 2019.

25. Funds "Travel" Regulations: Questions & Answers, Financial Enforcement Crime Network, FIN-2010-G004 (Nov. 8, 2010).

26. On October 23, the Board of Governors of the Federal Reserve System and FinCEN issued a proposed rule that would (1) reduce the threshold for the Recordkeeping and Travel Rules from $3,000 to $250 for transactions that begin or end outside of the United States and (2) clarify the application of these rules to CVCs and digital assets. At the time of this writing, that rule has not yet been finalized.

27. Application of FinCEN's Regulations to Certain Business Models Involving Convertible Virtual Currencies, Financial Enforcement Crime Network, FIN-2019-G001 (May 9, 2019).

unaware that cryptocurrency is being transferred to a financial institution, thereby triggering the rule. There are several industry groups working on a technology solution to the problem.

Transaction Monitoring

A financial institution must file a SAR for any transaction it "knows, suspects or has reason to suspect . . . involves funds derived from illegal activities or is intended or conducted in order to hide or disguise funds or assets derived from illegal activities. . . ."[28] Businesses subject to BSA/AML requirements, therefore, must monitor incoming and outgoing transactions to identify and report suspicious activity. A transaction monitoring program consists of processes and procedures an institution puts in place to identify transactions that may have origins in illegal activity, money laundering, financial crime, or terrorist financing and ensure that the potentially suspicious transactions are investigated and, if appropriate, reported to authorities in the form of SARs.[29] Transaction monitoring can be manual or automated, and the level of monitoring required and patterns of transactions that the monitoring attempts to identify, will be based on the business's risk.

Automated transaction monitoring is generally based on a set of "rules," largely dependent on the type of business involved, that identify transactions that show indications of possible suspicious activity (e.g., large transactions or patterns consistent with a typology of criminal activity). When a transaction is flagged as either meeting or diverging from the criteria defined in the monitoring rules, an automated system will generate an alert triggering a procedure for resolving the flagged transaction or set of transactions. The procedure for resolving the alert may include an investigation into the factors that triggered the flag, additional research, and consideration of any mitigating information. If the alert cannot be resolved and some indicia of suspicious or unusual activity remains, the organization is required to begin the SAR filing process and report the activity to the authorities.

Manual transaction monitoring applies the same principles of review as automated transaction monitoring but employs a less system-driven approach. A compliance officer reviewing daily reports or cash letter

---

28. 31 C.F.R. § 1020.320.

29. 31 C.F.R. § 1023.320.

transactions (e.g., checks) for review could be considered a manual monitoring process.

Businesses monitoring for suspicious activity relating to cryptocurrency should employ rules designed to capture traditional red flags, such as structuring, as well as red flags specific to digital assets. For example, businesses may want to investigate transactions involving privacy coins (e.g., Zcash and Monero), which are specifically designed to enhance the user's privacy by obfuscating the information on the blockchain. They should also closely scrutinize transactions involving a cash to privacy coin conversion, a common method of cryptocurrency money laundering. In addition, institutions wary of criminal activity involving cryptocurrency should consider incorporating know your transaction tools or blockchain tracing, discussed in greater detail later in this chapter, as part of a sound transaction monitoring program.

DIGITAL ASSETS' SUSCEPTIBILITY TO AML RISKS

To effectively combat money laundering involving cryptocurrency, it is important to understand the unique characteristics of digital assets that can both impede and enhance money laundering detection.

Three Stages of Money Laundering

Money laundering generally involves three distinct stages: placement, layering, and integration of illicit funds. The advent of cryptocurrency and associated technology has impeded investigators' ability to detect money laundering at each of these stages.

Placement

During the placement stage, illegal cash is introduced into the financial system or a legitimate business. The ease and speed with which users can open cryptocurrency wallets makes cryptocurrency a low-risk means of placing cash into the financial system.[30]

---

30. Daniel Holman & Barbara Stettner, *Anti–Money Laundering Regulation of Cryptocurrency: U.S. and Global Approaches,* Allen & Overy, LLP (June 12, 2018), https://www.allenovery.com/global/-/media/allenovery/2_documents/news_and_insights/publications/2019/5/anti-money_laundering_regulation_of_cryptocurrency.pdf?la=en-gb&hash=8493AD07139B6F753EBF20BBE332A552.

Layering

Next, money launderers will layer the transaction through a series of transactions intended to obfuscate the audit trail. Methods of layering cryptocurrency include the use of mixers/tumblers (discussed in greater detail later in this chapter) or participating in unregistered initial coin offerings (ICOs), both of which provide significant anonymity.

Integration

Finally, the money will be integrated back into the economy in a way that appears legitimate.[31] An increasing number of businesses are accepting cryptocurrency as a payment method, enabling money launderers to integrate the money back into the economy without a trace.

Cryptocurrency Characteristics that Facilitate Money Laundering

Certain unique characteristics of cryptocurrency and its supporting technology make cryptocurrency attractive to criminals seeking to conceal their identity and cover the trail of their illegal activity.

Peer-to-Peer Markets

One reason cryptocurrency has gained popularity is that transactions can be made on a peer-to-peer basis, rather than through a central institution. This decentralization cuts out the institutional intermediaries, such as banks, which are subject to regulations requiring them to scrutinize transactions for suspicious or illegal activity and perform know your customer (KYC) checks. Because peer-to-peer transfers lack these safeguards, it is easier to escape detection when conducting illegal activity. The government has nonetheless demonstrated its intent to crack down on this activity. In April 2019, FinCEN fined a peer-to-peer cryptocurrency exchanger Eric Powers $35,000 and barred him from providing money transmission services for buying and selling Bitcoin online without registering or reporting any suspicious activity.[32]

---

31. 2017 *Fraud Examiners Manual*, U.S. Edition.

32. *See* Press Release, FinCEN Penalizes Peer-to-Peer Virtual Currency Exchanger for Violations of Anti-Money Laundering Laws, Fin. Crimes Enforcement Network

Pseudonymous Transactions

Although cryptocurrency is known for its apparent anonymity, cryptocurrency can more accurately be described as pseudonymous. In a typical cryptocurrency transaction, the originating address, destination address, and amount of funds are permanently and, generally, immutably recorded on the blockchain. It is as if a dollar bill had a Global Positioning System tracker attached to it. There is, however, no personal identifying information, such as an individual's name, birth date, or social security number associated with the transaction. Despite the lack of personal identifiers, there are methods of ascertaining an address owner's identity. Since the blockchain is accessible to the entire network (which will vary, depending on whether the blockchain is public or private), anyone on the network can analyze blockchain activity for patterns that may provide insight into a user's identity or connect multiple transactions back to a single address. Further, analysis of the transactions broadcast to the blockchain can be employed to link an internet protocol (IP) address to the originating blockchain address. In addition, investigators can engage companies that have developed blockchain-tracing tools or leverage data obtained by regulated cryptocurrency exchanges in the United States and Europe that collect customer data in accordance with increasing KYC and AML regulations to determine the identity of the wallet holder.[33]

Privacy Coins with Greater Anonymity

Some cryptocurrencies, such as Monero, offer a greater level of anonymity. These coins make it challenging to discern the parties to a transaction through a series of steps designed to obfuscate the cryptocurrency trail. For example, when users initiate transactions involving Monero, the money is sent from the origin wallet address to a new address, where it is mixed with transactions originating from other unrelated wallet addresses.[34] The result is a "stealth" wallet address with no apparent

---

(Apr. 18, 2019), https://www.fincen.gov/news/news-releases/fincen-penalizes-peer-peer-virtual-currency-exchanger-violations-anti-money.

33. Douglas Heaven, *Sitting with the Cyber-Sleuths Who Track Cryptocurrency Criminals*, MIT Tech. Rev. (Apr. 19, 2018), https://www.technologyreview.com/s/610807/sitting-with-the-cyber-sleuths-who-track-cryptocurrency-criminals/.

34. *Risks and Vulnerabilities of Virtual Currency Cryptocurrency as a Payment Method*, 2017 Public-Private Analytic Exchange Program, https://www.dni.gov/files/PE/Documents/9—2017-AEP_Risks-and-Vulnerabilities-of-Virtual-Currency.pdf.

connection to the originator. This is enticing to bad actors as it further disconnects them from the transaction.

Multiple Wallet Addresses

Individuals can also obtain greater anonymity by using multiple wallet addresses. Owning multiple wallet addresses allows an individual to send money between those wallets, which have no apparent connection to one another. For example, someone involved in criminal activity seeking to disguise a $10,000 transaction could structure the transaction by using multiple wallets to make 100 $100 transactions and, subsequently, sending these smaller payments to multiple wallets all belonging to the same ultimate beneficiary of the transaction. Thus, even if investigators ascertained the owner of one of the wallets, they would not necessarily have insight into the owner of the other wallets and would therefore not be able to link the transactions to one another.

Mixers or Tumblers Obscuring Source of Funds

Every transaction on a cryptocurrency network is recorded on the blockchain so that when a transaction is conducted, other network members will have access to the wallet addresses and financial histories of the parties to the transaction and be able to monitor future transactions. To increase a customer's anonymity, tumblers sever this tie by mixing coins from one wallet address with coins from other wallet addresses, after which they provide new coins in new wallets to all those involved in the transaction. The tumbler can also randomize transaction amounts and add time delays for an enhanced level of anonymity. This is highly attractive for those seeking to launder money, as they can insert their coins into a mixer or tumbler and receive untraceable coins in return.

Crypto Dusting

Those engaging in illegal behavior may also engage in a type of attack referred to as *crypto dusting*, the purpose of which is to make money laundering activity untraceable.[35] In crypto dusting, a known mixer or

---

35. Ogwu Osaemezu Emmanuel, *"Crypto Dusting" Attack Sends Illegally Obtained Bitcoin to Random Cryptocurrency Wallets*, BTCMANAGER (Jan. 10, 2019), https://btcmanager.com/crypto-dusting-attack-sends-illegally-obtained-bitcoin

bad actor will send minuscule amounts of cryptocurrency to multiple cryptocurrency wallets, effectively tainting the reputation of all receiving addresses by creating the impression that the addresses are connected to money laundering.[36] In turn, this clouds the ability of blockchain analytic tools algorithms to detect money laundering,[37] thereby creating a smokescreen for actual illegal activity to occur.[38] As a result, cryptocurrency exchanges with strong AML regulations will monitor all these likely benign accounts on the suspicion of their involvement in illegal activity.[39]

Lightning Network Transactions

Another method of obscuring transactions is employing the *Lightning Network*. The Lightning Network is an added payment channel between two parties facilitating almost instant and unlimited transactions outside of the blockchain. In the Lightning Network, transaction data are only recorded on the blockchain once the channel is closed, and the data recorded include the initial and final balance, but none of the intermediary transactions. Once this technology becomes more widespread, the level of anonymity will be even further enhanced because, rather than setting up a private channel with each party to a transaction, the system will automatically leverage existing connected parties to facilitate the transactions.[40]

-to-random-cryptocurrency-wallets/?q=/crypto-dusting-attack-sends-illegally-obtained-bitcoin-to-random-cryptocurrency-wallets/.

36. Jake, *Crypto Dusting Is a New Type of Blockchain Spam that Corrodes Reputations and Impacts Cryptocurrency AML*, CipherTrace (Dec. 19, 2018), https://ciphertrace.com/crypto_dusting/.

37. *Cryptocurrency Anti–Money Laundering Report, 2018 Q4*, CipherTrace (Jan. 2019), https://ciphertrace.com/wp-content/uploads/2019/01/crypto_aml_report_2018q4.pdf.

38. Curtis Franklin Jr., *New "Crypto Dusting" Attack Gives Cash, Takes Reputation*, Dark Reading (Jan. 1, 2019, 7:00 PM), https://www.darkreading.com/vulnerabilities-and-threats/new-crypto-dusting-attack-gives-cash-takes-reputation/d/d-id/1333613.

39. Bitcoin Exchange Guide News Team, *New DarkReading Report on "Crypto Dusting" Highlights New Digital Asset Money Laundering Technique*, Bitcoin Exchange Guide (Jan. 11, 2019), https://bitcoinexchangeguide.com/new-darkreading-report-on-crypto-dusting-highlights-new-digital-asset-money-laundering-technique/.

40. *What Is the Lightning Network in Bitcoin and How Does It Work*, Cointelegraph, https://cointelegraph.com/lightning-network-101/what-is-lightning-network-and-how-it-works#what-is-the-lightning-network (last visited May 6, 2019).

Proxy Servers, Virtual Private Networks, and Tor to Obfuscate Internet Protocol Addresses

A virtual private network (VPN) is a valuable tool in further anonymizing a user's identity by masking their IP address. Typically, the IP address is the only identifying information in a cryptocurrency transaction. Cryptocurrency users living in countries such as China, where cryptocurrencies and associated websites have been banned or blocked,[41] can leverage a VPN to mask their geographic location by creating the facade that the internet activity is originating from a different country, providing them access to the blocked websites while hindering local government internet tracking.

Similarly, cryptocurrency users seeking greater anonymity can use a proxy server to hide their IP address. A proxy server serves as a middleman for people accessing a particular website. When using a proxy, the proxy IP address will appear to have accessed the website, rather than the actual user's actual IP address.[42]

Tor is a more sophisticated and secure proxy used widely in the criminal underworld. When a user employs Tor, the user's IP address is hidden, and the request to access a particular website will bounce off multiple servers globally, layering it with even more anonymity.

Identifying Information Challenges

The fact that a number of exchanges do not collect customer information creates an added layer of challenge for those investigating cryptocurrency activity. Some exchanges are designed to offer their users greater anonymity and allow customers to trade without creating an account or with an account requiring limited identifying information. Furthermore, wallet ownership may be ambiguous as multiple individuals could have the private key to a wallet address, providing each of them with equal access to the funds. Cryptocurrency that passes through an unregulated exchange or an exchange associated with ransomware payments or other criminal activity can be an indication of risk.

---

41. *Crypto Exchanges Are Evading China's Ban by Changing Domain Names*, CCN (Sept. 11, 2018), https://www.ccn.com/crypto-exchanges-are-evading-chinas-ban-by-changing-domain-names/.

42. *How to Use Proxies to Earn More Bitcoin*, Blazing SEO, https://blazingseollc.com/blog/use-proxies-earn-bitcoin/ (last updated 2016).

Cross-Border Transactions (Ease, Speed, and Ability to Circumvent Traditional Financial Crime Controls)

Blockchain runs on a decentralized system, which facilitates swifter transactions than those conducted through traditional banks. Traditional banks can take up to twenty-four hours or longer if the attempted transaction is international,[43] whereas Bitcoin transactions can take as little as ten minutes irrespective of geography.[44] Even sizable transactions can be completed swiftly. For example, a 30,000 Bitcoin ($120 million) transaction was reported to have been made in approximately thirty minutes.[45] Moreover, cryptocurrencies can conduct transactions spanning multiple countries, creating confusion regarding which jurisdiction's AML regime applies and adding an extra layer of complexity for law enforcement.[46]

Ability to Exchange for Fiat Currency or Other Cryptocurrencies

Another unique property of cryptocurrency is the ease and speed with which it is possible to exchange fiat currency for cryptocurrency, which can then be exchanged for other cryptocurrencies. This facilitates money laundering as users of cryptocurrency can place their illegal funds into the financial market by buying fiat currency with cryptocurrency. They can then layer that money by exchanging it for other cryptocurrencies and sending it to and from various wallets. The funds can subsequently be integrated back into the financial market by changing the cryptocurrency back into fiat currency. For example, an individual trying to disguise the source of illegal funds could exchange $10,000 of fiat currency for Bitcoin in multiple wallets and exchange some of the Bitcoin

---

43. Amanda Dixon, *How Long Does a Wire Transfer Take?* SMARTASSET (Nov. 20, 2018), https://smartasset.com/checking-account/how-long-does-a-wire-transfer-take.

44. Financial Action Task Force, *Guidance for a Risk-Based Approach* (June 2015), https://www.fatf-gafi.org/media/fatf/documents/reports/Guidance-RBA-Virtual-Currencies.pdf.

45. *30,000 BTC ($194M) Transaction Confirmed with $0.10 Fee in 30 Minutes,* BITCOIN CENTER NYC (Oct. 17, 2018), https://www.bitcoincenternyc.com/bitcoin-news/30000-btc-194m-transaction-confirmed-with-0-10-fee-in-30-minutes/.

46. Financial Action Task Force, *Guidance for a Risk-Based Approach* (June 2015), https://www.fatf-gafi.org/media/fatf/documents/reports/Guidance-RBA-Virtual-Currencies.pdf.

for other cryptocurrencies. While investigators may be able to track the movement of the funds, the ease and speed with which the transactions are executed impedes investigators' ability to keep up, providing the money launderers more time to conduct illegal activity or further layer their funds.

Lack of Governance and Consistent Regulation

As the cryptocurrency industry burgeoned, regulators began to call for AML standards, but implementation of these standards has been slow. Moreover, countries have widely varying approaches to the treatment of cryptocurrency due to its multifaceted nature.[47] While some countries have banned cryptocurrency, others accept it as legal tender. Where one country views it as a commodity, the next treats it as property. Further confusion stems from the fact that domestic regulators give cryptocurrency disparate treatment, simultaneously regulating it as money, property, a commodity, and a security. The lack of a uniform approach has prevented global regulators from uniting efforts to address the issues arising out of the cryptocurrency industry.

Some efforts are in motion to establish a consistent cryptocurrency regulatory framework. For example, in July 2018, Malta, "the world's first blockchain island," became the first country to pass a regulatory framework for blockchain, cryptocurrency, and distributed ledger technology (DLT).[48] Other interested players have also taken steps to create a more stable regulatory environment, including Gemini, the digital asset platform that introduced the self-regulatory organization, the Virtual Commodities Association, which Gemini hopes will promote sound practices in the virtual currency industry.[49]

---

47. Claire Groden, Edoardo Saravalle & Julia Solomon Strauss, *Unchartered Waters: A Primer on Virtual Currency Regulation Around the World,* Center on Law and Security NYU School of Law (updated July 2018), https://s3.amazonaws.com/files.cnas.org/documents/CNASReportWEB-Bitcoin.pdf?mtime=20181002093347.

48. Rachel Wolfson, *Maltese Parliament Passes Laws that Set Regulatory Framework for Blockchain, Cryptocurrency and DLT*, Forbes (Jul. 5, 2018, 8:00 AM), https://www.forbes.com/sites/rachelwolfson/2018/07/05/maltese-parliament-passes-laws-that-set-regulatory-framework-for-blockchain-cryptocurrency-and-dlt/#16e32e2449ed.

49. Cameron Winklevoss, *A Proposal for a Self-Regulatory Organization for the U.S. Virtual Currency Industry*, Gemini (Mar. 13, 2018), https://medium.com/gemini/a-proposal-for-a-self-regulatory-organization-for-the-u-s-virtual-currency-industry-79e4d7891cfc.

Cryptocurrency Characteristics that Assist with AML Detection and Prevention

Notwithstanding the wide array of features that make it difficult to detect and prevent criminal activity associated with cryptocurrency, certain characteristics of cryptocurrency can in fact enhance AML detection and prevention capabilities. Leveraging these has significantly improved investigators' ability to identify possible illegal activity.

Immutability of Blockchain

Once recorded and time stamped on the blockchain, it is virtually impossible to alter a transaction, which is why the blockchain ledger is considered immutable. For a transaction to be verified and processed, the user must input the correct origin and destination wallet addresses and cryptocurrency amount or the transaction will be blocked.[50] This mitigates criminals' ability to "cook the books" and enables investigators to track transactions and money flow.

On- and Off-Ramps for Transfer to Fiat Currency

Cryptocurrency is typically obtained via exchanges, which trade fiat currency for cryptocurrency, and vice versa. These exchanges therefore serve as a gateway for placing fiat currency into the financial system for money laundering purposes, as well as the medium through which money is integrated back into the financial system following the placement and layering money laundering stages. Ensuring exchanges have thorough identification verification processes is imperative for AML efforts as investigators can use this information to track bad actors.

PARTICIPANTS IN THE CRYPTOCURRENCY BUSINESS ECOSYSTEM

There are multiple players in the cryptocurrency arena, some of which pose more risk than others.

---

50. Pascal Sprenger & Franziska Balsiger, *Anti-Money Laundering in Times of Cryptocurrencies,* KPMG, (June 2018), https://assets.kpmg/content/dam/kpmg/ch/pdf/anti-money-laundering-in-times-of-cryptocurrency.pdf.

Cryptocurrency Miners

Many cryptocurrencies are created through the "proof of work" mining process. In this process, miners verify the accuracy of transactions and then race to add the transactions to the blockchain, using computers to solve complex math problems that are built into the encryption mechanism. The first miner to solve the problem is rewarded with newly created digital tokens in the applicable cryptocurrency. Some miners create cryptocurrency to exchange it for US dollars or for other fiat or virtual currency. While mining itself is not illegal, those involved in criminal enterprises can invest in mining to disguise the actual source of funds. Miners are not required to register as an MSB unless mining to sell or trade on behalf of a third party.[51]

Cryptocurrency Exchanges

A user can buy cryptocurrency with US dollars or convert one cryptocurrency into a different cryptocurrency using a cryptocurrency exchange platform. The cryptocurrency-to-cryptocurrency exchange may be problematic because if the cryptocurrencies use different blockchains, the cryptocurrency exchange could be an attempt to conceal the source of funds. Also, if the user converts the cryptocurrency to US dollars, the details of the cryptocurrency exchange will not be available to banks without further inquiry. One possible mitigating factor is that many cryptocurrency exchanges operating in the United States must register as MSBs with FinCEN, in which case, as discussed earlier, they are subject to certain requirements, including an AML program and recordkeeping and reporting requirements. Depending on the state, there may be state requirements as well. Certain exchanges, however, continue to allow users to trade anonymously.[52]

Bitcoin Teller Machines

Bitcoin teller machines (BTMs) are used to exchange fiat currency for cryptocurrency, and vice versa. Certain machines will only exchange cryptocurrency for fiat currency, but others will also accept fiat currency

---

51. Fin. Crimes Enforcement Network, FIN-2014-R001, Application of FinCEN's Regulations to Virtual Currency Mining Operations (Jan. 30, 2014).

52. *Best Bitcoin Exchange*, http://www.bestbitcoinexchange.net/anonymous/ (last visited Jan. 28, 2019).

for cryptocurrency. There are currently over 3,000 BTMs in seventy different countries, [53,54] providing a seamless medium for exchanging cryptocurrency to and from fiat currency. One of the ramifications of these machines is that criminals can easily launder their money by depositing or withdrawing fiat currency at BTMs. Although BTMs are MSBs and therefore subject to FinCEN registration, in addition to any applicable state registration requirements,[55] some BTMs lack robust quality customer identification verification, or have no customer identification verification whatsoever, providing criminals the anonymity to launder money.[56]

Cryptocurrency Structuring and Mixers/Tumblers

A user can send cryptocurrency through a mixer/tumbler service, which is a type of exchange. The mixer/tumbler combines the cryptocurrency with other users' transactions or distributes it among hundreds of thousands of wallets that belong to the mixer/tumbler. Once the process is complete, "clean" cryptocurrency is transferred back to the sender or to the new owner. Mixers/tumblers are a risk because users can employ these services to circumvent the blockchain, which would otherwise provide a record of each individual transaction and relevant data and conceal the true originator of the transactions. This impedes the ability to trace the cryptocurrency on the blockchain.

Digital Commodities and Securities

Some cryptocurrency exchanges offer derivatives, including futures trading. This service is likely to become more popular over time. For example, the parent company of the New York Stock Exchange, Intercontinental

---

53. Peter Terlato, *There Are Almost 2,000 Bitcoin ATM's in USA*, Finder (May 2018), https://www.finder.com/almost-2000-bitcoin-atms-in-usa (last visited Jan. 28, 2019).

54. *International Bitcoin Teller Machines: Another Money-Laundering Vehicle or Legitimate Enterprise?* Thomson Reuters (Nov. 27, 2019), http://www.legalexecutiveinstitute.com/bitcoin-teller-machines/.

55. *Bitcoin ATM Regulatory Requirements in USA*, Coin ATM Radar Blog (Feb. 13, 2018), https://coinatmradar.com/blog/bitcoin-atm-regulatory-requirements-in-usa/.

56. *Bloomberg, Coinsource Report Indicates Bitcoin ATMs Are Money Laundering Vehicles,* Bitcoin Exchange Guide (Dec. 17, 2018), https://bitcoinexchangeguide.com/bloomberg-coinsource-report-indicates-bitcoin-atms-are-money-laundering-vehicles/.

Exchange,[57] and the NASDAQ have both announced plans to launch their own Bitcoin futures platform.[58] The risks associated with US dollar transactions involving futures trading are different than those associated with mixers/tumblers or standard exchanges because they do not actually involve the purchase or selling of a cryptocurrency.

Digital Asset Managers

Asset managers have taken varied approaches to cryptocurrency. Some are avoiding investing in cryptocurrency altogether due to concerns that it is too speculative.[59] Others have made efforts to incorporate digital asset trading into their platform. For example, in December 2020, cryptocurrency start-up Bitwise's Asset Management's Crypto Index Fund became available to US investors in over-the-counter markets. It is the first cryptocurrency index fund available to investors and tracks the Bitwise 10 Large Cap Crypto Index, a market-cap-weighted index of the ten largest cryptocurrencies that is rebalanced monthly.[60] A major challenge, however, is that cryptocurrency can be difficult to price and is susceptible to market manipulation, which is compounded by the uncertain regulatory environment. Cryptocurrency has been highly volatile since its inception because its value is determined by market perception, making it vulnerable to large price fluctuations. Consequently, cryptocurrency trading has been plagued by fraud, prompting the US Securities and Exchange Commission to issue alerts about cryptocurrency investment red flags to encourage investors to be cautious when trading in this space.[61]

---

57. Nathaniel Popper, *Bitcoin Sees Wall Street Warm to Trading Virtual Currency*, NEW YORK TIMES (May 7, 2018), https://www.nytimes.com/2018/05/07/technology/bitcoin-new-york-stock-exchange.html.

58. Teuta Franjkovic, *Bitcoin and Ethereum Indices to Be Added to NASDAQ's Global Data Service This Month*, COINSPEAKER (Feb. 14, 2019, 8:33 AM), https://www.coinspeaker.com/bitcoin-ethereum-nasdaq-global-data/.

59. *Six of the World's Largest Asset Managers Rule Out Bitcoin*, FINANCIAL NEWS, https://www.fnlondon.com/articles/six-of-the-worlds-largest-asset-managers-rule-out-bitcoin-20180115 (updated Jan. 10, 2018).

60. Muyao Shen, *Bitwise's Crypto Index Fund Becomes Available to US Investors*, COINDESK (Dec. 9, 2020), https://www.coindesk.com/bitwise-crypto-index-fund-us-investors.

61. Ponzi Schemes Using Virtual Currencies, SEC Office of Investor Education and Advocacy Investor Alert Pub. No. 153 (July 2013).

Buyers and Sellers of Digital Assets

As interest in cryptocurrency surged, ICOs became a popular way to finance cryptocurrency/blockchain projects.[62] However, in the absence of adequate regulatory oversight, ICOs quickly became notorious as a means for fraudsters to scam investors. Furthermore, ICOs, which generally accept other cryptocurrencies as a means of payment, can pose an AML threat as there is no way to tell whether the cryptocurrency originated from illicit activity.[63]

Ransomware Firms

Businesses such as digital forensics and incident response companies and cyber insurance companies that support victims of ransomware attacks and facilitate ransomware payments to cybercriminals on behalf of victims typically use cryptocurrency in a large number of transactions, as it is the preferred payment method of ransomware perpetrators. While not traditionally considered cryptocurrency firms, FinCEN has opined that these companies and other ransomware firms may have to register as money transmitters because they make payments in cryptocurrency on behalf of their customers. The US Department of the Treasury's Office of Foreign Assets Control, FinCEN, and law enforcement officials are concerned because these companies inevitably make payments in cryptocurrencies to malicious cyberactors and possibly to sanctioned entities.[64]

Financial Institutions' Adoption of Cryptocurrency

Traditional financial institutions initially took a cautious approach toward cryptocurrency and were slow to incorporate it into their business models. In December 2018, however, NYDFS granted its first BitLicense

---

62. Saheli Roy Choudhury, *It's a Very Good Time to Be a Money Launderer, and You Can Thank Cryptocurrencies*, CNBC (Aug. 4, 2017, 5:18 AM), https://www.cnbc.com/2017/08/04/icos-may-be-seen-as-securities-by-u-s-and-singapore-regulators.html.

63. Tom Robinson, *ICO Risk: Why AML Compliance Matters*, Elliptic (Apr. 23, 2018), https://www.elliptic.co/our-thinking/ico-risk-why-aml-compliance-matters.

64. U.S. Department of the Treasury, *Advisory on Potential Sanctions Risks for Facilitating Ransomware Payments* (Oct. 1, 2020), https://home.treasury.gov/system/files/126/ofac_ransomware_advisory_10012020_1.pdf.

to a bank that adopted a digital payments platform using blockchain.[65] Since then, there has been more interest in cryptocurrencies by traditional banking institutions. For example, Fidelity Investments launched Fidelity Digital Assets, which offers services such as custody and trade execution of cryptocurrency assets to institutional investors. Likewise, BNY Mellon announced in February 2021 that it will be rolling out a digital custody unit to custody clients' crypto assets. In addition, payment providers such as PayPal have announced that customers will be able to use cryptocurrencies to shop at merchants in their networks,[66] and certain banks have announced the introduction of their own internal stablecoin,[67] based on the US dollar as a way to increase efficiency and reduce costs.[68]

Stablecoins

On January 4, 2021, the Office of the Comptroller of the Currency (OCC) issued an interpretive letter allowing federally regulated banks to use stablecoins or cryptocurrencies with relatively stable prices to conduct payments and other permissible activities.[69] This update will reduce transaction costs, improve efficiency, and reduce the transaction completion time, benefits typically associated with digital currencies, but,

---

65. Nikhilesh De, *Signature Bank Wins New York Approval for "Real-Time" Blockchain Payments*, CoinDesk (Dec. 4, 2018, 3:20 PM), https://www.coindesk.com/signature-bank-wins-new-york-approval-for-real-time-blockchain-payments.

66. Andrey Shevchenko, *PayPal to Offer Crypto Payments Starting in 2021*, Cointelegraph (Oct. 21, 2020), https://cointelegraph.com/news/paypal-to-offer-crypto-payments-starting-in-2021.

67. A stablecoin is a digital currency that maintains a stable value as it is backed by an underlying asset or a benchmark, such as the U.S. dollar.

68. Hugh Son, *JP Morgan Is Rolling Out the First US Bank-Backed Cryptocurrency to Transform Payments Business*, CNBC (Feb. 14, 2019, 5:59 AM), https://www.cnbc.com/2019/02/13/jp-morgan-is-rolling-out-the-first-us-bank-backed-cryptocurrency-to-transform-payments--.html.

69. OCC Interpretive Letter 1174, OCC Chief Counsel's Interpretation on National Bank and Federal Savings Association Authority to Use Independent Node Verification Networks and Stablecoins for Payment Activities (Jan. 4, 2021).

unlike digital currencies, the stablecoin will also offer the stability of its underlying asset.[70]

RISKS FOR FINANCIAL INSTITUTIONS

Digital assets can pose unique threats to traditional financial institutions, which have long been subject to AML regulations and generally have a lower risk tolerance than many digital assets companies, which are relatively new to the financial industry.

Money Laundering in Cryptocurrency Transactions

The explosive growth of cryptocurrencies has outpaced market regulations and controls and exposed the industry to a number of risks,[71] ranging from market volatility, to fraud, to money laundering, to a variety of other types of financial crime. The regulatory response has been primarily focused on illegal transactions, consumer protection, and fraud. Within the industry, however, concerns about the risk of money laundering and terrorist financing persist due to the anonymous nature of the transactions and limited amount of identification required of cryptocurrency users.[72]

Financial institutions should assess cryptocurrency carefully. As previously noted, several of the blockchain's core features can be misused by criminal enterprises, which explains why cryptocurrency is attractive to the criminal community. There are multiple security threats that criminals can exploit—they can hack into crypto exchanges, empty crypto wallets, and even infect individual computers with malware that

70. Mengqi Sun, *OCC Says Banks Can Use Stablecoins in Payments*, Wall Street J. (Jan. 7, 2021, 8:15 PM), https://www.wsj.com/articles/occ-says-banks-can-use-stablecoins-in-payments-11610068515.

71. Billy Bambrough, *IMF Issues Stark Warning Over Bitcoin and Crypto "Rapid" Growth*, Forbes (Oct. 9, 2018, 3:08 AM), https://www.forbes.com/sites/billybambrough/2018/10/09/imf-issues-stark-warning-over-bitcoin-and-crypto-rapid-growth/#68a6904c3544.

72. John Thackeray, *5 Inherent Risks of Cryptocurrency*, FEI (July 17, 2018), https://daily.financialexecutives.org/FEI-Daily/July-2018/5-Inherent-Risks-of-Cryptocurrency.aspx.

steals cryptocurrency. Cryptocurrency is also highly reliant on unregulated companies and start-ups, including some that may not yet have developed mature internal controls and are therefore more susceptible to fraud and theft than established regulated financial institutions. In addition, because many financial institutions do not understand how cryptocurrency works, they may not implement adequate controls to mitigate the risk.

From the criminal's perspective, cryptocurrency has increasingly become a favorable method for hiding or laundering funds, serving as an often-employed alternative to wiring of funds to offshore locations that offer banking secrecy.[73] While bearer-share bonds or a Swiss bank account were once the preferred method of hiding money, the added benefits of cryptocurrency, including the elimination of overhead costs of intermediaries and the risk that intermediaries might be forced to release account information, make cryptocurrency an equally, if not more, attractive option.

Over the past several decades, financial institutions have gradually acquired techniques and processes for combating financial crime and money laundering in cash and traditional transactions. Cryptocurrency, however, has only been a relevant market and product since around 2008, and techniques to detect and prevent money laundering involving cryptocurrencies are therefore in their infancy. Moreover, cryptocurrencies were designed to allow coin holders to avoid financial institutions, which have traditionally taken on the role of intermediaries in the global anti–money laundering effort.

Today, it is almost impossible to attribute an anonymous digital wallet to a particular user to determine whether the user is a criminal, a money launderer, or subject to sanctions. The blockchain does not store information such as IP addresses or KYC information that can be used to identify the account holder. Even if the blockchain did retain such information, there are several options users can take advantage of to conceal their identity and IP addresses. As previously discussed, VPN blocks, use of multiple wallets, multiple email addresses, and proxy networks are all methods that can provide further anonymity. The use of mixers or tumblers, privacy coins, and unregulated cryptocurrency exchanges can

---

73. Alfred Ng, *Cryptocurrency Like Bitcoin Is Easy Money for Criminals*, CNET (Feb. 14, 2018, 5:00 AM), https://www.cnet.com/news/cryptocurrency-cybercrimes-mean-easy-money/.

further obfuscate identifying information. In a blockchain transaction, financial institutions typically can only identify their own clients.

Despite these obstacles, certain characteristics of digital currency can be useful to those trying to spot criminal activity. For example, most current digital currencies operate using DLT. Each transaction that transpires in a particular currency is tracked and recorded in a permanent, transparent log. Theoretically, because every transaction is publicly recorded on the ledger, there is potential for transactions to be linked to a particular person and, in effect, "de-anonymized."

Understanding Cryptocurrency Risk

Financial institutions must take special care when dealing with cryptocurrency transactions or customers involved with digital assets. They must develop a full understanding of the various parties involved and identify and address any heightened risks.

Customer Risk

As noted earlier, KYC/CDD procedures traditionally involve a careful review and verification of a customer's information so the institution can understand the nature and purpose of the customer relationship and assign the customer an appropriate risk rating. The anonymous nature of cryptocurrency, however, impedes a traditional assessment of customer risk. This, combined with the fact that cryptocurrency can facilitate and is frequently used for criminal activity, means that the customer risk of businesses dealing in cryptocurrency is often higher. Moreover, certain businesses within the cryptocurrency industry present more inherent risk than others.

Business Risk

A financial institution applies business risk principles to identify areas of vulnerability, changes in the regulatory landscape and risk environment, and appropriate controls. Key considerations in making this evaluation are (1) the direction of the business, (2) the institution's risk tolerance, and (3) whether the institution is willing to assume a particular risk. The institution should ensure that it has appropriately defined risk and that its assessment of risk is comprehensive and adequately tailored to the institution's products, services, customer base, and geographic locations.

Institutions involved in cryptocurrency face a high level of business risk due to the still nascent market's susceptibility to criminal activity, regulatory uncertainty, and volatility. These businesses should tailor their risk framework accordingly.

Geographic Risk

Geographic risk is an evaluation of risk based on the countries in which the institution does business. Countries considered high risk for money laundering and financing terrorism are those with one or more high risk factors, including, for example, a high corruption index, unsecure economic or political systems, an inefficient legal system, or being known for trafficking drugs and weapons.

It is almost impossible for financial institutions to determine whether an anonymous digital wallet or a transaction involving cryptocurrency is associated with a user or an entity in a high-risk country. Users can easily hide their locations using VPNs. Moreover, users of cryptocurrency have the ability to physically store significant amounts of digital currency in hardware. Hardware wallets are considered one of the most secure ways to store cryptocurrency as they allow the owner to process transactions and subsequently store coins offline. In general, there are several methods to access and conduct digital transactions without revealing geographic location. Thus, institutions dealing in cryptocurrency must account for the high degree of geographic risk to which they are inherently disposed.

MITIGATING CRYPTOCURRENCY RISK

On October 8, 2020, the US Department of Justice (DOJ) Office of the Deputy Attorney General's Cyber-Digital Task Force published *Cryptocurrency: Enforcement Framework*.[74] The framework highlights the emerging criminal and national security threat that cryptocurrency use poses to the United States and provides detailed information about the DOJ's approach to combating the illicit use of cryptocurrency and related technologies.

74. U.S. Department of Justice, Office of the Deputy Attorney General, Cyber-Digital Task Force, *Cryptocurrency: Enforcement Framework* (Oct. 2020), https://www.justice.gov/archives/ag/page/file/1326061/download.

One of the primary facets of the DOJ's response strategy is promotion of close cooperation between the public and private sectors to advance mutual goals in the fight against emerging threats to the virtual asset marketplace.[75] Digital asset companies and financial institutions can familiarize themselves with the most effective ways to manage and address the risks of cryptocurrencies, from specific considerations for their AML programs to tools and techniques they can apply to identify and respond appropriately to cryptocurrency transactions.

Risk Assessment

While increased anonymity and privacy are attractive to users in the cryptocurrency space, these traits pose a challenge to those charged with combating financial crime, as there is minimal insight into the identity of the parties involved in a transaction. A comprehensive risk assessment that is informed by an understanding of the industry and its players and pinpoints applicable cryptocurrency business risks will allow the business to focus its efforts on appropriate mitigation and is critical to managing cryptocurrency risk.

Know Your Customer

To comply with applicable AML laws and regulations, digital asset companies and financial institutions should ensure they have a strong KYC program to verify the identity of customers and determine whether clients are involved in illegal activity.

Within the cryptocurrency industry, conformity with and application of KYC rules currently vary based on company type, products and services offered, and the company's perceived standing under the BSA. Some companies do not require any KYC,[76] others collect basic customer information, such as email addresses and phone numbers,[77] that are difficult to verify due to the lack of an official standard for proving an associated identity, and a few have robust KYC programs in place.

75. *Id.*

76. *AML/KYC*, Changelly, https://changelly.com/aml-kyc (last updated Oct. 2019).

77. Hacken Club, *Is There Real KYC in the Crypto Industry?* Cryptocurrency-Hub (Nov. 23, 2018), https://cryptocurrencyhub.io/https-cryptocurrencyhub-io-cer-is-there-real-kyc-in-the-crypto-industry-2212f405a0ac.

Training

Institutions should periodically conduct training related to cryptocurrencies. Training topics should include the following:

- Characteristics of cryptocurrencies and their susceptibility to sanctions risks
- Money laundering and sanctions-evasion typologies unique to cryptocurrencies
- Reinforcement of reporting requirements for money laundering and sanctions-related violations that may include cryptocurrencies
- Regulator guidance and industry best practices related to cryptocurrencies

AML Controls

A crucial question that companies in the cryptocurrency industry should ask is whether they can reasonably manage the business's AML risk. A proper assessment of the risk posed can help ensure these institutions have adequate controls and facilitate the design of policies and procedures specific to cryptocurrencies and digital assets. These policies, procedures, and controls will provide assurance that the company is capable of meeting relevant AML requirements. The following are some examples of AML controls to minimize cryptocurrency risk:

- Appropriate request for information procedures that call for analysts to obtain detailed information about transactions with cryptocurrency indicia
- A case management system that adequately captures information relevant to the escalation of financial crime involving digital assets
- Periodic training related to typologies specific to digital assets

Regulator Engagement

Traditional banks and financial institutions are required to implement AML compliance programs to control financial crime and money laundering risk. Although the regulatory landscape for cryptocurrency is beginning to take shape, some digital currency companies are not yet subject to the same explicit rigorous requirements.

It is recommended that cryptocurrency firms develop an ongoing dialogue with regulators to discuss the evolution of the digital asset industry and associated regulations. In New York, for example, multiple entities that have obtained an NYDFS BitLicense did so in close collaboration with the agency.[78]

Identifying Red Flags in Cryptocurrency Transactions

Institutions must ensure that their filter technology solution is capable of generating alerts on cryptocurrency-related identifiers. Institutions should also be proactive in using blockchains to analyze patterns behind how sanctioned entities use digital assets. Technology marketed by detection solution providers can trace activity by individual wallet addresses to identify activity obscured by mixers and tumblers. Blockchain analysis should be incorporated into policies, procedures, and training.

Cryptocurrency firms can apply specialized tools and analysis to detect red flags in cryptocurrency transactions. Blockchain tracing software or connector tracking allows investigators researching a blockchain transaction to trace the source and route of blockchain tokens. The goal of blockchain tracing is to "de-anonymize" cryptocurrency transactions and users. Additionally, companies that offer tracing services can link or tag digital wallets that are confirmed to have been tied to criminal activity.

A blockchain explorer is essentially a browser for the blockchain and can search the blockchain similarly to how users can search the internet with Google. Blockchain explorers are limited to platforms related to a particular type of token—in other words, a user can use an explorer to search a Bitcoin platform or an Ethereum platform, but not both, not both at the same time—but a user can access any information that is on the platform's blockchain. Although inherently anonymous or pseudonymous, the open-source, public nature of the blockchain allows for transparency into the movement of cryptocurrency. Therefore, once bad actors are confirmed and identified, their transaction activity is visible on the blockchain. Many cryptocurrency communities keep lists of fraudulent or scam IP addresses and wallets that are known for illegal activity.

---

78. Ana Alexandre, *New York Digital Investment Group Subsidiary Acquires New York BitLicense*, COINTELEGRAPH (Nov. 15, 2018), https://cointelegraph.com/news/new-york-digital-investment-group-subsidiary-acquires-new-york-bitlicense.

Other methods of detecting red flags include obtaining customer IP addresses at customer onboarding and during periodic reviews to analyze a user's digital footprint and plain text analysis, which can be used to sort and filter data in intelligent ways to see patterns indicative of unusual activity. Companies can also use various methods of identification (ID) verification to reduce the anonymity of cryptocurrency. Cryptocurrency firms that would prefer to outsource this task can employ third-party vendors that will process KYC information and verify documentation. The primary verification documents required by cryptocurrency firms and exchanges are a passport, photograph, and written certificate. However, application of the ID requirement is inconsistently applied across the most recognizable cryptocurrency exchanges, and, as previously noted, some do not follow any KYC procedures.[79]

Prohibition/Blocking of Anonymous Trading Tools

Authorities have expressed interest in identifying effective ways to reduce the anonymity of blockchain transactions. Some jurisdictions, such as Taiwan and South Korea, have introduced regulations that ban anonymous cryptocurrency trading outright.[80] In late 2018, The Financial Action Task Force announced forthcoming updates to their recommendations, global standards for anti–money laundering, and alluded to a requirement that all jurisdictions ensure that cryptocurrency providers are subject to AML regulations and registration and licensing. These measures would eliminate the use of anonymous trading tools such as mixers and tumblers, privacy coins, and VPNs, enhancing cryptocurrency transaction monitoring.

CONCLUSION

The emergence of virtual currencies and increased growth in the cryptocurrency market has given rise to a need for a clear regulatory framework applicable to digital asset businesses. Businesses involved in virtual

---

79. Hacken Ecosystem, *Is There Real KYC in the Crypto Industry?* CRYPTOCURRENCYHUB (Nov. 23, 2018), https://cryptocurrencyhub.io/https-cryptocurrencyhub-io-cer-is-there-real-kyc-in-the-crypto-industry-2212f405a0ac.

80. Rosie Perper, *South Korea Will Ban Anonymous Cryptocurrency Trading to Help Boost Transparency*, INSIDER (Jan. 23, 2018, 6:31 PM), https://www.businessinsider.com/south-korea-bans-anonymous-cryptocurrency-trading-2018-1.

currency must be aware of applicable BSA requirements and, if applicable, must design and implement a risk-based program to ensure compliance with its provisions. Businesses must also understand the unique characteristics of digital assets that make them susceptible to AML risks, as well as those that can enhance money laundering detection. Then digital asset businesses can design and implement effective risk-based BSA/AML compliance programs and prevent their businesses from abuse by criminals and terrorists.

7 | Sanctions Compliance for Cryptocurrency Transactions

Alma Angotti, Adam Klauder, and Elizabeth Sisul

SANCTIONS—OVERVIEW

Economic sanctions are a tool to aid in accomplishing a nations' foreign and security policy goals. The state-sponsored use of cryptocurrencies to evade sanctions poses a serious risk to the efficacy of economic sanctions. As discussed later in this chapter, many of the nation-states targeted by US comprehensive sanctions are involved in cryptocurrency-related activities, some for the stated purpose of evading sanctions. This chapter provides an overview of the application of US economic sanctions generally and in the context of cryptocurrencies.

Economic sanctions are the "withdrawal of customary trade and financial relations for foreign and security policy purposes."[1] In the United States, economic sanctions are primarily administered and enforced by the US Department of the Treasury's Office of Foreign Assets Control (OFAC).[2] All "US persons" must comply with OFAC regulations. US persons include US citizens and permanent resident aliens regardless of where they are located, all persons and entities within the United States, and

1. Jonathan Masters, *What Are Economic Sanctions?*, Council on Foreign Relations Backgrounder (Aug. 7, 2017), https://www.cfr.org/backgrounder/what-are-economic-sanctions.

2. Although this chapter will focus on OFAC, it is worth noting that other U.S. governmental agencies also help administer and enforce U.S. sanctions (e.g., the U.S. Department of Commerce's Bureau of Industry and Security, the U.S. Department of Justice, etc.).

all US incorporated entities and their foreign branches.[3] For some OFAC sanctions programs, foreign subsidiaries that are owned or controlled by US persons must also comply with US sanctions regulations. Compliance with sanctions laws and regulations, therefore, does not depend on whether a cryptocurrency business is a regulated entity in the traditional sense, such as a broker-dealer registered by the US Securities and Exchange Commission or a federally chartered bank or money transmitter.

Economic sanctions may take the form of comprehensive sanctions, which are geographically targeted, or selective sanctions, which target specific persons and entities. Unless authorized by an OFAC license or exempted by statute,[4] US persons are prohibited from transacting with governments and nationals of the sanctioned jurisdiction and are prohibited from transacting with the individuals and entities found on OFAC's list of Specially Designated Nationals and Blocked Persons (SDN List).[5]

In November 2018, OFAC took an important step in both acknowledging and addressing how cryptocurrencies can be used to circumvent US sanctions. OFAC used its cyber-related sanctions to sanction two Iranian cryptocurrency exchangers for using cryptocurrencies to facilitate the exchange of ransomware payments into fiat currency. Importantly, OFAC also, for the first time, listed cryptocurrency addresses as identifiers associated with the individuals. In its press release, OFAC explained that the cryptocurrency addresses "should assist those in the compliance and digital currency communities in identifying transactions and funds that must be blocked and investigating any connections to these addresses."[6] OFAC has taken additional cryptocurrency-related

---

3. U.S. Department of the Treasury, *OFAC Frequently Asked Questions: General Questions*, https://www.treasury.gov/resource-center/faqs/Sanctions/Pages/faq_general.aspx#basic (last visited Feb. 25, 2019).

4. An OFAC license is an authorization from OFAC to engage in an otherwise prohibited transaction.

5. U.S. Department of the Treasury, *OFAC Frequently Asked Questions: General Questions*, https://www.treasury.gov/resource-center/faqs/Sanctions/Pages/faq_general.aspx#basic (last visited Feb. 25, 2019).

6. Press Release, U.S. Department of the Treasury, *Treasury Designates Iran-Based Financial Facilitators of Malicious Cyber Activity and for the First Time Identifies Associated Digital Currency Addresses* (Nov. 28, 2018), https://home.treasury.gov/news/press-releases/sm556.

actions since November 2018. These actions are discussed in greater detail in the sections that follow.

Effective sanctions compliance requires adequate due diligence and ongoing screening.[7] If an organization identifies a person or transaction that is related to a sanctioned jurisdiction, individual, or entity, it may be required to block or reject related accounts and other property.[8] If an institution blocks or rejects a transaction, it is required to file a report with OFAC within ten business days.[9] In addition, the organization is required to file an Annual Report of Blocked Property (ARBP) with OFAC. The ARBP is a list of all blocked property held as of June 30 of the current year.[10] Cryptocurrency-related transactions are not exempt from these requirements.[11]

CRYPTOCURRENCY'S SUSCEPTIBILITY TO SANCTIONS RISKS

Bitcoin was created in part to eliminate the need for financial intermediaries (i.e., banks) in payment transactions.[12] It accomplished this task by creating a system that allows for (1) direct peer-to-peer transactions and (2) consensus among all participants about the current state of all transactions. Blockchain is the technology that underpins this system and forms the immutable "ledger" on which transactions are recorded.

---

7. *Office of Foreign Assets Control—Overview,* Federal Financial Institutions Examination Council Bank Secrecy Act/Anti–Money Laundering InfoBase: Bank Secrecy Act/Anti–Money Laundering Examination Manual, https://bsaaml.ffiec.gov/manual/OfficeOfForeignAssetsControl/01.

8. In certain circumstances, OFAC may grant a license to allow otherwise prohibited transactions.

9. U.S. Department of the Treasury, *OFAC Frequently Asked Questions: Sanctions Compliance*, https://www.treasury.gov/resource-center/faqs/Sanctions/Pages/faq_compliance.aspx#reports (last visited Feb. 25, 2019).

10. U.S. Department of the Treasury, *OFAC Recent Actions: Reminder for the Annual Report of Blocked Property*, https://www.treasury.gov/resource-center/sanctions/OFAC-Enforcement/Pages/20180702.aspx (last visited Apr. 30, 2019).

11. OFAC FAQ 560.

12. Satoshi Nakamoto, *Bitcoin: A Peer-to-Peer Electronic Cash System*, WWW.BITCOIN.ORG, https://bitcoin.org/bitcoin.pdf (last visited Feb. 25, 2019).

In general, public blockchains work as follows:[13]

1. A user initiates a peer-to-peer transaction.
2. Transactions are grouped into blocks to await validation.
3. Network participants validate blocks of transactions for some form of compensation.
4. A validated block of transactions is added to the previous chain of blocks.
5. Participants in the network conduct all subsequent transactions with the understanding that the newly added block is the most current state of the ledger.[14]

A more detailed discussion of blockchain protocols is outside the scope of this chapter (and is discussed in more detail in Chapter 1), but it is important to understand how blockchains operate to appreciate the characteristics of cryptocurrencies that make them susceptible to sanctions risk. Some of these characteristics are discussed in greater detail in the sections that follow.

Pseudo-anonymity

Many of the most popular cryptocurrencies transact over blockchains that provide "pseudo-anonymity," or the ability to link transactions to a specific cryptocurrency address but not to real-world individuals.[15] The ability to link transactions to a specific cryptocurrency address is related to how transactions on a blockchain are verified. Since there are no financial intermediaries, network participants must be able to trust that the cryptocurrency they are receiving has not already been spent elsewhere. To accomplish this, in a typical cryptocurrency transaction,

---

13. A discussion of public versus private blockchains is outside the scope of this chapter.

14. Nolan Bauerle, *How Does Blockchain Technology Work?* CoinDesk, https://www.coindesk.com/learn/how-does-blockchain-technology-work/(last visited Feb. 24, 2019); *see also* Annika Feign, *What Is Blockchain Technology?* CoinDesk (Jul. 22, 2021), https://www.coindesk.com/learn/what-is-blockchain-technology/.

15. Toshendra Kumar Sharma, *How Is Blockchain Verifiable by Public and Yet Anonymous?* Blockchain Council (Jul. 10, 2018), https://www.blockchain-council.org/blockchain/how-is-blockchain-verifiable-by-public-and-yet-anonymous/.

the system broadcasts wallet origin, destination address, and the amount of funds related to each transaction to the network to be verified. When that transaction is verified and becomes part of a block on a blockchain, the information that is associated with that transaction is permanently and, generally, immutably recorded on the blockchain. There are commercially available cryptocurrency monitoring tools that analyze the blockchain to connect transaction activity back to a known wallet address.

Although linking transactions to a specific cryptocurrency address is a useful tool for monitoring transactions on a blockchain, difficulties in connecting a cryptocurrency address to a real-world individual or entity create significant sanctions compliance risk. More concerning, and discussed later in this chapter, some blockchains are now able to facilitate completely anonymous cryptocurrency transactions.

Cross-Border Transactions

Traditional sanctions regimes enable nations to regulate transactions between borders. One of the most important characteristics of cryptocurrencies that make them susceptible to sanctions risks is the ease and speed with which users can make cross-border transactions. The requirements for effecting a cross-border cryptocurrency transaction are the same as those for a domestic transaction—internet access.

Cryptocurrency transactions rely on public key cryptography. "Public-key cryptography, or asymmetric cryptography, is an encryption scheme that uses two mathematically related, but not identical, keys—a public key and a private key. . . . The public key is used to encrypt and the private key is used to decrypt."[16] A user must have the private key associated with the funds they are trying to send. Like public keys, private keys are strings of alphanumeric characters. Users can store private keys in many ways, including as a Quick Response code, in cold storage wallets often no more than the size of a Universal Serial Bus stick, or simply written down on a piece of paper. The ability to physically move private keys across borders is as easy as keeping a piece of paper in your pocket.

16. *What Is Public-Key Cryptography?* GlobalSign, https://www.globalsign.com/en/ssl-information-center/what-is-public-key-cryptography/ (last visited Feb. 25, 2019).

Exchanges and a Path to Fiat Currency

Online trading platforms/exchanges enable buyers and sellers to trade cryptocurrencies for other assets, including fiat currencies and other cryptocurrencies, and take a fee from each transaction. Some platforms, known as "peer-to-peer exchangers," enable individual persons to trade in virtual currencies online or through in-person meetups.[17]

A primary objective of most sanctions regimes is restricting access to a particular fiat currency (e.g., US dollars). Given their position as a gateway to the traditional financial system, robust sanctions controls at trading platforms and peer-to-peer exchangers are particularly important. In its May 2019 "Advisory on Illicit Activity Involving Convertible Virtual Currency," the Financial Crimes Enforcement Network (FinCEN) highlighted the risks posed by darknet marketplaces, peer-to-peer exchanges, foreign-located money service businesses, and convertible virtual currency kiosks.[18] FinCEN stressed that without "sufficient controls in place, financial institutions cannot reasonably assess and mitigate the potential risks posed by a customer's source of funds or a customer's counterparty, and criminals can exploit the US financial system by engaging in illicit transactions."[19]

Immutability

One of the most important aspects of blockchains are their immutability—or inability to be changed.[20] In order for the network of participants to form a consensus about the current state of the ledger, participants must be able to trust that the ledger cannot be changed in any way. Once a sanctioned entity or individual is sent or sends money

---

17. U.S. Department of the Treasury, *Advisory on the Iranian Regime's Illicit and Malign Activities and Attempts to Exploit the Financial System*, FinCEN Advisory FIN-2018-A006 (Oct. 11, 2018), https://www.fincen.gov/sites/default/files/advisory/2018-10-11/Iran%20Advisory%20FINAL%20508.pdf.

18. U.S. Department of the Treasury, *Advisory on Illicit Activity Involving Convertible Virtual Currency*, FinCEN Advisory FIN-2019-A003 (May 9, 2019), https://www.fincen.gov/sites/default/files/advisory/2019-05-10/FinCEN%20Advisory%20CVC%20FINAL%20508.pdf.

19. *Id.*

20. Immutability of blockchains is not certain. In some instances, the network can collectively agree to change the previous state of the ledger, or a bad actor can launch an attack that changes the previous state of the ledger.

to a wallet that they control, there is no way to reverse the transaction. This limits the ability to freeze assets and block transactions.[21]

Privacy-Focused Cryptocurrencies

Over time, blockchains have become more sophisticated, leading to wider adoption of privacy-focused cryptocurrencies. These cryptocurrencies offer the user ways to hide their identities and transaction histories.

Listed in the following table are examples of some of the most popular privacy-focused cryptocurrencies.

Cryptocurrency	Privacy Offered
Monero[22]	Hides sending address, receiving address, and transaction amount
Dash[23]	Automatically mixes coins before completing a transaction
Verge[24]	Obscures IP addresses using Tor
Zcash[25]	Uses zero-knowledge proofs to encrypt sending address, receiving address, and transaction amount

On September 10, 2020, OFAC listed Zcash and Dash addresses as identifiers associated with two individuals that were added to the SDN list.[26]

Ability to Be Mixed or Tumbled to Obscure the Source of Funds

Mixers (or "tumblers") are services that combine cryptocurrencies from different wallet addresses into one and then redistribute the mixed coins into various cryptocurrency wallet addresses. This often makes it more

21. Yaya Fanusie, *Seeking Sanctions Resistance Through Blockchain Technology*, Forbes (Oct. 11, 2018), https://www.forbes.com/sites/yayafanusie/2018/10/11/seeking-sanctions-resistance-through-blockchain-technology/#7c4e701f6392.

22. Monero, https://www.getmonero.org/ (last visited: Feb. 24, 2019).

23. Dash, https://www.dash.org/ (last visited: Feb. 24, 2019).

24. Verge, https://vergecurrency.com/ (last visited: Feb. 24, 2019).

25. Zcash, https://z.cash/ (last visited: Feb. 24, 2019).

26. U.S. Department of the Treasury, *Cyber-Related Designations; Foreign Interference in U.S. Election Designations* (Sept. 10, 2020), https://home.treasury.gov/policy-issues/financial-sanctions/recent-actions/20200910.

difficult to trace the transactions to or from a particular wallet address and may make it difficult to identify whether a sanctioned entity is the true originator or beneficiary of a transaction.

Ease of Creating New Cryptocurrencies

New cryptocurrencies can be created simply by launching a blockchain, or some other form of distributed ledger technology. Many countries are exploring how the blockchain can change the way national currencies are tracked, distributed, and monitored.[27] Some are interested in the blockchain's ability to increase transparency and efficiency, while others seek to use cryptocurrencies to avoid US sanctions. The state sponsorship of cryptocurrencies is discussed in greater detail later in this chapter.

Online Activity

Users send cryptocurrency transactions to the network via an online connection making it possible to track users via internet protocol (IP) addresses. Sanctions evaders often use proxy servers, virtual private networks, and Tor, however, to obfuscate IP addresses.

FOREIGN NATIONS' USE OF CRYPTOCURRENCY TO EVADE US SANCTIONS

As noted previously, some countries are exploring how to use the blockchain and cryptocurrencies to evade US sanctions. This section includes a discussion of Iran, Venezuela, Russia, and North Korea and their approaches to leveraging cryptocurrencies for this purpose. It is also worth noting that these countries may benefit from other countries' increasing acceptance of digital assets as a form of currency. For example, several sanctioned countries have close ties to China, which is the first country to officially launch its own digital currency. In November 2020, the People's Bank of China began trial runs of China's digital currency, the Digital Currency Electronic Payment (DCEP).

27. Yogita Khatri, *Swiss Startup to Produce "Banknotes" for Marshall Islands' Official Cryptocurrency*, CoinDesk (Jan 29, 2019), https://www.coindesk.com/swiss-startup-to-produce-banknotes-for-marshall-islands-official-cryptocurrency.

Once implemented, DCEP could be a means for sanctioned entities to bypass the US financial system.

Iran

In October 2018, the FinCEN issued guidance that includes information about Iran's use of cryptocurrency and, in particular, its use of cryptocurrency in evading sanctions. The guidance notes that while the Central Bank of Iran has "banned domestic financial institutions from handling decentralized virtual currencies," Iranians can still access cryptocurrencies through exchanges based inside and outside of Iran, as well as through peer-to-peer exchangers.[28] In November 2018, the use of cryptocurrencies to facilitate the exchange of ransomware payments into fiat currency prompted the OFAC to sanction two Iranian cryptocurrency exchangers.[29]

As Iran's ability to leverage cryptocurrency to evade sanctions becomes clearer, it appears that its government is softening its stance toward its citizens' use of cryptocurrencies. The relatively cheap cost of energy in Iran has contributed to the growth of Bitcoin mining operations in the country.[30] In addition, based on information from the most recent report from its central bank, Iran "will not directly restrict anyone from personally holding or transferring small amounts of approved cryptocurrency."[31]

Iran is also exploring the idea of creating its own state-backed cryptocurrency. Iran expects to use a rial-backed token to "facilitate payments between Iranian banks and other Iranian institutions active in the

---

28. U.S. Department of the Treasury, *Advisory on the Iranian Regime's Illicit and Malign Activities and Attempts to Exploit the Financial System*, FinCEN Advisory FIN-2018-A006 (Oct. 11, 2018), https://www.fincen.gov/sites/default/files/advisory/2018-10-11/Iran%20Advisory%20FINAL%20508.pdf.

29. Press Release, U.S. Department of the Treasury, *Treasury Designates Iran-Based Financial Facilitators of Malicious Cyber Activity and for the First Time Identifies Associated Digital Currency Addresses* (Nov. 28, 2018), https://home.treasury.gov/news/press-releases/sm556.

30. Thomas Erdbrink, *How Bitcoin Could Help Iran Undermine U.S. Sanctions*, New York Times (Jan. 29, 2019), https://www.nytimes.com/2019/01/29/world/middleeast/bitcoin-iran-sanctions.html.

31. Leigh Cuen & Stan Higgins, *Iran Could Ban Bitcoin for Payments, Central Bank Report Suggests*, CoinDesk (Jan. 29, 2019), https://www.coindesk.com/iran-could-ban-bitcoin-for-payments-central-bank-report-suggests.

crypto space, and later possibly as an instrument for the Iranian public to pay for local goods and services."[32]

Venezuela

In 2018, the government of Venezuela created a state-sponsored cryptocurrency (the "Petro"). The creation of Petro in the context of US sanctions is illustrated in the following timeline.

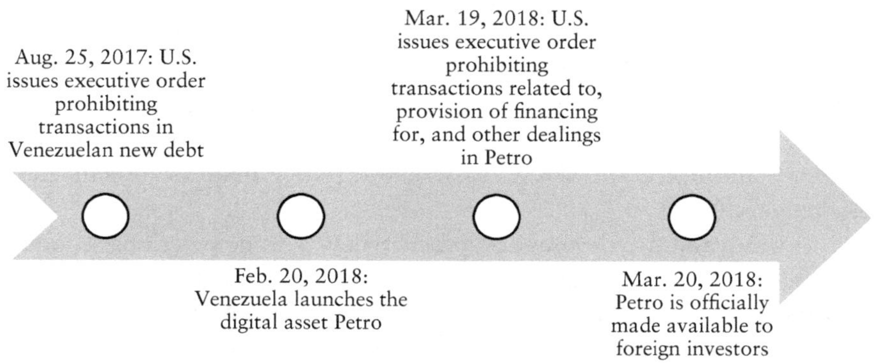

Former Venezuelan President Maduro claims that the Petro is backed by Venezuela's oil reserves and was made available for purchase by foreign investors in euros, dollars, Bitcoin, or Ethereum.[33] While government officials touted the success of Petro, it is unclear whether those assertions were true.[34] According to a Reuters investigation, the Petro "is not sold on any major cryptocurrency exchange . . . [and] [n]o shops are known to accept it."[35]

32. Maziar Motamedi, *Iran Inches Closer to Unveiling State-Backed Cryptocurrency*, Al Jazeera (Jan. 27, 2019), https://www.aljazeera.com/news/2019/01/iran-inches-closer-unveiling-state-backed-cryptocurrency-190127060320571.html.

33. Jack Karsten & Darrell M. West, *Venezuela's "Petro" Undermines Other Cryptocurrencies—And International Sanctions*, Brookings (Mar. 9, 2018), https://www.brookings.edu/blog/techtank/2018/03/09/venezuelas-petro-undermines-other-cryptocurrencies-and-international-sanctions/.

34. Brian Ellsworth, *Special Report: In Venezuela, New Cryptocurrency Is Nowhere to Be Found,* Reuters (Aug. 30, 2018), https://www.reuters.com/article/us-cryptocurrency-venezuela-specialrepor/special-report-in-venezuela-new-cryptocurrency-is-nowhere-to-be-found-idUSKCN1LF15U.

35. *Id.*

Since the launch of the Petro, the US government has taken steps to address Venezuela's use of cryptocurrency to evade US sanctions. On March 11, 2019, OFAC designated Evrofinance Mosnarbank. According to the press release, "Evrofinance emerged as the primary international financial institution willing to finance the Petro. Early investors in the Petro were invited to buy the cryptocurrency by wiring funds to a Venezuelan government account at Evrofinance."[36] In addition, Joselit de la Trinidad Ramirez Camacho, Venezuela's superintendent of cryptocurrency, is currently on the US Immigration and Customs Enforcement's Most Wanted List.[37]

Russia

In the past, Russia appeared hesitant to publicly embrace cryptocurrencies. The Russian Central Bank has issued warnings against the use of cryptocurrencies and expressed relief that the excitement around cryptocurrencies has diminished.[38,39] Privately, however, the Russian government may be more supportive than previously thought. A 2018 report from *TIME* asserted that Venezuela's Petro cryptocurrency was "a half-hidden joint venture between Venezuelan and Russian officials and businessmen, whose aim was to erode the power of US sanctions."[40,41]

---

36. Press Release, U.S. Department of the Treasury, *Treasury Sanctions Russia-Based Bank Attempting to Circumvent U.S. Sanctions on Venezuela* (Mar. 11, 2019), https://home.treasury.gov/news/press-releases/sm622.

37. U.S. Immigration and Customs Enforcement, *Most Wanted: De La Trinidad Ramirez Camacho, Joselit (Wanted for Money Laundering; Sanctions Evasion)*, https://www.ice.gov/most-wanted/de-la-trinidad-ramirez-camacho-joselit.

38. Nikhilesh De, *Russian Central Bank Issues New Warning Against Cryptocurrencies*, CoinDesk (Nov. 29, 2017), https://www.coindesk.com/russian-central-bank-issues-new-warning-against-cryptocurrencies.

39. Ana Berman, *"Cryptocurrency Fever" Has Begun to Diminish, Russian Central Bank Head Says*, Cointelegraph (Oct. 18, 2018), https://cointelegraph.com/news/cryptocurrency-fever-has-begun-to-diminish-russian-central-bank-head-says.

40. Simon Shuster, *Exclusive: Russia Secretly Helped Venezuela Launch a Cryptocurrency to Evade U.S. Sanctions*, TIME (Mar. 20, 2018), http://time.com/5206835/exclusive-russia-petro-venezuela-cryptocurrency/.

41. Press Release, U.S. Department of the Treasury, *Treasury Sanctions Russia-Based Bank Attempting to Circumvent U.S. Sanctions on Venezuela* (Mar. 11, 2019), https://home.treasury.gov/news/press-releases/sm622.

More recently, it appears that Russia's public approach to cryptocurrencies is softening. It has been reported that the central deposit for the Moscow Exchange "is developing a blockchain platform to provide deposit and settlement services for digital assets and cryptocurrencies. . . . The platform would enable Russia's National Settlement Depository, a non-bank financial institution that provides securities depository and settlement services, to issue a cryptocurrency and cryptocurrency wallet, available for banks, pension funds, and retail investors, that would also enable the exchange of those assets for fiat currencies."[42] In January 2019, Bitcoinist.com reported that the Russian government may begin investing in Bitcoin as a way to reduce its dependence on the US dollar and to avoid US sanctions.[43]

In July 2020, Russia passed a law that establishes cryptocurrencies as "assets [that] can be sold, purchased, exchanged, and pledged. The law, however, which came into effect on January 1, 2021, does not permit cryptocurrency to be used as a means of payment."[44]

North Korea

North Korea's strategy is focused primarily on leveraging its cyber capabilities to obtain various cryptocurrencies. Its known activities include the following:

- Hacking cryptocurrency exchanges
- Launching ransomware attacks
- Mining cryptocurrency

North Korean state actors have repeatedly been identified as responsible for hacking cryptocurrency exchanges. The first known attack against a South Korean exchange occurred in 2017, when state-backed

---

42. Wolfie Zhao, *Russia's Central Depository Plans to Build Its Own Cryptocurrency Wallet*, CoinDesk (Aug. 11, 2017), https://www.coindesk.com/russias-central-depository-plans-build-cryptocurrency-wallet (last updated: Oct. 24, 2017).

43. Osato Avan-Nomayo, *Russia Plans to Ditch US Dollar for Bitcoin, Says University Professor*, Bitcoinist.com (Jan. 8, 2019), https://bitcoinist.com/russia-ditch-usd-bitcoin-prof/.

44. Kevin Helms, *Putin Signs Law Giving Cryptocurrency Legal Status in Russia*, Bitcoin.com (Aug. 2, 2020), https://news.bitcoin.com/putin-signs-law-cryptocurrency-legal-russia/.

North Korean actors stole $7 million from Bithumb.[45] Since then, North Korea has been identified as the culprit in additional attacks on South Korean cryptocurrency exchanges.[46]

North Korea has also been active in developing ransomware. Ransomware "blocks access to a computer or its data and demands money to release it."[47] The WannaCry ransomware attack demanded payment in the form of Bitcoin. WannaCry was particularly successful, and victims included the National Health Service in the United Kingdom.[48] On December 19, 2017, the United States attributed the WannaCry attack to North Korea.[49] In September 2018, the United States filed criminal charges against Park Jin Hyok, a member of the North Korean–sponsored Lazarus Group, for his involvement in multiple ransomware-related attacks.[50] Since then, Lazarus Group has been implicated in a range of criminal activity relating to cryptocurrency. On February 17, 2021, the US Department of Justice (DOJ) announced the unsealing of a federal indictment that charged three North Korean programmers with ties to Lazarus Group for their role in a criminal conspiracy that included multiple cyberattacks, schemes to steal or extort money and cryptocurrency from banks and other businesses, creation of malicious cryptocurrency

---

45. Juan Andres Guerrero-Saade & Priscilla Moriuchi, *North Korea Targeted South Korean Cryptocurrency Users and Exchange in Late 2017 Campaign*, Recorded Future (Jan. 16, 2018), https://www.recordedfuture.com/north-korea-cryptocurrency-campaign/.

46. Rhett Jones, *North Korea Is Main Suspect in Ruinous Hack of South Korean Bitcoin Exchange*, Gizmodo (Dec. 21, 2017), https://gizmodo.com/north-korea-is-main-suspect-in-ruinous-hack-of-south-ko-1821498942.

47. Alex Hern & Samuel Gibbs, *What Is WannaCry Ransomware and Why Is It Attacking Global Computers?* The Guardian (May 12, 2017), https://www.theguardian.com/technology/2017/may/12/nhs-ransomware-cyber-attack-what-is-wanacrypt0r-20.

48. *Id.*

49. The White House, *Press Briefing on the Attribution of the WannaCry Malware Attack to North Korea* (Dec. 19, 2017, 9:09 AM EST), https://kr.usembassy.gov/121917-press-briefing-attribution-wannacry-malware-attack-north-korea/.

50. Press Release, U.S. Department of Justice, *North Korean Regime-Backed Programmer Charged with Conspiracy to Conduct Multiple Cyber Attacks and Intrusions* (Sep. 6, 2018), https://www.justice.gov/opa/pr/north-korean-regime-backed-programmer-charged-conspiracy-conduct-multiple-cyber-attacks-and.

applications,[51] and development and marketing of a fraudulent blockchain platform designed to evade US sanctions.[52]

North Korea actively uses its cyber capabilities to mine cryptocurrencies. In 2017, North Korean state actors hacked a South Korean server and used it to mine Monero.[53]

REGULATORY REGIME GUIDANCE

OFAC requires that institutions abide by the laws that it administers, but it does not have specific requirements regarding what, if any, type of sanctions compliance program institutions must implement. It will take into consideration, however, "the existence, nature and adequacy" of a subject's sanctions compliance program when determining the appropriate response to a sanctions violation.[54]

OFAC has provided guidance in which it defines key terms relating to digital assets and clearly asserts that organizational and individual sanctions compliance obligations extend to cryptocurrency activity. The guidance states that the agency will consider cryptocurrency addresses as identifiers on the SDN list, and that blocking and reporting requirements are the same for cryptocurrency transactions as they are for fiat transactions. In addition, if an organization or individual identifies other associated identifiers, the organization should share that information with OFAC. To comply with these requirements, organizations should review

---

51. The same day the DOJ announced the unsealed indictment, the Federal Bureau of Investigation, the Cybersecurity and Infrastructure Security Agency, and the Department of Treasury issued a Joint Cybersecurity Advisory in which they warned the public of malware, which it refers to as "Apple Jeus," to facilitate cybersecurity theft. *See* Joint Cybersecurity Advisory, *AppleJeus: Analysis of North Korea's Cryptocurrency Malware* (Feb. 17, 2021), https://us-cert.cisa.gov/sites/default/files/publications/Joint_Cybersecurity_Advisory_AppleJeus%E2%80%93Analysis%20of%20North%20Korea%E2%80%99s%20Cryptocurrency%20Malware.pdf.

52. Press Release, U.S. Department of Justice, U.S. Attorney's Office, Central District of California, *3 North Korean Military Hackers Indicted in Wide-Ranging Scheme to Commit Cyberattacks and Financial Crimes Across the Globe* (Feb. 17, 2021), https://www.justice.gov/usao-cdca/pr/3-north-korean-military-hackers-indicted-wide-ranging-scheme-commit-cyberattacks-and.

53. Sam Kim, *North Korean Hackers Hijack Computers to Mine Cryptocurrencies*, Bloomberg (Jan. 1, 2018), https://www.bloomberg.com/news/articles/2018-01-02/north-korean-hackers-hijack-computers-to-mine-cryptocurrencies.

54. 31 C.F.R. § 501, Appx. A (2009).

their screening systems and reporting procedures to ensure appropriate coverage of cryptocurrency activity.[55]

On October 8, 2020, the DOJ's Office of the Deputy Attorney General's Cyber-Digital Task Force published *Cryptocurrency: An Enforcement Framework*.[56] The framework highlights the emerging criminal and national security threat that cryptocurrency use poses to the United States, including cryptocurrencies' potential use in evading sanctions. In addition to presenting the current cryptocurrency regulatory landscape, the framework identifies the types of business models and activities that may facilitate cryptocurrency-related criminal activity as well as strategies that DOJ expects to deploy in response.

Also in October 2020, OFAC issued an Advisory Notice highlighting sanctions compliance risks associated with ransomware payments involving malicious cyber-enabled activities. OFAC has designated numerous malicious cyber actors under its cyber-related sanctions program and other sanctions programs, including perpetrators of ransomware attacks and those who facilitate ransomware transactions. Ransomware payments with a sanctions nexus threaten US national security interests; as a result, facilitating ransomware payments on behalf of a victim may violate OFAC regulations.

Finally, on October 15, 2021, OFAC published compliance guidance for the virtual currency industry.[57] This guidance, which acknowledges the prominent role that virtual currencies play in the global economy and in payments, consolidates OFAC's previous guidance in this area (e.g., FAQs, enforcement actions, and other statements) and details regulatory expectations for sanctions compliance in the virtual currency industry.

Enforcement Actions

On December 30, 2020, OFAC announced a settlement with BitGo for 183 apparent violations of multiple sanctions programs. According to

55. U.S. Department of the Treasury, *OFAC Frequently Asked Questions: Sanctions Compliance*, Questions 559–63, 594, 646–47, https://www.treasury.gov/resource-center/faqs/Sanctions/Pages/faq_compliance.aspx#reports (last visited May 6, 2019).

56. Press Release, U.S. Department of Justice, *Attorney General William P. Barr Announces Publication of Cryptocurrency Enforcement Framework* (Oct. 8, 2020), https://www.justice.gov/opa/pr/attorney-general-william-p-barr-announces-publication-cryptocurrency-enforcement-framework.

57. U.S. Department of the Treasury, *Sanctions Compliance Guidance for the Virtual Currency Industry* (Oct. 15, 2021), *https://home.treasury.gov/system/files/126/virtual_currency_guidance_brochure.pdf.*

the enforcement release, BitGo tracked its users' IP addresses for security purposes related to account logins but did not use this information for sanctions compliance purposes. As a result, OFAC found that BitGo had "failed to prevent persons apparently located in the Crimea region of Ukraine, Cuba, Iran, Sudan, and Syria from using its non-custodial secure digital wallet management service."[58]

On February 18, 2021, OFAC announced a settlement with BitPay, Inc., for 2,102 apparent violations of multiple sanctions programs. BitPay is a digital currency payment processing solution for merchants. According to OFAC's enforcement release, BitPay had failed to conduct appropriate due diligence, including analyzing IP addresses and other location data, for its merchants' buyers. As a result, OFAC determined that BitPay had facilitated payments for buyers from sanctioned locations, including Crimea, Cuba, North Korea, Iran, Sudan, and Syria.[59]

Cryptocurrency Addresses as Identifiers

In November 2018, OFAC for the first time listed two cryptocurrency addresses as identifiers associated with individuals added to the SDN list. According to the OFAC press release, the two individuals added to the OFAC list, Mohammad GHORBANIYAN and Ali KHORASHADIZADEH, were responsible for exchanging the proceeds of a ransomware attack called SamSam into Iranian rial and depositing the rial into Iranian banks. To facilitate the exchange, the two individuals processed over 7,000 transactions through two cryptocurrency addresses.

The OFAC individuals added to the OFAC list are copied as follows (associated cryptocurrency addresses are bolded and underlined):

1. GHORBANIYAN, Mohammad (a.k.a. GHORBANIAN, Mohammad; a.k.a. "EnExchanger"; a.k.a. "Ensaniyat"; a.k.a. "Ensaniyat_Exchanger"), Iran; DOB 09 Mar 1987; POB Tehran, Iran; nationality Iran; Website www.enexchanger.com;

58. Enforcement Release, U.S. Department of the Treasury, *OFAC Enters Into $98,830 Settlement with BitGo, Inc. for Apparent Violations of Multiple Sanctions Programs Related to Digital Currency Transactions* (Dec. 30, 2020), https://home.treasury.gov/system/files/126/20201230_bitgo.pdf.

59. Enforcement Release, U.S. Department of the Treasury, *OFAC Enters Into $507,375 Settlement with BitPay, Inc. for Apparent Violations of Multiple Sanctions Programs Related to Digital Currency Transactions* (Feb. 18, 2021), https://home.treasury.gov/system/files/126/20210218_bp.pdf.

Email Address EnExchanger@gmail.com; alt. Email Address Ensaniyat1365@gmail.com; Additional Sanctions Information—Subject to Secondary Sanctions; Gender Male; **Digital Currency Address—XBT 1AjZPMsnmpdK2Rv9KQNfMurTXinscVro9V;** Identification Number 008-046347-9 (Iran); Birth Certificate Number 32270 (Iran) (individual) [CYBER2].

2. KHORASHADIZADEH, Ali (a.k.a. "Iranvisacart"; a.k.a. "Mastercartaria"), Iran; DOB 21 Sep 1979; POB Tehran, Iran; nationality Iran; Email Address iranvisacart@yahoo.com; alt. Email Address mastercartaria@yahoo.com; alt. Email Address alikhorashadi@yahoo.com; alt. Email Address toppglasses@gmail.com; alt. Email Address iranian_boy5@yahoo.com; Additional Sanctions Information—Subject to Secondary Sanctions; Gender Male; **Digital Currency Address—XBT 149w62rY42aZBox8fGcmqNsXUzSSt-Keq8C;** Passport T14553558 (Iran) issued 28 Oct 2008 expires 29 Oct 2013 (individual) [CYBER2].

Since 2018, OFAC has continued to list cryptocurrency addresses as identifiers for designated individuals and to target individuals that use cryptocurrencies to launder proceeds of illegal activity.[60]

STRATEGIES FOR COMPLIANCE

To avoid becoming the subject of an enforcement action, it is imperative that US organizations utilizing or otherwise involved with cryptocurrencies build and maintain a robust sanctions program that includes the following:

- Screening of all customers, including beneficial owners of entities, during the onboarding process and on a periodic and ongoing basis
- Documenting, implementing, and maintaining procedures and internal controls necessary to detect and prevent sanctions violations
- Reporting any sanctions-related violations, attempted sanctions violations, or attempts to circumvent sanctions to OFAC

60. Press Release, U.S. Department of the Treasury, *Treasury Targets Chinese Persons Involved with Drug Trafficking Organization Moving Fentanyl* (July 17, 2020), https://home.treasury.gov/news/press-releases/sm1063.

This section explores strategies for building and maintaining a robust sanctions program.

Risk Assessment

Institutions should conduct or update an OFAC risk assessment to identify how cryptocurrencies may impact the organization's risk for sanctions violations. When conducting a risk assessment, it is important to understand the types of cryptocurrency actors and how they may interact with your own institution. Common cryptocurrency actors include the following:

- Administrator—". . . a person engaged as a business in issuing (putting into circulation) a virtual currency, and who has the authority to redeem (to withdraw from circulation) such virtual currency"[61]
- Miner—an entity or individual that is generating income by selling newly minted digital assets
- Exchanger—". . . a person engaged as a business in the exchange of virtual currency for real currency, funds, or other virtual currency"[62]
- Mixer—an entity or individual generating income by charging commissions to obscure the source of digital assets

Know Your Customer Assessment and Update

It may be necessary to conduct a know your customer (KYC) refresh to include additional information related to cryptocurrency activity. In addition, institutions should update their KYC procedures to ensure that the additional information is captured in the future. Additional information they should consider capturing includes the following:

- Wallet addresses
- IP addresses

---

61. U.S. Department of the Treasury, *Application of FinCEN's Regulations to Persons Administering, Exchanging, or Using Virtual Currencies*, FinCEN Guidance FIN-2013-G001 (Mar. 18, 2013), https://www.fincen.gov/sites/default/files/shared/FIN-2013-G001.pdf.

62. *Id.*

- Expected cryptocurrency activity, including types of cryptocurrencies expected to be used
- Expected counterparties

Transaction Screening and Surveillance

An institution must ensure that its filter technology solution is capable of alerting on cryptocurrency-related identifiers. An institution should also be proactive in using blockchains to analyze patterns behind how sanctioned entities use digital assets. Technology marketed by detection solution providers can trace activity by individual wallet addresses to identify activity obscured by mixers and tumblers and to identify wallet addresses with potential sanctions exposure. Any blockchain analysis should be incorporated into policies, procedures, and training.

Training

Institutions should periodically conduct training related to cryptocurrencies. Training topics should include the following:

- Characteristics of cryptocurrencies and their susceptibility to sanctions risks
- Sanctions evasion typologies unique to cryptocurrencies
- Reinforcement of reporting requirements for sanctions-related violations that may include cryptocurrencies
- Regulator guidance and industry best practices related to cryptocurrencies

CONCLUSION

The use of cryptocurrency, especially by rogue nations, presents an ongoing sanctions threat. This threat is constantly evolving and requires a focused effort from governments and corporations to ensure that this new type of currency is not used for illicit or sanctioned purposes.

8 | Selected Issues in Litigation

Michael Fluhr and Deborah Meshulam

INTRODUCTION

As discussed in the beginning of this book, blockchain technology is merely a medium. A particular blockchain use may implicate any number of laws, regulations, or types of litigation. In other chapters, we have set forth the regulatory schemes and related litigation most commonly applied to blockchain technology. But while these are the legal regimes most commonly applied to blockchain technology, they are not exclusive. In this section, we survey a number of cases involving application of existing laws to blockchain technology. The purpose and content of this chapter is not a comprehensive or necessarily cohesive treatment of blockchain technology in litigation, rather it is a sample of some of the more interesting litigation issues that concern blockchain technology.

FRAUD, CONVERSION, AND MISAPPROPRIATION OF TRADE SECRETS

I am Nakamoto: *Kleiman v. Wright*, No. 18-cv-80176 (S.D. Fla.)

As discussed in Chapter 1 the true identity of Bitcoin inventor Satoshi Nakamoto remains unknown. Many candidates have been proposed but none confirmed. Probably the most well-known candidates, albeit self-identified and of dubious reliability, are the duo David Kleiman (now deceased) and Craig Wright.

In 2018, the Estate of Kleiman filed suit against Wright in the US District Court for the Southern District of Florida, alleging that in 2008 the duo created Bitcoin under the pseudonym Satoshi Nakamoto.[1] According to the operative Second Amended Complaint, between 2008 and before Kleiman's death in April 2013, the two allegedly worked together on Bitcoin, including through a company called W&K Info Defense Research LLC that they had created, mining coins and developing certain blockchain-related intellectual property.[2] During this period, they allegedly mined significant amounts of Bitcoin.[3] Plaintiffs Kleiman and W&K alleged that Wright perpetrated a complicated, extended fraudulent scheme to appropriate plaintiffs' Bitcoin.[4] The scheme included Wright's alleged production of fraudulent documents and forging of Kleiman's signatures on documents to purportedly show transfer of Bitcoin to Wright.[5] Based on these allegations, Kleiman's Estate and W&K asserted claims against Wright for various causes of action, including conversion, unjust enrichment, misappropriation, and trade secret theft.[6] Trial concluded in December 2021, with a jury finding Wright liable on only the conversion claim and awarding W&K $100 million.

Outside of trial, the possibility that Craig Wright and Ira Kleiman actually invented Bitcoin has been fiercely debated. On December 8, 2015, *Wired* published an article posing whether Wright might be Nakamoto.[7] When published, *Wired* reported that "the strongest evidence yet of Satoshi Nakamoto's true identity . . . point[s] to Craig Steven Wright."[8] *Wired* claimed that "either Wright invented bitcoin, or he's a brilliant hoaxer who very badly wants us to believe he did."[9] The evidence cited included an August 2008 post on Wright's blog mentioning his intention to release a "cryptocurrency paper," a leaked July 2008 email from Wright

1. Kleiman v. Wright, No. 18-cv-80176, 2020 WL 5632654, at *2 (S.D. Fla. Sep. 21, 2020) (adjudicating cross-motions for summary judgment).

2. *Id.*

3. *Id.*

4. *Id.*

5. *Id.*

6. *Id.*

7. Andy Greenberg & Gwern Branwen, *Is Bitcoin's Creator This Unknown Australian Genius? Probably Not*, Wired (Dec. 12, 2015), https://www.wired.com/2015/12/bitcoins-creator-satoshi-nakamoto-is-probably-this-unknown-australian-genius (last visited Mar. 6, 2021).

8. *Id.*

9. *Id.*

to his lawyer in which Wright imagines a "P2P distributed ledger," an anticipated paper called "Electronic Cash Without a Trusted Third Party," and an email to David Kleiman before Bitcoin's January 2009 launch to discuss a paper they had been working on together.[10] But *Wired* also noted problems, inconsistencies, and red flags in Wright's story. *Wired* subsequently updated the piece to note the fraudulent nature of certain evidence offered and clarify that the magazine "no longer believes Wright is likely to be the creator of Bitcoin."[11]

After the trial, Dr. Wright's lawyers issued a statement asserting that the jury verdict reinforces the view that Dr. Wright is the sole creator of Bitcoin and blockchain technology. The lawyers for the other side asserted that the verdict was a great win for the Kleinman estate and for justice.[12] Ultimately, however, the origins of Bitcoin remain a mystery. The trial in *Kleiman v. Wright* may be more entertaining than enlightening.

The Fall of Mt. Gox

In 2011, Mark Karpeles, a programmer and Bitcoin enthusiast,[13] purchased the Mt. Gox website mtgox.com, rewrote its software, and turned Mt. Gox into the world's most popular and highly trusted Bitcoin trading platform.[14] Behind the scenes, however, the infrastructure was crumbling. Insiders reported a host of shoddy software development practices.[15] By fall 2013, US federal agents had seized $5 million from the company because it had failed to register as a money transmitter.[16] It was being sued for $75 million by former business partner CoinLab.[17] And customers were experiencing substantial delays withdrawing currency from the platform.[18]

---

10. *Id.*

11. *Id.*

12. https://www.zdnet.com/article/craig-wright-to-pay-100-million-in-kleiman-v-wright-56b-case/

13. *Id.*

14. *Id.*

15. *Id.*

16. *Id.*

17. *Id.*

18. *Id.*

The issues came to a head in February 2014, when a leaked Mt. Gox document revealed that hackers had been skimming money from the company for years and that the company was missing 850,000 Bitcoins, then worth nearly half a billion dollars.[19] On February 28, 2014, Mt. Gox filed for a form of bankruptcy protection in Tokyo, claiming that it had liabilities of approximately $65 million against $38 million in assets.[20]

As expected, a raft of litigation followed. Several Mt. Gox customers filed class actions against both Karpeles and against a bank that had processed fiat currency wire transfers to and from Mt. Gox accounts and held custody of the underlying fiat deposits in those accounts.[21] Plaintiffs alleged that the bank had facilitated Karpeles's fraud and wrongfully failed to process fiat withdrawals from customer accounts.[22]

The bank had a number of successes in these cases, defeating class certification and prevailing on motions to dismiss for lack of personal jurisdiction. In contrast, Karpeles enjoyed less success. Courts have denied his motions to dismiss for lack of personal jurisdiction, reasoning that Karpeles generally targeted individuals throughout the United States and that Mt. Gox had thousands of users in Illinois specifically.

Several of these cases remain active. As a platform, Mt. Gox is defunct now but remains a cautionary tale for those selecting a trading platform or custodian of cryptocurrency.

BLOCKCHAIN AND TRADEMARK

As more new businesses and ventures enter the blockchain space, there has been a land grab for trade names. This has given rise to some interesting trademark disputes.

---

19. *Id.*

20. *See* Yoshifumi Takemoto & Sophie Knight, *Mt. Gox Files for Bankruptcy, Hit with Lawsuit*, Reuters (Feb. 28, 2014), https://www.reuters.com/article/bitcoin-mtgox-bankrtupcy-idUSL3N0LX36C20140228.

21. *See* Greene v. Mizuho Bank, Ltd., 169 F. Supp. 3d 855 (N.D. Ill 2016) (describing involvement of Mizuho Bank, Ltd.); *see also* Lack v. Mizuho Bank, No. 18-cv-617, 2018 WL 5906849 (C.D. Cal. June 19, 2018); Pearce v. Mizuho Bank, Ltd., No. 18-306, 2018 WL 4094812 (E.D. Pa. Aug. 27, 2018); Babiak v. Mizuho Bank, Ltd., No. 18-cv-352, 2018 WL 4473584 (E.D. Va. Sept. 17, 2018); Carmel v. Mizuho Bank, Ltd., No. 18-2483, 2018 WL 6981840 (C.D. Cal. Nov. 13, 2018).

22. *See Greene*, 169 F. Supp. 3d at 858–59.

Trademarks are words, names, symbols, devices, or combinations thereof used by a manufacturer or merchant to identify the source of products and distinguish them from those manufactured or sold by others.[23] A trademark owner can prevent others from using an identical or similar mark in certain situations. To obtain ownership of a trademark and the accompanying legal protection, one must actually use the mark in commerce.[24]

Trademark law protects only against "use" in commerce. Courts have addressed the issue of whether a token issuer has "used" the token name in commerce so as to qualify for trademark protection. This issue arose in a recent case involving Telegram. Telegram had begun creating a new blockchain network called TON and in 2017 adopted the name "Gram" for its native token.[25] At roughly the same time, on September 18, 2018, a company called Lantah announced on its website an intention to sell a token also called Gram.[26] In January 2018, Telegram began entering into purchase agreements with persons and firms who paid money in exchange for the right to receive Grams when the TON blockchain launched.[27] Then on March 9, 2018, Lantah sold its Gram tokens.[28] Telegram believed that its use of the name Gram preceded Lantah's and sued Lantah in the Northern District of California for trademark infringement.[29] On Telegram's motion, the court preliminarily enjoined Lantah from using the Gram mark, holding that Telegram was likely to succeed on the merits of its trademark claims.[30] Responding to Lantah's claim that Telegram's sale of contracts for future token distribution did not constitute use of the tokens in commerce, the court acknowledged that preliminary steps do not constitute such use.[31] Nevertheless, the court held that Telegram's contract for future distribution of Grams was

23. *See, e.g.*, Bd. of Supervisors for Louisiana State Univ. Agric. & Mech. Coll. V. Smack Apparel Co., 550 F.3d 465, 475 (5th Cir. 2008).

24. *See, e.g.*, Telegram Messenger Inc. v. Lantah, LLC, No. 18-cv-2811, 2018 WL 3753748, at *3 (N.D. Cal. Aug. 8, 2018).

25. *Lantah*, 2018 WL 3753748, at *1.

26. *Id.*

27. *Id.* at *2.

28. *Id.*

29. *Id.*

30. *Id.* at *3–6.

31. *Id.*

akin to the taking of an order prior to fulfillment, which courts in other contexts had held to constitute use in commerce.[32]

The Southern District of New York addressed a similar question in *Alibaba Group Holding Limited v. Alibabacoin Foundation.*[33] In that case, plaintiff Alibaba Group sued Alibabacoin Foundation and other related companies (collectively, "Alibabacoin"), asserting claims sounding in trademark infringement based on Alibabacoin's creation of a cryptocurrency called Alibabacoin, which would purportedly function as currency for an online marketplace.[34] Defending a motion for preliminary injunction, Alibabacoin argued that it had only sold the coin to private investors, had not actually sold the token publicly or listed it on a public exchange, and thus had not used it in commerce.[35] The court rejected this argument, holding that Alibabacoin had failed to explain why its private sales (through "initial coin offerings") did not constitute sales in commerce.[36]

Another issue that has arisen is whether a trade name using common blockchain terminology can be "distinctive" and thus eligible for trademark protection. The Southern District of New York considered this question in *Blockchain Luxembourg S.A. v. Paymium, SAS.*[37] Plaintiffs (collectively "BLK") purported to be a leading provider of various digital currency services, including wallet services, mobile application services, web services, and suite services.[38] BLK claimed ownership in a number of word marks, including BLOCKCHAIN, BLOCKCHAIN.INFO, BLOCKCHAIN.COM, BLOCKCHAIN MERCHANT, BLOCKCHAIN PRINCIPAL STRATEGIES, BLOCKCHAIN COMPASS FUND, and BLOCKCHAIN ASCENT FUND, as well as in a design mark comprising the word BLOCKCHAIN.[39] Defendant Paymium announced it

---

32. *Id.* at *5–6.

33. No. 18-cv-2897, 2018 WL 2022626 (S.D.N.Y. Apr. 30, 2018).

34. *Id.* at *1.

35. *Id.* at *3.

36. *Id.* Alibabacoin made this argument in the context of a motion to dismiss for lack of subject-matter jurisdiction. *Id.* at *2–3. The court appropriately rejected this argument on the independent ground that the "use in commerce" requirement is an element of the claim but not a jurisdictional requirement. *Id.*

37. No. 18-cv-8612, 2019 WL 4199902 (S.D.N.Y. Aug. 7, 2019).

38. *Id.* at *1–2.

39. *Id.* Word marks protect only the actual characters against identical or similar infringement use while design marks incorporate protection for the look and feel of a logo, which may or may not incorporate words in it.

would launch www.blockchain.io as a new platform for certain digital currency services under the word mark BLOCKCHAIN.IO and under a design mark incorporating that text string.[40] BLK filed suit alleging various claims of infringement upon its various marks.[41] Paymium moved to dismiss, arguing, among other things, that by using the term BLOCKCHAIN, BLK's marks were merely descriptive of the services it provided and thus not entitled to trademark protection.[42] The court denied Paymium's motion, holding that BLK had adequately alleged that the marks were inherently distinctive and that even if they were only descriptive, BLK had alleged sufficient examples of public use of its marks to allow a factfinder to find they had acquired secondary meaning.[43] As of early 2021, the case remains pending.

As blockchain businesses mature and terminology standardizes, additional disputes over the distinctiveness and protectability of various names can be expected.

CONTRACT ISSUES: FORKED CURRENCIES

Currency "forks" present interesting issues concerning property ownership that have arisen in at least two cases. A fork can be created by modifying the software used by a currency's miners and users and publicly distributing the modified versions to anyone who wants to use or help operate the forked currency.[44] Holders of the preforked currency can then initiate transfers of amounts held in their account prefork through the new, forked blockchain, through a continuation of the

40. *Id.* at *2.

41. *Id.* at *3.

42. *Id.* at *5. Marks that are merely "descriptive" of underlying services and do not require an inferential leap to connect the mark with the service are not distinctive and do not receive trademark protection, unless they have achieved "secondary meaning" in the marketplace (i.e., a particular association in the marketplace between the mark and the product). *See id.* at *6. In contrast, marks that are "suggestive" of underlying service with such an inferential leap are distinctive. *See id.* The location of the line between descriptive and suggestive generates much legal dispute, particularly as courts may be reluctant to resolve it on a motion to dismiss. *See id.* at *6.

43. *See id.* at *5–7.

44. *See, e.g.*, Zack Voell, *Bitcoin's Forks Have Trounced Bitcoin This Year*, COINDESK (June 8, 2020), https://www.coindesk.com/returns-for-bitcoins-forks-have-trounced-bitcoin-this-year.

original blockchain, or both. In practical terms, after a fork an account password-holder can theoretically access the prefork amount of both the original currency and the forked currency, the two, forked blockchains now operating wholly independently. While there are examples of widely adopted cryptocurrency forks,[45] forks are relatively easy to initiate and can occur at any time with varying levels of publicity or secrecy,[46] so many if not the majority of forks will go unknown and unnoticed.

As many cryptocurrency holders buy and store currencies on exchanges or other trading platforms, a question has arisen as to the obligation of those trading platforms to provide access to any or all forks.

In at least two cases, courts have held that the issue is governed by the contract between the user and trading platform and have rejected a per se entitlement to forked currencies. In *BDI Capital, LLC v. Bulbul Investments LLC*, plaintiff BDI Capital had a certain amount of Bitcoin held in an account with cryptocurrency exchange CampBX.[47] CampBX closed and, after some back and forth, returned all custodied Bitcoin to BDI.[48] But BDI contended that CampBX unlawfully retained certain Bitcoin forked currencies and sued CampBX for violation of the Commodities Exchange Act and various state laws.[49] On summary judgment, the court dismissed BDI's claims for entitlement to forked currencies.[50] The court reasoned that accessing each new forked currency would require an exchange, such as CampBX, to download and integrate into its software stack the new, modified software and that this would impose "a major new duty on all cryptocurrency exchanges operating in Georgia to affirmatively honor every single bitcoin fork."[51]

Relying on *BDI*, the California First District Court of Appeal reached a similar conclusion in *Archer v. Coinbase, Inc.*[52] Plaintiff Darrell Archer

45. *See, e.g.*, *Asset Directory*, Coinbase, https://help.coinbase.com/en/supported-crypto (last visited Dec. 12, 2021) (exchange Coinbase listing several major forked currencies for trading, including Bitcoin Cash ["BCH"] and Bitcoin Satoshi Vision ["BSV"]).

46. *See* Jordan Baczuk, *How to Fork Bitcoin—Part 1*, Medium (May 24, 2019), https://www.medium.com/@jordan.baczuk/how-to-fork-bitcoin-part-1-397598ef7e66.

47. BDI Capital, LLC v. Bulbul Inv. LLC, 446 F. Supp. 3d 1127, 1131 (N.D. Ga. 2020).

48. *Id.* at 1131–34.

49. *Id.* at 1131–34.

50. *Id.* at 1138–41.

51. *Id.*

52. 53 Cal. App. 5th 266 (2020).

had 350 Bitcoin in an account with trading platform Coinbase when on October 23, 2017, a forked currency called Bitcoin Gold was released.[53] Coinbase had previously evaluated the anticipated Bitcoin Gold fork and notified its customers it would not support withdrawals of the forked currency, citing security concerns.[54] Coinbase's concerns proved prescient; in 2018, the Bitcoin Gold network was attacked by hackers who stole millions of dollars in the currency from trading platforms and others on the network.[55] Nevertheless, Archer sued Coinbase for breach of contract, negligence, and conversion.[56] The trial court dismissed Archer's claims on summary judgment, and on appeal the First District Court of Appeal affirmed.[57] The court reasoned that Coinbase's obligations were governed by the user agreement between the parties, and Archer had failed to identify a breached provision thereof.[58]

Both *BDI* and *Archer* rested heavily on the contractual obligations between the parties. Trading platforms and other custodians typically make quite clear that they have no obligation to provide access to forked currencies, so where such custodians are concerned, the issue may already be firmly resolved. Perhaps a more interesting question will arise where the custodian and accountholder have no such express agreement, as this may raise deeper issues of property ownership in the context of blockchain-based assets.

ANONYMITY ON THE BLOCKCHAIN

One of the touted benefits of public blockchains as payment systems is anonymity.[59] The blockchain contains only account numbers (public addresses) and payment records.[60] There is no direct way to determine who owns or controls each account. But in practice, the privacy afforded by public blockchains has limitations. In some limited set of

53. *Id.* at 269.

54. *Id.* at 270.

55. *Id.*

56. *Id.*

57. *Id.* at 279.

58. *Id.* at 272–79.

59. *See* Satoshi Nakamoto, *Bitcoin: A Peer-to-Peer Electronic Cash System*, WWW.BITCOIN.ORG, https://www.bitcoin.org/bitcoin.pdf.

60. *Id.*

circumstances, there are ways to tie the "on-chain" anonymous information to the account owner's "off-chain" identifying information, and there are businesses that specialize in this sort of investigation. Also, if an individual wants to transact in cryptocurrency through an exchange or other trading platform, they will have to submit to that entity a variety of identifying information for anti–money laundering and other compliance purposes.[61]

The privacy that blockchains attempt to provide has been addressed in several cases, such as *United States v. Gratkowski*.[62] In *Gratkowski*, federal agents identified a number of Bitcoin addresses controlled by a website containing child pornography.[63] The agents served a subpoena on a cryptocurrency trading platform for information about customers whose accounts had sent Bitcoin to any account controlled by the website, and defendant Richard Gratkowski was identified as such a customer.[64] Gratkowski was charged with receipt and access of child pornography.[65] He moved to suppress the evidence obtained through the subpoena as an illegal search in violation of the Fourth Amendment, but the district court denied the motion, and the Fifth Circuit affirmed.[66] The court analogized Gratkowski's account information on the cryptocurrency trading platform to bank records, which the Supreme Court had held lacked an expectation of privacy as records exposed to financial institution employees in the ordinary course of business.[67] The court also reasoned that any information on the Bitcoin blockchain was public and thus not subject to any privacy interest.[68]

A related issue has arisen multiple times in another context: class certification. To obtain certification of a class, a plaintiff must show, among other things, that the proposed class is "readily ascertainable" and specifically that "there is a reliable and administratively feasible mechanism for determining whether putative class members fall within

61. *See* Chapter 6.

62. 964 F.3d 307 (5th Cir. 2020).

63. *Id.* at 309.

64. *Id.*

65. *Id.*

66. *Id.*

67. *Id.* at 311.

68. *Id.*

the class definition."[69] Several courts have held that public blockchains may provide assistance in this process. In *Balestra v. Cloud With Me*, named plaintiffs sued defendants on behalf of a class that allegedly purchased unregistered security tokens called CLD from defendants during the class period.[70] Class members allegedly purchased CLD with Bitcoin, Ethereum, and other virtual currencies.[71] On plaintiffs' unopposed motion for class certification (defendants did not appear), the court held that the class members were ascertainable because, among other things, "there is publicly-available information through public blockchains for cryptocurrencies invested."[72] The court also reasoned that "investor trading records and records from virtual currency exchanges may provide an adequate method of identifying members."[73] This result raises some questions and possibly concerns not addressed in the opinion, likely because the motion was unopposed. Without records from defendants, how would the court or plaintiffs identify the Bitcoin, Ethereum, or other addresses used to purchase CLD or the owners of such addresses? The court made reference to a "Token Purchase Certificate" that each investor received but did not explain how these could be used to identify investor class members.[74]

Another court was more skeptical of a similar motion for class certification, raising exactly these questions. In *Rensel v. Centra Tech, Inc.*, plaintiffs also filed a class action complaint against defendant Centra Tech alleging securities law violations arising from the unregistered sale of CTR tokens.[75] In an unopposed motion for class certification, plaintiffs argued they could meet the ascertainability requirement by using "'currency exchanges' as a mechanism for identifying plaintiffs."[76] The

69. *See* Balestra v. Cloud With Me Ltd., No. 18-cv-804, 2020 WL 4370392, at *4 (W.D. Pa. July 2, 2020) (report and recommendation by magistrate); Balestra v. Cloud With Me Ltd., No. 18-cv-804, 2020 4368153 (W.D. Pa. July 30, 2020) (adopting report and recommendation by magistrate).

70. *Balestra*, 2020 WL 4370392, at *1.

71. *Id.* at *1.

72. *Id.* at *5.

73. *Id.*

74. *Id.* at *5.

75. Rensel v. Centra Tech, Inc., No. 17-24500, 2019 WL 7376759, at *1 (S.D. Fla. Sept. 17, 2019).

76. *Id.* at *4.

court rejected this argument and denied class certification, reasoning that "[t]he Plaintiffs do not explain how currency exchanges would help identify potential class members."[77] The court stated that "[t]he world of cryptocurrency and currency exchanges is a highly technical area and the Plaintiffs would need to explain to the Court how currency exchanges work, what information is stored, and how the Plaintiffs would access this information to identify potential class members."[78]

Although the full details of a dispute do not always come through in a single motion opinion, the *Rensel* court likely has the better view. It may be possible in certain circumstances to use public information on a blockchain, trading platform accountholder information, or both to identify the originator of various transfers, including for purposes of a class action ascertainability analysis. But practitioners should provide clear explanations of any such processes, and courts should view generalized, blanket assertions about blockchain technological capability through a critical lens.

VALUING CRYPTOCURRENCY LOSS

Like other assets with floating value, such as stocks, the changing value of cryptocurrency can raise issues as to the appropriate measure of damages in certain cases. One such case is *Ox Labs, Inc. v. Bitpay, Inc.*[79] On July 10, 2015, plaintiff Ox Labs, an exchange, inadvertently credited customer BitPay with 200 Bitcoins.[80] Evidence suggested that BitPay sold the 200 Bitcoins that day for $57,216.56.[81] Ox Labs did not discover the error for several years, by which time the value of Bitcoin had increased substantially.[82] After receiving notice of the error, on July 12, 2017, two years after the inadvertent transfer, BitPay sent Ox Labs a

77. *Id.*

78. *Id.*

79. No. 18-5934, 2019 WL 6729667 (C.D. Cal. Sept. 27, 2019).

80. *Id.* at *1.

81. *Id.*

82. *Id.*

check for $57,216.56, but Ox Labs rejected it and sued for conversion.[83] On summary judgment, the court addressed the appropriate measure of damages for conversion under California law, noting that the default measure is the value of the property at the time of conversion, with interest, at least absent special circumstances.[84] The court stopped short of resolving the question definitively on summary judgment but expressed skepticism that any such special circumstances could be found here, citing to California cases holding that damages for the conversion of stock shares are the value at the time of conversion plus interest.[85]

The US District Court for the District of New Jersey addressed the valuation issue in a wholly different context in *Gordon v. Dailey*.[86] The facts are sparse, but it appears that plaintiffs purchased certain bonds from defendants using Bitcoin.[87] Plaintiffs claimed to have been induced to purchase the bonds by fraud and sued defendants for a variety of claims, including securities fraud in violation of state and federal law.[88] On a motion to dismiss, the court evaluated its subject-matter jurisdiction under the federal diversity jurisdiction statute, 28 U.S.C. § 1332.[89] The court held that with respect to the amount in controversy as measured by the Bitcoin investment, as of the time a recent motion to amend was filed (July 13, 2016), the value of Bitcoin was $664.84, while at the time the opinion was written, the value was $1,047.89.[90] The court declined to decide the appropriate valuation as both would cause the amount in controversy to exceed the minimum $75,000 threshold.[91] But *Gordon* reminds that the valuation timing can have important consequences, and it is easy to imagine a case where it would have a dispositive impact on subject-matter jurisdiction.

---

83. *Id.* at *1–2.

84. *Id.* at *5.

85. *Id.* at *5–6.

86. No. 14-7495, 2017 WL 1181577 (D.N.J. Mar. 30, 2017).

87. *Id.* at *1; *see also* Gordon v. Dailey, No. 14-7495, 2016 WL1509080 (D.N.J. June 21, 2016).

88. *Gordon*, 2016 WL 1509080, at *1.

89. *Gordon*, 2016 WL 1181577, at *3.

90. *Id.* at *3 n. 5.

91. *Id.*

LOCATION OF BLOCKCHAIN TRANSACTIONS

Where geographically can blockchain transactions be said to occur? They are often initiated by a human or legal entity from one geographic location, the transaction may be added to the blockchain by a miner in nearly any geographic location, the nodes that verify and record the transaction are legion and located nearly everywhere, and the recipient is yet another human or legal in another geographic location. Given this, is it possible to assign a geographic location to a blockchain transaction? Must they be considered interstate?

The Ninth Circuit addressed this question in *United States v. Costanzo*.[92] Thomas Costanzo was indicted and convicted on multiple counts of money laundering for operating a cash-for-Bitcoin exchange business allegedly used to conceal or disguise the nature, location, source, ownership, or control of money from unlawful activity.[93] On appeal, Costanzo argued that the government had failed to prove that the transactions affected interstate commerce, an element of the crimes charged.[94] The Ninth Circuit disagreed, holding that the government had presented sufficient evidence, including of "the transfer of bitcoin through a digital wallet, which by its nature invokes a wide and international network."[95] The court cited to cases recognizing that the internet generally is an instrumentality of and intimately related to interstate commerce.[96]

Costanzo was perhaps an easier case. The requisite nexus with interstate commerce sufficient for criminal need not be extensive; the prosecution need only show that the transaction affected interstate or foreign commerce "in any way or degree."[97] A more interesting issue may arise when a litigant must tie a blockchain transaction to a particular jurisdiction, such as for purposes of personal jurisdiction.

---

92. 956 F.3d 1088 (9th Cir. 2020).

93. *Id.* at 1089–91.

94. *Id.* at 1091.

95. *Id.* at 1092.

96. *Id.*

97. *Id.*

WHAT DO THESE CASES MEAN?

This small sampling of cases involving blockchain and blockchain assets show that as the industry expands, litigation will also increase. While blockchain presents a new way to transact business, the issues that arise as a result relate to traditional issues such as damages, contract disputes, and other common claims. Blockchain may add some novel twists, but in many cases, the more things change, the more they remain the same.